Cuba in the Shadow of Change

CONTEMPORARY CUBA

UNIVERSITY PRESS OF FLORIDA

Florida A&M University, Tallahassee
Florida Atlantic University, Boca Raton
Florida Gulf Coast University, Ft. Myers
Florida International University, Miami
Florida State University, Tallahassee
New College of Florida, Sarasota
University of Central Florida, Orlando
University of Florida, Gainesville
University of North Florida, Jacksonville
University of South Florida, Tampa
University of West Florida, Pensacola

Contemporary Cuba

Edited by John M. Kirk

Afro-Cuban Voices: On Race and Identity in Contemporary Cuba, by Pedro Pérez-Sarduy and Jean Stubbs (2000)

Cuba, the United States, and the Helms-Burton Doctrine: International Reactions, by Joaquín Roy (2000)

Cuba Today and Tomorrow: Reinventing Socialism, by Max Azicri (2000); first paperback edition, 2001

Cuba's Foreign Relations in a Post-Soviet World, by H. Michael Erisman (2000); first paperback edition, 2002

Cuba's Sugar Industry, by José Alvarez and Lázaro Peña Castellanos (2001)

Culture and the Cuban Revolution: Conversations in Havana, by John M. Kirk and Leonardo Padura Fuentes (2001)

Looking at Cuba: Essays on Culture and Civil Society, by Rafael Hernández, translated by Dick Cluster (2003)

Santería Healing: A Journey into the Afro-Cuban World of Divinities, Spirits, and Sorcery, by Johan Wedel (2004)

Cuba's Agricultural Sector, by José Alvarez (2004)

Cuban Socialism in a New Century: Adversity, Survival and Renewal, edited by Max Azicri and Elsie Deal (2004)

Cuba, the United States, and the Post–Cold War World: The International Dimensions of the Washington-Havana Relationship, edited by Morris Morley and Chris McGillion (2005)

Redefining Cuban Foreign Policy: The Impact of the "Special Period," edited by H. Michael Erisman and John M. Kirk (2006)

Gender and Democracy in Cuba, by Ilja A. Luciak (2007); first paperback edition, 2009

Ritual, Discourse, and Community in Cuban Santería: Speaking a Sacred World, by Kristina Wirtz (2007)

The "New Man" in Cuba: Culture and Identity in the Revolution, by Ana Serra (2007)

U.S.-Cuban Cooperation Past, Present, and Future, by Melanie M. Ziegler (2007)

Protestants, Revolution, and the Cuba-U.S. Bond, by Theron Corse (2007)

The Changing Dynamic of Cuban Civil Society, edited by Alexander I. Gray and Antoni Kapcia (2008)

Cuba in the Shadow of Change: Daily Life in the Twilight of the Revolution, by Amelia Rosenberg Weinreb (2009)

Cuba in the Shadow of Change

Daily Life in the Twilight of the Revolution

Amelia Rosenberg Weinreb

University Press of Florida
Gainesville/Tallahassee/Tampa/Boca Raton
Pensacola/Orlando/Miami/Jacksonville/Ft. Myers/Sarasota

Copyright 2009 by Amelia Rosenberg Weinreb
Photographs courtesy of Alex Weinreb
Printed in the United States of America. This book is printed on Glatfelter Natures Book,
a paper certified under the standards of the Forestry Stewardship Council (FSC). It is a
recycled stock that contains 30 percent post-consumer waste and is acid-free.

14 13 12 11 10 09   6 5 4 3 2 1

Library of Congress Cataloging-in-Publication Data
Weinreb, Amelia Rosenberg.
Cuba in the shadow of change : daily life in the twilight of the revolution / Amelia
Rosenberg Weinreb.
p. cm. — (Contemporary cuba)
Includes bibliographical references and index.
ISBN 978-0-8130-3369-3 (alk. paper)
1. Ethnology—Cuba. 2. Economic anthropology—Cuba. 3. Social classes—Cuba.
4. Social change—Cuba. 5. Consumption (Economics)—Cuba. 6. Cuba—History—
Revolution, 1959. 7. Cuba—Economic conditions—21st century. 8. Cuba—Social life
and customs. I. Title.
GN564.C9W45   2009
306.097291—dc22
2009011121

The University Press of Florida is the scholarly publishing agency for the State University
System of Florida, comprising Florida A&M University, Florida Atlantic University,
Florida Gulf Coast University, Florida International University, Florida State University,
New College of Florida, University of Central Florida, University of Florida, University
of North Florida, University of South Florida, and University of West Florida.

University Press of Florida
15 Northwest 15th Street
Gainesville, FL 32611-2079
www.upf.com

This book is dedicated to the memory of my parents,
Don and Jeanine Rosenberg,
who no longer share in my earthly adventures,
but encouraged me to experience them.

Contents

List of Figures   ix
List of Tables   xi
Acknowledgments   xiii

Introduction   1
1. Historical Overview: Tracing Discontent   19

Part I. Private   35

2. Private Space   39
3. Private Experience   52

Part II. Means   63

4. Words and Means: The Special Period Lexicon   65
5. What Goods Mean in Cuba   83
6. Dollars, Means, and the New Cuban Class System   98

Part III. Free   115

7. Un-migration   117
8. Freedom Offstage   142
9. Conclusion: Citizens, Consumers, and Shadow Publics in Time and
   Space   160
   Epilogue   180

Appendix: Informant Profiles   191
Notes   197
Literature Cited   219
Index   245

Figures

0.1. The author with her children 12

1.1. Cubans wait in line to enter a dollar store 24

1.2. Poster advertising the socialist revolution hangs in a car showroom 30

1.3. Schoolchildren buy snacks in Old Havana 33

I.1. *Uso particular*: a "private use" vehicle 36

2.1. José Martí towers over *Plaza de la Revolución* 40

4.1. An empty shop window touting "Offers in National Currency" 73

4.2. Vintage American car rolls by 77

6.1. Full circle: the logic of Afro-Cuban poverty in late-socialist Cuba 111

7.1. Havana at twilight, looking toward the Florida Straits 117

9.1. Types of citizen-state relationships 163

9.2. A Havana primary school pays homage to Fidel 179

Tables

6.1. Cuba's Late-Socialist Social Classes   105
6.2. Advantages of Dollars/CUCs over Pesos for Gaining Personal
     Freedoms   106

Acknowledgments

For their encouragement and critical comments on earlier drafts, I am indebted to Asif Agha, Sheldon Garon, Peggy Reeves Sanday, Deborah Thomas, Greg Urban, a hawk-eyed anonymous reviewer for the University Press of Florida, and my husband, Alex Weinreb, who also provided never-ending company and loyal support at every stage, as well as all photographs that appear in this book. I thank Katherine Gordy and Megan Tracy for their electronic camaraderie and feedback, Kristina Wirtz for her inspiration, and John Kirk and Archibald Ritter for their gallant intellectual endorsement. I am grateful to Jan Trasen and Leon Weinreb for editing away my typographical blind spots, and to Leon also for help with graphics. I thank copyeditor Kirsteen Anderson for her excellent work at the manuscript's final stages. That said, the errors that remain in this book are mine alone.

I would like to acknowledge the Andrew W. Mellon Foundation, whose award for field research through the University of Pennsylvania's Population Studies Center made the core of this research possible in 2003, and the support of the Ben-Gurion University's Blaustein Center for Scientific Cooperation, whose postdoctoral fellowship enabled me to complete final work on the manuscript against the unlikely backdrop of a small desert town in the Negev Highlands of Israel.

I must thank my children, Maya, Max, and Boaz Weinreb, for creating the bridges during fieldwork that allowed me to connect with people who might otherwise have mistrusted me. I am indebted to my Cuban informants, who opened up a world to me that I did not know existed, and did so generously and with goodwill, despite the threat of government reprisal. Finally, I extend special thanks to my key informant, whom I call "David," without whose perceptions, analysis, and ongoing friendship, this book would not exist.

A brief essay that contains some of the ethnographic detail in this book recast for a general audience appeared in *Expedition* (vol. 50, no. 1, Spring 2008: pp. 26–33); and sections of chapter 6 were published in *Transforming Anthropology* (vol. 16, no. 6, Fall 2008). I gratefully acknowledge permission to reprint those materials here.

Introduction

Summer morning
Residential neighborhood
Havana, Cuba

Garments dry quickly in the morning sun, and are best brought indoors by midday to avoid the daily frenzy of unpegging at the first roll of afternoon thunder. This is when women call out, announcing the arrival of rain and, as a neighborly gesture, yank down all nearby laundry from the communal clothesline. Cubans, who excel at guarding their private lives from one another, and who take care not to air their dirty laundry in public, still engage in a lot of friendly handling of other people's clean laundry. They also spend a lot of time sharing lines—not only clotheslines, but also phone lines, ration lines, pharmacy lines, shopping lines, faltering factory production lines, and one-party lines.

I am privy to certain conversations because I share a clothesline with Tatiana and Petra, who have been living two doors down from each other on the same passageway for five years, and who do trust each other—as far as Cuban neighbors ever do. Squinting and starting to sweat, I listen to them chat as clothes go up for the day, about the influence of their astrological signs on their personalities, the going rate for home manicures and pedicures, the declining quality of public school lunches, and—quite aggravating to Tatiana—the fact that the price of Nestlé Nesquik flavored milk has just gone up, yet again. Her complaint does not resonate with nostalgic images of Cubans receiving communist no-brand rations in tin cups. In fact, Tatiana regards chocolate-flavored Nesquik (a Mexican import) as a household staple for her school-aged daughter, and the price hike is going to place an added strain on the family purse. "But," she adds, lowering her voice, a Cuban citizen's ritual indexing the moment when a political problem enters the arena, "I can't say anything," she hisses in frustration, "Who would I complain to?" She throws up her hands, shrugs, and then slaps her cutoff jeans.

Unsatisfied Citizen-Consumers

The protagonists of this book are ordinary Cuban families quietly in search of a life with basic luxuries. Their search appears unremarkable, since neither their poverty nor their desires are extreme. They do not live terribly, they are not starving, but they work hard, and they want to live better. They long for affordable, quality goods and services that they believe are available elsewhere, they are frustrated with nationalized systems offering less than ever before, and they harbor resentment over their hard and unrewarded work. However, they explicitly avoid political activism as a tool to raise their standard of living. They prefer ritualized civic participation (or civic withdrawal), engagement in the informal economy, and undocumented migration as practical, clandestine strategies that circumvent or extend beyond the reach of state control.

Despite state achievements like low infant mortality and high literacy rates, this group, whom I call "unsatisfied citizen-consumers," wants something more, and they believe they can get it somewhere else. They often have remarkable firsthand details about specific types of goods and services they would like to access, for example Johnson's Baby Shampoo No More Tears formula, queen-sized pantyhose, home mortgage deals, fast Internet connections, and short lines at well-stocked medical centers.

The imported products increasingly available on shelves in shops in Havana remain prohibitively expensive for most Cubans, but as before, they continue to obtain awareness of consumer goods through hand-delivered gifts, visits and phone calls from family abroad, commercials broadcast on illegal satellite TV, conversations with tourists, and even videotaped footage of loved ones enjoying life in other countries. Such consumer details are politically symbolic, igniting vivid imaginings of life elsewhere and fueling subdued anger against the state. Ordinary citizens unavoidably experience stress and secrecy in trying to make ends meet in Cuba's authoritarian bureaucratic structure,[1] obtain basic luxuries under the table, and discreetly plan their escape. These desires and pressures lie at the core of their lived experience.

I argue that unsatisfied citizen-consumers' political silence, underground economic activity, and secret identity as prospective migrants mark the boundaries of a significant "shadow public." This term plays on the common, parallel phrase "shadow economy," as it also indicates informality and underground activity. Unlike what is generally considered "the public," however, a shadow public is a large group with common interests and concerns, but one that is non-united and seeks invisibility as its members look to improve their lot. Throughout this book, I explore and conceptualize the unsatisfied citizen-consumer in relationship to the state and the creation of the shadow public in Cuba's changing circumstances.

And Cuba's circumstances are changing. Everything I describe is unfolding in Cuba's era of late socialism: a confluence of socialist bureaucracy with a social, economic, and cultural turn towards capitalist modes of consumption and production.[2] I will define late socialism in more detail in the historical overview in chapter 1, and throughout the book, by illuminating the lived experience in this era, which first became clearly visible in Cuba after the fall of the Soviet Union. Late socialism serves as the backdrop for both a local sense of transformation and an unending stagnation that leads to citizen-consumer dissatisfaction and, consequently, to the development of a shadow public in Cuba.

Neighborhood Context

There is nothing shadowy about the neighborhoods of the shadow public. Informants directed me to and gave me tours of residential areas they recommended as economical, safe, decent, and "authentic." There was a simple code. By "economical, safe, and decent," informants were referring to communities that broke the stereotypical portrait of regional poverty: dirt, crime, delinquency, and marginality. Rather, they reflected a sort of "Middle America," Cuban style. These neighborhoods were further marketed to me, a prospective renter with a young family in tow, as populated by *buena gente* (families of respectable, kind, quality people, and in this context implicitly "white"),[3] who would be good neighbors to us and would welcome us because we were, ostensibly, like them. "Es un barrio muy Cubano" (It's a very Cuban neighborhood), they would say, describing areas relatively unfrequented by tourists.

Consequently, many of the events in this book take place in a leafy, middle-income, primarily residential neighborhood I will call "Los Árboles,"[4] which contains modest and mostly shabby apartment buildings and houses, and is located just outside the capital city center. Like most Havana neighborhoods, this one has its own small shopping strip with "dollar" stores (where goods must be purchased in U.S. dollars),[5] a small outdoor farmers market, a *consultorio* (medical practice) with a family doctor, pharmacies, schools, *bodegas* (ration distribution centers), and municipal headquarters. It is tied to Havana's city center, which is within easy traveling distance, for taking care of bureaucratic transactions, obtaining consumer supplies, and for some, going to work each morning. Yet Los Árboles and its residents lie outside both the popular and scholarly imagination of Cuban life. The area is described dismissively in travel guides in such terms as "it doesn't offer much to persuade you to linger" and "you wouldn't miss anything if you didn't drive through." Nor does the neighborhood represent an obvious center of "socialist exotica"

(Hernandez-Reguant 2005, 2006) or the "fallen grandeur" of *solares*, the Spanish colonial structures battered by the tropical elements where tourists feel they have stumbled upon the "real" Cuba (Whitfield 2006).

If urban and suburban communities like Los Árboles are unremarkable, they are also pleasant in their unremarkability. Los Árboles is clean and tree-lined, and its longer-term residents are friendly and do not cause one another trouble. No matter the relative size or exterior condition of the dwellings (sometimes neighboring houses are in quite different states of repair), and despite socialist or egalitarian principles, the tidy interiors of these relatively modern, nuclear family homes usually feature a TV/VCR, a stereo, a pantry stocked with food and household cleaning products from the supermarket, and a bathroom cupboard containing a stash of pharmaceuticals and beauty aids. On their walls are framed photos of family members, mass-produced artwork, and sometimes a cross, expressing a moderate connection to Catholicism. They also typically have a modest collection of clothing and children's toys and other trappings of the modern "bourgeois" household—*electrodomésticos* such as blenders, air conditioners and washing machines—even if such trappings have unusual origins or histories of acquisition, which they almost always do.

This veneer of comfortable living belied the fact that most of my informants were cyclically cash poor and expended what they considered unreasonable amounts of time and energy perfecting the art of finding more, stretching their resources, and milking national systems. During hard times, employment provided them with a sense of legitimacy as rightful citizens and frustration as consumers with what they felt were punitively tight limitations, fueling negative feelings about how they lived, where they lived, and who was to blame for their situation.

Providing for the Family

Determining who is at fault becomes a particularly heated issue when parents are unable to provide what they want for their children. This inability shapes parents' worldview painfully and profoundly, making families with children more likely to fit the characterization of unsatisfied citizen-consumers. In Cuba, as in most countries, families are the primary focus of national laws protecting and providing for citizens; the Código de Familia (Family Code) specifically outlines, among other things, the rights and responsibilities of families regarding their own children, and informs families of what the state is obligated to provide in turn. Guarantees of health care and education outlined in national constitutions are particularly valued by families, but unsatisfied citizen-consumers generally regard these provisions as just one crucial means of stretching their income. These benefits are not what citizens live on, they are not what they used to be, and they are not sufficient reason to show excessive deference to the state; on the other hand, nor are they considered an appropriate reason to organize collectively against the state.

Providing for their children means that families are forced to live in the present moment, taking care of immediate emotional and material needs, while also thinking about their children's futures. These citizen-consumers intentionally keep their families small. Regardless of the number of children they would ideally like, unsatisfied citizen-consumers commonly prevent further hardship by adhering strictly to birth-control regimens (and occasionally abortions funded by state clinics), unconfident that they could provide materially for more than one or two carefully spaced children in any dignified way, given their insecure personal financial circumstances and national economic realities. Sharing many consumption practices, they commiserate over line items on their budget and a special set of economic burdens and stressful financial cycles as they scrape together funds for birthdays, holidays, and school-related events.

When they have insufficient funds to provide for their children, they become more inventive, often engaging in illegal activities, which heighten their awareness of the state as an oppositional watchdog. Thus, families become embroiled in a cycle of vertical responsibility: their responsibilities to their children, and those the state has toward them.

Staying Afloat

Despite these frustrations, the unsatisfied citizen-consumers were quick to admit that others had it worse than they did. Informants would distinguish themselves from the truly poverty-stricken, saying things like, "¡Pero imagínete si yo fuera pobre!" (But imagine if I were poor!), or more often, "Si yo no tuviera dólares . . ." (if I didn't have dollars), expressing relief not to be in that category, which would provoke even more hardship. Indeed, because of a combination of legal and clandestine employment, state subsidies, and remittances and other gifts from abroad, none of the unsatisfied citizen-consumer families I discuss experienced extreme or prolonged difficulty subsisting, and they worked diligently to keep it that way.

In fact, at least one of the adults in each of the households I describe held gainful employment, even if only in a constitutionally guaranteed state position. More typically, the head of household (usually but not always the husband) held some sort of full-time work, and at least one family member also contributed to family income *por la izquierda* (literally "on the left"), meaning through self-employment in the form of small off-the-books, untaxed jobs, such as baking and selling cakes from home; peddling clothing, farm-fresh food, or bootleg CDs door-to-door; or running a hair salon out of a back room of their home. Other times, the family were *bisneros* (slang for black marke-teers), with much more extensive engagement in a black-market business such as running a lucrative home-based restaurant with lobster on the menu, or selling bottles of rum pilfered from a state factory line.

Even if the combination of activities and income sources helped them and their families stay afloat, many felt that they were wasting their training and education; many had earned state-subsidized university degrees, and occa-sionally even higher degrees. Instead of applying their skills in a fruitful, legal job market, these unsatisfied citizen-consumers lived with the daily stress of maintaining an underground enterprise, facing the contradiction of wanting to provide a decent lifestyle for themselves and their families and of wanting to earn their own keep, but having no choice but to do so extralegally. Their aspirations were chronically frustrated, and they rendered themselves without the possibility of building a satisfying life, and therefore *sin futuro* (without a future), at least in Cuba.

Ordinary Outlaws

While unsatisfied citizen-consumers sometimes do not know specifically who the other members are—their constituency is very large and its boundaries very unclear—individual members of the group still share a general sense that they are normal and that they represent a majority.[6] They refer to themselves and their condition as those of *la gente de la calle* (the "man on the street," or "everyday people"). Furthermore, most unsatisfied citizen-consumers, despite their involvement in illegal activities, are otherwise "clean-living"—they have immaculate homes; ironed clothing; well-scrubbed children; strong moral orientation in the areas of generosity, manners, propriety, thrift, industrious-ness, and conscientiousness; a desire for self-reliance; intense family loyalty; and sometimes (but not always) religious belief and observance.

Although Cuban unsatisfied citizen-consumers did not fit the typical por-trait of outlaws, they were aware that they had excluded honesty and rule-following from their moral universe in the interest of coping materially. They were also troubled by certain elements of these choices. They described experiencing a dissonance between their personal values and the strategies they employed in order to earn a living informally or illegally—talking about how they had become largely numb to corruption and living outside the law, and how the constraint and apprehensions of their lives were fatiguing. They also described how their personal identities, against their will, had become wrapped up in thrift and stress related to maintaining financial security by illegal means, at the expense of all other individual interests.

I introduce, in short, an analytic category of people who are a key pres-ence in Cuba but who remain a missing piece of the puzzle for understanding its transition into late socialism. This may be in part because anthropologists have tended to overlook "un-alluring," or majority, groups "hidden in plain sight" (Di Leonardo 1998) even when their views and experiences are remarkably important for theorizing a concept.[7] Middle-class non-elites do not "deserve" or warrant research like the poor do, and therefore there is little moral imperative to investigate their interests, as is made evident by their near-invisibility in publications and academic discourse, particularly in contrast with the abundant anthropological literature and discourse on poverty in Latin America.[8]

By defining the unsatisfied citizen-consumer, I approach citizen discontent in Latin America differently from the way anthropologists traditionally have done. The existing repertoire of analytic paradigms for Latin American citizen discontent remains derivative of either structural Marxism and world systems theory, or new social movement (NSM) theory.[9] Both models seek out a valiant and vocal minority—members of peasant uprisings, pockets of urban grassroots organizing, or participants in labor and indigenous movements—while ignoring the backdrop of the broadest and most stable base: the quiet majority of "ordinary" citizens who are not moved to organize because they do not share a clearly articulated ideological struggle, because they are waiting for political change to develop gradually with time, or because they fear state menace (see Gutmann 2002 and García 2005, who also address this issue).

Therefore, throughout the book, many of my points of reference are not to other Latin American and Caribbean countries, nor to the experiences of Latin American and Caribbean citizens, but—particularly since I am framing my topic in terms of late socialism—to those in the post-Soviet Eastern-bloc countries who have undergone socialist transitions in their own right and have striking ethnographic similarities with Cuban citizen-consumers, and perhaps share political and economic trajectories with them.

Blurring Citizens and Consumers

The term *citizen-consumer* blurs the conceptual distinction between "individuals in a political relationship with government" and individuals who are "concerned with satisfying private, material desires" (L. Cohen 2003: 8). Blending *citizen* and *consumer* within the same conceptual frame (whether or not the hyphenated term is used) has been a recent project in consumer studies, cultural studies, and political and social science, focusing primarily on the industrialized West.[10]

The stream of literature invokes questions about morality, choice, and the importance of consumption in modern society, in particular a consumption that jockeys for a place next to the more classical forms of democratic and civic participation. This stream of literature is useful not only in the analysis of the permeability of political and economic spheres, but also the connections between private spending and the public good in a transforming socialist society. In addition, this scholarship reflects the anxiety that consumers will come to *replace* citizens, that citizens will be reduced to consumers, that citizenship and civic participation will become commodified, or that the power of markets will replace the power of states. Despite the importance and flexibility of the citizen-consumer as a concept, it has rarely been applied to analysis in the welfare state, the late-socialist state, or the developing world, arenas where I believe it takes on special significance because of the type of material coping mechanisms applied in such contexts.[11]

By tagging the word *unsatisfied* to the phrase *Cuban citizen-consumer*, I hope to capture the mutually constitutive frustration over unfulfilled government obligations and over chronic difficulties achieving private material fulfillment. Part of our understanding of the customer, or consumer, is based on the everyday discourse of "consumer satisfaction," "consumer dissatisfaction," and "consumer loyalty" in the market context, particularly in relation to emotional responses, expectations, products, and the consumption experience (ideas used to describe the consumer's responses after consumption, after choice, based on accumulated experience, and so on, as described in Giese and Cote 2000). Responses, choice, and cumulative experience regarding consumption are important in the context of the welfare state, where welfare-state "clients," or citizens of the welfare state, are also *consumers* of public goods and services, also making them citizen-consumers in this sense. For example, when rationing, long waits for nationalized services, or low, state-fixed salaries stir discontent, is it ultimately a citizen right or a consumer interest at stake? This is a fundamental question in the late-socialist era.

Late socialism, by definition, suggests the increasing centrality of consumers in moves towards capitalism, as well as declining commitment among socialist citizens to the socialist state. I consider whether there is such a thing as pure *citizen* satisfaction and dissatisfaction and how it functions in an increasingly consumer-driven world. What is citizen loyalty if citizens know that if they are not satisfied, they may be able to take their citizenship elsewhere? When does it happen, and what does it lead to? A discussion that involves citizen dissatisfaction, migration, and a shadow economy, such as the one I present here, brings into question not only definitions of "good" citizenship, but also of citizenship itself (see also chapter 7 on migration).

While I use *citizen-consumer* throughout the book to emphasize the connection between citizen and consumer, there are times when it is clearer to separate the roles. Examples are when I describe how the dissatisfactions of my informants are specifically political, in terms of citizen dissatisfaction with national policy; shortcomings of the late-socialist welfare state;

and problems such as lack of personal liberties, perceptions of heavy taxation, and absence of venues for complaint. On the other hand, these "citizen problems" often blend with consumer dissatisfactions, such as unpredictable household income expenditures and access to basic foodstuffs and articles of daily use, shortages, inconveniences, and low quality of local services, which often figure more prominently than citizen issues in everyday discourse. Together, the blended citizen and consumer complaints reflect on the welfare state's inability to provide, and lead to a collective disenchantment with home, lack of motivation to abide by the law, disengagement with the state, and ultimately migration.

Documenting Dissatisfaction

I recognize that consumer dissatisfaction outside the market mechanism is difficult to gauge empirically, but it can be partly captured in discourses of complaint, or in the products and services offered on the black market. Likewise, citizen dissatisfaction, like any collective attitude, is difficult to capture and measure. This is compounded by the fact that the historical record contains "few reliable traces of people's inner dialogs, hidden fantasies, suppressed anxieties or unstated preferences" (Tilly 1983: 462)—all trappings of a shadow public. Without the benefit of social movements, public records of visa applications, or even reliable surveys or elections in the Cuban case, what trail of evidence exists for dissatisfaction? Tilly suggests that historical evidence is nevertheless marked by "interests, complaints, demands and aspirations—by attitudes in the loose sense of the word" (p. 462).[12] I hope I have captured these in the ethnographic present, providing a historical record of shadow public opinion.

I argue that dissatisfaction can be captured in the ethnographic present through a set of questions that bring elements of *doxa* and cultural practice of the collectivity to the fore: What assumptions about the citizen-state contract go unstated? What is citizens' collective memory, and how does it constrain and become modified by practice? What form does citizens' indignation take? What form does the corrective action take (based on Tilly's 1997 "Primer on Citizenship")? This set of questions about citizenship suggests the existence of "penetrations" between social-structural form and location versus "lived" assessments of their possibilities or everyday culture (Willis 2000). I address these questions and this process of penetration in more detail throughout the book. But at the very least, these questions point to an undeniable reality that the rules and expectations of the state shape daily life, and that, in turn, the practices of daily life place constraints on the absolute power of the state.

Methods and Routes to Analysis

These reflections on the links among citizenship, consumption, and the shadow public come from field visits to Cuba in 1994, 2001, 2003, and 2008, and from correspondence with informants throughout those years, which provided me with opportunities to absorb the increasingly market-driven policies and ethnographic realities during that time frame.

Local perspectives on the rapidly developing U.S. dollar economy as the alternative to dependence on a crumbling welfare state, and on the erosion of ideals of the socialist revolution, kept moving to the center of conversations, swallowing whole any other research agenda I had. I was also unable to ignore the outpouring of talk concerning how access to dollars was affording new economic freedoms and creating private impatience, but not collective action, to gain political liberties. Ordinary people were saying dramatic, desperate, and gripping things about their household economic situations and the country's political failings, leading me down new paths of interpretation and analysis. It became clear to me that Cuba was in the throes of a slow but dramatic transition—what I eventually came to realize was a particular type of late socialism.

My methodology reflects that of classic urban or suburban ethnography. I lived as a resident in a community, establishing rapport with key informants through open-ended conversations, unstructured interviews, and participant observation. As with most ethnographic research, there were a small number of households within walking distance of my apartment with which I had intensive, daily interaction. Therefore, in the scope of this book, I present the contextualized stories and opinions of several informants with whom I developed close and long-term relationships. Although ethnographers always run the risk of inaccurate extrapolation from a small sample, I argue that in Cuba personal relationships are the best, if not the only, way of gaining insider access to, reliable information about, and a deep understanding of a clandestine world that is usually guarded from the public eye. I argue that the experiences of key informants were not idiosyncratic, but rather representative of those of most middle-class Cubans living on the island during the years of my research. Nevertheless, to enrich my perspective, I purposively selected several other informants in other neighborhoods with contrasting socioeconomic characteristics. All together, my informant pool totaled around fifty families (see the appendix for complete profiles of individuals). The diversity within that pool, in terms of both personal and neighborhood characteristics, exposed me to a wider cross-section of micro-enterprises and social and migration networks. In turn, this helped me to define the boundaries of unsatisfied citizen-consumers as a group.

I conducted fieldwork almost exclusively with families either in their homes or home-based businesses or as I accompanied them during their daily tasks. During participant observation I most commonly accompanied informants with whom I had daily contact—and with whom I became close friends—as they did laundry, went grocery shopping, prepared meals, ran errands, took care of children, enjoyed extended family visits on Sundays, exercised, or spent time at home in the afternoon and evening hours. Much of the time, and especially with informants whom I saw less frequently, I also was hosted as a guest for coffee, refreshments, or meals and I in turn hosted similar events in my rented apartment.

Desconfianza

In order to conduct ethnographic research in Cuba, one has to make concessions. I had to build trust with informants who realized that I, like anyone they met, could be a government informer, international spy, or reporter, and that a piece of recorded data could be used against them. Therefore, I did not audiotape, photograph, videotape, or even take handwritten notes during participant observation or conversations with informants in public spaces or even inside their homes.[13]

While this method compromises the capture of certain kinds of highly detailed data (particularly the exact words used in a conversation), it remained essential not only for avoiding state surveillance or confiscation of my recorded materials, but also as the only way to collect any credible data whatsoever from mistrustful informants. I found that what was lost by not electronically recording participant observations and interviews was compensated for by the quality of relationships with informants and by the wealth and reliability of the information I gathered. Not recording during interactions also allowed for more natural interactions that enhanced relationship building in general.

I adjusted to this compromise by taking "scratch notes" of my conversations upon my return home, and then typing up highly detailed field notes as soon as possible after a field session. I structured my daily schedule in order to allow for two sessions of typing up field notes during each twenty-four hour period. As a result, unless otherwise noted, when I place quotation marks around a statement, I am indicating post-facto documented speech, not directly transcribed speech, though I have made every effort to capture the tone, nuance, and specificity of word choice of the speaker. I found that I did not generally sacrifice thoroughness or density of the documentation—especially since I never came to rely on piles of recorded interactions requiring later transcription as a crutch for conjuring up details long after the fact (see also Lancaster 1992 and Ries 1997).

As in all ethnographic work, but especially in the case of Cuba, where state retribution remains a threat for many of the people whose activities or beliefs are reported here, I worked to protect my informants' anonymity. During fieldwork, I encoded all names and places when writing, and I stored the only copy of my field notes in a secure (double password protected) computer "vault," sending compressed files out weekly to a secure server in the United States. In addition to using pseudonyms for person- and place-names in the book, I occasionally have made slight changes to substantively irrelevant details in order to obscure the identity of individuals.

Family Fieldwork

What I call "family fieldwork" helped enormously in climates of *desconfianza* (mistrust),[14] in that the presence of my spouse, and particularly of my children, served as a "guarantee of good intentions" (Cassell 1987: 260) in the field (fig. 0.1). After my initial trip to Cuba in 1994, I deviated from the "Lone Ranger approach" to fieldwork (Erickson and Stull 1998), that is, the "solitary" (and historically male) fieldworker model as critiqued by Rosaldo (1989), seeing the benefits of family in the field in Cuba.

Family fieldwork increased the ease and speed with which I established rapport, gained entrée into intimate spaces of people's homes and businesses, obtained gendered perspectives, and developed relationships of trust, thus

Figure 0.1. The author enjoys ice cream in Havana with her children, who increased the ease and speed of establishing rapport during ethnographic fieldwork.

providing my greatest advantage in data collection concerning sensitive topics. What I am calling "family fieldwork" is not new. In addition to the many anthropologists who have benefited from conducting fieldwork while accompanied by family members who receive little or no mention, contemporary narratives and analyses of anthropologists with children and families in the field have granted serious scholarly attention to the methodological and theoretical impact of "accompanied" fieldwork (Butler and Turner 1987; Cassell 1987; Flinn, Marshall, and Armstrong 1998; and Cupples and Kindon 2003).

Although my two children were "out of the way" attending child care during the morning hours—which were normally dedicated to writing round one of my daily field notes—during the remainder of my day in the field, I almost always had at least one child with me. Occasionally, my whole family accompanied me during participant observation.[15]

Motherhood Persona

Having my family with me enhanced my data collection in three apparent ways. First, rather than perceiving me as merely a foreign researcher or any other dubious individual, Cubans found my identity easily comprehensible: I was a mother of very small children and a hapless neighborhood newcomer.

My persona was benign and vulnerable—someone in need of information about local life rather than someone formally present to extract a certain kind of data. My field persona also allowed me to meet my key informant family, not by introducing myself as an anthropologist, but through a pressing family hygiene need: finding someone to launder piles of dirty cloth diapers. This need ensured daily contact through morning diaper drop-off and evening diaper pick-up, and also allowed me to enter a network of citizens engaged in similar forms of untaxed labor.

Although I still had to make an effort to establish trust and rapport, the process was made easier as I was invited inside the intimate spaces of people's homes and was having open-ended conversations about local life within a day of my arrival to the site. My motherhood persona facilitated the depth with which I was incorporated into daily community life, especially through our use of local child care, schools, clinics, grocery stores, ration centers, and underground enterprises. In this way, "family fieldwork" facilitated capturing the types of sensitive personal data that made this study possible, especially regarding income, involvement in the black market, and private family plans.

When I toted children in public, I was showered with unsolicited information, often in the form of advice, by neighbors who came to know me, and also sometimes even by passersby. The most common topics regarded shopping, properly caring for children, schools, ways to save money, the quality of products and services, safety tips, recipes, home remedies, local services, untrustworthy types of people to avoid, and the relative suitability for children of upcoming local events—all details which provided priceless contextual data that shaped my topic.

The local families with whom I spoke in depth generously provided extensive guidance, I believe, not only because they saw me as sharing something basic in common with them, but also because of our difference—I was an eccentric and incapable "housewife" in need of indigenous expertise. Because of my distracting and "charming" characteristics, people who did not know me well rarely questioned why I was in the country, and many people assumed it was my husband who had some sort of position, and that I had merely accompanied him.

People were generally curious and impressed when someone reminded them of my professional reason for being in Cuba, but usually seemed to forget about it and just want to talk about "something else"—a more immediately pressing personal or political topic. There were also instances when informants would humbly request that I accompany them (for example, to take a bus to seek medical treatment, to wait in an hours-long line at a state pharmacy, to shop at the grocery store), paradoxically thinking they might be imposing upon me by "taking time away" from my busy schedule to keep them company, and I had to convince them they were providing me with precious insider experiences and data without my even having to ask.

These responses to my presence in the communities convinced me I was perceived as unthreatening and trustworthy. In other words, motherhood and a busy family life provided a consistently connective, humanizing mantle over my researcher's role and blended seamlessly with my research style. I base this self-characterization as nonthreatening also on the more objective measure of my ability to obtain the type of sensitive data that it typically takes researchers a much longer period of time to access (see Renzetti and Lee 1992; Lee 1993; Bernard 2000).

Second, my own children also needed to use local services in a way that I, as an adult, did not, allowing for "pure" participant observation in the community. For example, I never had to cut through any red tape to obtain permission as a foreign researcher to observe a day care, school, or clinic. Rather I was *using* clinics because my kids were patients, and as a potential client I was invited to attend trial sessions at several different schools and child-care centers, selected one with the help of neighbors' advice, and then documented the experience of having children actually enrolled as "insiders."

Informants did not want our kids to miss birthday or holiday parties or other special local events, and the invitations were extended to me, providing me with access to family events at which we were sometimes the only non-kin present, embedding me deeply in extended family and community life.

Eyes and Ears

Finally, while in the end I was the only designated researcher, I undeniably had extra eyes and ears in the field. While children's reports are not a reliable source of data, I had a source of interesting details or gossip from child-care centers or around the neighborhood that I otherwise would have been blind to and about which I could then follow up. But perhaps more revealing than reports was observing the development of language and play. What vocabulary and concepts do children first learn? What games or behaviors did my daughter pick up from other children? What was the specific content of fantasy play or mimicking of adults? These provided not only amusing stories to share with other adults in conversation, but also allowed me to gather an unusual type of data on cultural transmission that I could later investigate or have key informants help me interpret.

My husband was also a vital presence in the field. More commonly recognized than the advantages of having children in the field is how one's sex determines access to gender-segregated activities and social spheres, and the ability for men and women to synergistically fill in knowledge gaps and answer gender-related questions that they would not discuss with someone of the opposite sex (Golde 1986; Ariens and Strijp 1989; Bell, Caplan, and Karim 1993).

My experience bore out this observation; my husband was able to have conversations with men, develop relationships with husbands in key informant families in which different kinds of information was exchanged than was shared with me, and was invited to different types of events than I was (watching sports on television, sharing rum and cigarettes, watching late-night videos, and chatting), therefore capturing a different quality of information than I did. In some cases, we had simultaneous, parallel fieldwork experiences in different parts of the neighborhood (or just different parts of the same room at a gathering), or he would be engaged in "after-hours" fieldwork while I was minding sleeping children during my late-night write-up sessions (in either case, my husband would occasionally contribute his field notes to my file or dictate "head notes" to me). His relationships maximized our time, breadth of connections, experiences, and documentation in the field sites (see Oboler 1986 on husbands in the field, and Valentine 1999 on interviewing couples together and apart).

I have showcased what I see as the tremendous advantages of family fieldwork here, but in reality, there are tiring disadvantages, too. I endured the stressors of simultaneously managing a professional life and "adventures" in the field with young children, or as Flinn, Marshall, and Armstrong (1998: 10) call it, the tensions stemming from the "role conflicts between 'parent' and 'researcher.'" This balancing act meant negotiating the "uncontrollables"—teeth-gnashing irritation and fatigue, long workdays and late nights, unpredictable delays, and uncomfortable journeys, along with the memorable relationships with other families and sense of local community support.

Furthermore, because children afford ethnographers less privacy due to their noise, needs, and indiscretion, neighborhood informants, in my case, had more access to my "back region" than they would have had, had I been a lone fieldworker (see discussion of Goffman's impression management in the field as filtered by Berreman 1962). With access to the back region, the host society can also watch us interacting with members of our own culture (Gilmore 1998: 35), just as we can watch them interacting with members of theirs. This reveals to informants things about the ethnographer that would otherwise remain private, and therefore allows for a "more egalitarian" form of fieldwork through two-way self-disclosure (Cassell 1989: 259). In truth, I found "egalitarian" field methods, along with my open-door policy, to be quite stressful and invasive at times. It required that I develop faith that the pace and price of being a "whole human being" in the eyes of informants was a worth-while investment (Goodenough 1998: 34). In retrospect, I am convinced that it was.

I have taken the time to foreground family fieldwork in order to be intel-lectually honest about the generation of, and undeniable backdrop to, the data on whose basis I make my claims. While family fieldwork details will reappear when relevant to the integrity of the text, context, and cultural analysis, it will not again receive this degree of detailed attention. I have categorized family fieldwork as a "method," but perhaps it is more accurately a way of life in the field or an epistemology. In either case, I cannot imagine having done success-ful fieldwork on this topic, during this era in Cuba, in any other way.

Book Overview

A primary impetus for writing this book is to introduce a population that, un-til now, has been un-theorized and under-described, despite their importance for any full understanding of contemporary Cuba. I call this group unsatisfied citizen-consumers. I argue that they are a shadow public whose activity il-luminates the cultural shifts and social and economic transformations taking place in Cuba in an era of late socialism. Virtually all scholarly work on Cuba has tended to ignore this population and their dissatisfaction. Instead, schol-ars have argued that Cubans accept material scarcity as part of revolutionary sacrifice; that the absence of ideal public spheres, elections, or freedom of as-sembly provides an alternative landscape upon which to explore agency; and that Cubans are part of a naturally participatory and expressive culture. These are, I think, problematic assumptions, and certainly describe a quite different Cuba than the one that my informants showed and described to me. Their Cuba—and the one that I describe in this book—highlights the importance of purposeful obscurity, rather than activism, as a coping mechanism during the liminal years of a prolonged Special Period. Rather than sidelining consumer desire as superficial or apolitical, it places it at the center of significant social change and citizen-state relationships. And rather than intellectualizing or relativizing citizen liberty, it illustrates the emotional and cultural elements of deeply unsatisfying citizenship in daily life.

In establishing the historical foundation for this argument, chapter 1 proceeds with an overview of citizen-consumer discontent as it has developed in Cuba, focusing particularly on events since the collapse of the Soviet bloc in 1989 and through what is known as the Special Period to the present. It then defines the late-socialist period within a global context.

Part I, "Private," describes what constitutes the private in the context of heavy state control and economic dependence on the welfare state, and engages with current theoretical literature on the problem of "socialist binaries." Specifically, chapter 2 illustrates how, despite arguments against socialist binaries, private space shifts power towards citizens and consumers and away from the state. Chapter 3 expands the argument to include ethnographic cases of private enterprise and private forms of communication and protest.

Part II, "Means," is about means of speaking, means of obtaining consumer products, and means of earning in late-socialist Cuba. Specifically, chapter 4 introduces the "Special Period lexicon" and some key words with reappropriated meanings. Chapter 5 focuses on the means of obtaining goods and information about goods in the late-socialist era: state-issued brand-name goods and goods in a state of shortage. It describes the role of external influences, particularly global media, hand-delivered gifts, and family abroad, in provoking a sharp sense of relative deprivation based on intimate knowledge about goods. Chapter 6 explores how the division of the population through differential access to dollars has spawned social changes related to race, types of employment, social and discursive networks, relationship to the state, and the laws or philosophies that govern lifestyle.

Part III, "Free," relates to reaching out, being trapped, and critiquing and complaining in the contemporary Cuban context. Chapter 7 is about feeling trapped within the confines of the island of Cuba: the near impossibility of obtaining exit permits that leads to separations from family outside the island, the role of memories of travel, and metaphors—particularly that of asphyxiation—for being trapped, that circulate among citizen-consumers. It considers not only migration, the exit option to perceived freedom, but also the more common "un-migration," the frustrating fate of a Cuban shadow public who never make it to their imagined destination, and the genesis and quality of that unfulfilled state of being. Chapter 8 describes representation and resistance, Cuban-style. It focuses in particular on common forms of "off-stage," "backstage," and at-home criticism, building on the improbability of large-scale protest or the development of powerful interest groups. This chapter also explains how forms of protest do not represent a unified, national opposition movement of any sustained potency. In chapter 9, the conclusion, I propose a definition of citizenship and publics based on the Cuban case. Pulling away from the national specificity of Cuba, I then question whether this citizen type is a Latin American–Caribbean regional phenomenon—a new "public face" of Latin America—and if so, how it relates to other international trends. Finally, the coda, rather than focusing on Cuba's imminent future, offers an ironic discussion of the future of nostalgia for the citizen-consumers and the shadow public, using current cultural trends in post-socialist states as a guide and bringing the citizen-consumer desire full circle, back to the future.

1

Historical Overview

Tracing Discontent

How did citizen-consumer dissatisfaction emerge, and when? In this chapter, I describe relevant contemporary history and national conditions in Cuba, particularly its role as a welfare state and its transition from Special Period to late socialism in the last fifteen years. I emphasize the way that information about contemporary difficulties is repeatedly circulated by Cubans in local discourse, paying particular attention to those political and economic details that most buffet urban and suburban citizen-consumers.

Here, in summary and introductory form, I speak of "ordinary Cubans," which is a variously defined and contested term. This is so particularly because ordinary Cubans are not a monolithic group that has formed a consensus about their country, although at times Havana's overwhelming mood of collective frustration and its widely circulating discourse on problems can create this perception. Throughout the book I use the phrase *ordinary Cubans* to refer most generally to those Cubans without leadership roles in the Communist Party or a mass organization, and without special status as elite performing artists, musicians, entertainers, or athletes. Many times, ordinary Cubans also fit the definition of unsatisfied citizen-consumers, those with whom I spent my time and whom I think are overlooked and under-analyzed, and whom this book therefore features.

Sources and Perspectives

While the perspective I present is arguably both ordinary and important for understanding contemporary Cuba, I must emphasize that I also spent time with people who continue to heartily support the revolution, the Castros, and the Communist Party (see the appendix). Their crucially important minority point of view is woven into this book, as they remain essential to the makeup of Cuban national culture, although I argue that their numbers are dwindling and they are disproportionately composed of people over fifty years of age and those with close Party connections.

I draw surprisingly little on existing ethnographic texts, for the simple reason that so few exist. While Cuba is written about extensively—even excessively—if one judges by the number of journalists and travel writers who have been able to cobble together colorful stories about their visits in the last fifteen years, the informant pool of these authors draws heavily on people they meet on the street: hustlers and prostitutes and those related in some way to the tourist industry and Cuba's salsa-rich nightlife (T. Miller 1992; Hunt 1998; Codrescu 1999; Corbett 2002; Chiang 2004; Aschkenas 2006).[1] These narratives drown out more mundane, less flashy struggles taking place in residential areas, and the voices of families whose stories are harder to access if only because they perceive greater personal and financial risk in disclosing their stories to outsiders (such as having to pay fines or payoffs to officials to protect themselves and their families).

Ethnographies by researchers entrenched in ordinary, everyday life in postrevolutionary Cuba, such as the Lewis, Lewis, and Rigdon trilogy (1977–78) and Rosendahl (1997), are now outdated.[2] Since that time, writing has focused on "safer" topics, highlighting revolutionary accomplishments and such aspects of Cuban culture as sports (Price 2002); medicine (Feinsilver 1993); Santería (Wedel 2003; M. Clark 2005; Wirtz 2004); or music, dance, and the arts (Daniels 1995; Kirk and Padura Fuentes 2001; Perna 2005; Fernandes 2006; R. Moore 2006)—although, increasingly, no topic is actually safe from penetration by issues related to the Special Period crisis, as most of these books reveal. Nevertheless, they do not focus on what I claim are ordinary Cuban citizens' changing and increasingly negative relationship to the state, their unattainable aspirations, and their disappointments.

Like any summary of a country's history, the summary I present here is not disinterested. On the contrary, the information and tone I communicate are influenced by the interests and perspectives of my informants; I could not and would not have written this section in the same way prior to my fieldwork. As I am the filter of citizen-consumer dissatisfaction, this profile is not particularly promotional or even balanced when reporting the accomplishments of the Cuban state (though see Levinson and Brightman 1971; Randall 1974, 1981; Cole 1998; August 1999; Azicri 2000; Erisman 2000; Hernández 2003; Azicri and Deal 2004; for contrasting or supplementary views). I also recognize that opinions regarding Cuban politics and "structural adjustment," are contested in Latin America and the Caribbean.[3] Therefore, I write with the acute awareness that "gain for one group must be considered in the context of cost to another" and that "action is always in the interest of some publics and not others" (Sanday 2005: 1). For example, that which is in the interest of the U.S. business lobby and exiles in Miami is not always in the interest of Cuba's national sovereignty. More specifically to this thesis, what is in the interest of unsatisfied citizen-consumers and is connected to their "norms, values hopes and dreams of the future" (Sanday 2005: 4) may not, or some would say distinctly is not, in the interest of the very poor in their own country, or of the taxpaying public of the host countries that potentially absorb them.

While in this book I do not advocate one policy or political program over another, using an ethnographic lens, I do implicitly ask a slippery question: How free a market? Or, what is usually on the flip side of the coin: How wide a social safety net? I address these questions, in part, through decoding how markets—free, black, informal, gray, mixed, and global—operate in the daily lives of ordinary citizens in late-socialist Cuba. I will provide a rare glimpse into how everyday people manage and acquire goods, and the meanings they give to their search, not only as consumers, but also as citizens.

From Socialist Revolution to Special Period

Cuba's revolutionary government is often categorized as a socialist authoritarian regime, but it was not always that way, and it was not explicitly designed as such.[4] Fidel Castro's revolutionary government was established in January 1959, after the overthrow of Fulgencio Batista, who had been the leading figure in Cuban politics (through either direct or indirect leadership) since his military coup of 1934. The new Castro government was loosely designed by its leaders to be a "Dictatorship of the Proletariat"—a state in which the workers would hold exclusive rule. Castro did not declare it unequivocally a Marxist-Leninist state until 1961, and enjoyed relatively widespread popular support among poor families; rural families; idealists who hoped for freedom, independence, and services for all Cubans; and those who were drawn to Fidel's charisma and apparent passion for a new Cuba.[5]

Today, nearly a half-century has passed since the "triumph of the revolution" (most Cubans use the term "the triumph," *el triunfo*, no matter what their political stance concerning the current regime). Yet one of Cuba's most prominent political features is instead the exclusive rule of the country's single party—El Partido Comunista (PCC, locally referred to as just El Partido, "The Party")—led by Fidel Castro Ruz, and currently, since Fidel's emergency surgery and ceding of power, by his younger brother Raúl Castro Ruz.[6] Fidel Castro has maintained a centrally planned, or "command," economy since the first year of the revolution, making Cuba (along with North Korea) one of the world's last two enclaves of classical communism and centrally planned economies. In such an economy the state in theory controls wages, property ownership, and the circulation of goods within and across its borders, and most of the means of production are owned and run by the government. By some accounts, it is a state characterized by its "secrecy, monopoly and protectionism" (Gaidar 1990:

4). According to Cuban government statistics, around 75 percent of the labor force is employed by the state and another 10 percent work in government-run agricultural cooperatives (U.S. Department of State 2001).

Until 1990, the Cuban government alternately tightened and then loosened control over the economy—in terms of land, goods, services, and modes of production—through four key pieces of legislation. The Agrarian Reform Act of 1961 nationalized most foreign landholdings. In 1968, all sectors of the Cuban economy were nationalized, and free enterprise no longer existed legally in any form. It was also at this time that Castro began to formally embed Cuba in the economy of the Soviet Union and joined the CMEA (Council for Mutual Economic Assistance, or Comecon).[7] In 1977, the economy decentralized somewhat when farmers markets temporarily opened to free enterprise. Later, in 1986, the Rectification once again limited free enterprise (Mesa-Lago 2000; Corbett 2002: 92–94).

Global changes, in particular the collapse in 1990 of the CMEA—with which 80 percent of Cuba's trade was conducted at that time—precipitated an economic crisis in Cuba that forced Castro to declare the Período Especial en Tiempo de Paz (Special Period in Time of Peace), the official name given to the economic crisis in a speech by Castro in February 1990. The early phases of the Special Period, in the first half of the 1990s, were marked by austerity measures in tandem with a mandate to citizens to work hard and be patient in the face of shortages of food, medicine, clothing, shoes, paper, soap, gasoline, and other basic supplies at levels that they had not experienced under the revolutionary government. Desperation led to the *balsero* (rafter) crisis in 1994, when 35,000 Cubans took to the open sea in homemade rafts, heading for the United States, willing to risk death in order to escape material scarcity and political stagnation (for a review of scholarly literature on the crisis in the first half of the 1990s, see Pastor 1996; see also Erisman and Kirk 2006).

The U.S. trade embargo against Cuba (or *bloqueo*, "blockade," as it is referred to locally, emphasizing its extreme effects), was tightened by the Torricelli Act in 1992, then by the Helms-Burton Act in 1996, resulting in further Special Period reforms.[8] The ideological foundations of the self-proclaimed Marxist-Leninist state—or at least the policies reflecting those foundations—had been rocked. Ironically, many of the reforms drew on features of capitalist societies[9]—representing what has been called "timid but dramatic" moves towards the market (Mesa-Lago 2000). These included de-penalizing the dollar, opening free markets for agricultural products, allowing certain forms of self-employment, increasing foreign investment, and emphasizing tourism as the most important means of rebuilding the Cuban economy.

While shortages improved with economic recovery, and the worst of the Special Period was over by the mid-1990s, it was the ironic means of economic recovery that had the most lasting impact for Cuba's citizen-consumers. All liberalizing reforms, new to revolutionary Cuba, were meant to increase state revenue by any means necessary in order to ensure the egalitarian society established by the revolution. The Special Period reforms were justified by Castro as temporary measures that responded to the national state of emergency.[10] While socialism is still declared to be thriving in official state discourse, most of the market reforms are still in place, to a greater or lesser extent, and for an undesignated time. As a result, Cuba is still officially in a Special Period, though the worst of the austerity is over and it has moved into what I am calling late socialism—an awkward and ironic blend of capitalist and socialist strategies for national development and economic recovery.

Cubans themselves now often use the start of the Special Period and the disturbing paradoxes it presented—no longer the revolution itself—as a historical "ground zero," or reference point, of change, and there is a national discourse of *antes de* (before) the Special Period. That is, *antes de* in daily speech indexes the era before personal household economic crises and the population's loss of its basic luxuries: "*Antes de* we used to throw big birthday parties for our kids when they turned one. Not now." "*Antes de* you used to be able to get bras and underwear annually on the ration book. Not anymore." And more than any other specific reform of the Special Period, they see "dollarization" as having affected them profoundly and personally.[11] They explain that while access to dollars has afforded them new consumer freedoms, it has also created citizen-consumer dissatisfaction and, more than anything else, has permanently altered Cuban society by ushering in the twilight of the socialist revolution.

Specifically, Cuba has developed an unruly, two-tiered economy in the wake of dollarization (see Kildergaard and Orro Fernández 2000). As Cubans describe it, one can legally hold only one job, at low, state-controlled wages payable in pesos. Frustrating to Cuban consumers, however, is that most useful household products are available only in dollars in dollar stores (officially called TRDs—*tiendas de recuperación de divisas,* or "dollar recovery stores"), where prices are often inflated beyond their means (figure 1.1).

The Cuban government captures dollars and dollar remittances by allowing Cuban citizens to shop in state-run dollar stores, which sell clothing, food, and household items at high markups averaging more than 240 percent of face value by some estimates (Barberia 2002: 19). Local people told me they had heard all goods in dollar stores carried at least a 12 percent tax, but to their frustration there was no known way to confirm this, or to know where the money went. There were wild stories in circulation about a US$17 cabbage, a $13 box of dry cereal, and a $30 pack of twenty-four disposable diapers. While these are extremes, they nevertheless make pricing seem unpredictable

Figure 1.1. Cubans wait in line to enter a dollar store. The blue placard on the door reads: "Revolution is to emancipate ourselves and through our own efforts" (a quotation from Fidel's speech on International Workers Day, 2000). To the right, the logo indicates Visa credit cards are accepted.

and hyperbolic to ordinary shoppers earning, on average, the equivalent of US$17–19 (as of this writing) a month from their state salaries.

The merchandise in dollar stores is restricted, state-selected, and does not follow the laws of supply and demand. Furthermore, lack of access to dollars and the limited goods most Cubans can buy have "sharpened the longing for material abundance. The visibility of the new, consuming sectors, whether native Cubans or tourists, only served to increase many Cubans' dissatisfaction with their humble lifestyles" (Chomsky, Carr, and Smorkaloff 2003: 637). This phenomenon is central to the emergence of a broad base of unsatisfied citizen-consumers and to their acute sense of relative deprivation.

It is not feasible for Cuban citizens to organize or protest publicly concerning the ongoing difficulties of these changes or the frustrations they provoke. To their distaste, they are regularly required to attend state-organized marches under a particular banner. Socialist "civil society" is purportedly available through mass organizations (*organizaciones de masas*). Such organizations, such as the Committee for the Defense of the Revolution, the Federation of Cuban Women, and the Confederation of Cuban Workers, are millions of members strong (see Dilla 2003: 654), but the shadow public eschews active involvement in these organizations because of too tight an association with El Partido and the fear that involvement might further embroil them in the network of surveillance.

At syndicate election time citizens are accustomed to raising their hands unanimously for the first candidate mentioned—a silent agreement among attendees, so that the ritual will be over quickly and everyone can just go home as soon as possible.[12] For many years they have not expected to be able to express opinions freely in the press; they have disengaged from the national media, and do not see state press organs as a venue for more than receiving announcements. Most citizens are inured to these limitations, go through the motions, and view them as a fact of national life. Despite this backdrop, there was an attempt, known as Proyecto Varela (the Varela Project), to exercise the right of popular sovereignty in 2002, through gathering signatures on a petition to amend the national constitution, a project that ended in the incarceration of its organizing leaders and the harassment and expulsion from jobs and universities of those who openly supported it.[13]

"And come on," informants would say, "have you ever seen the names on the list? These were no ordinary people. They were people with connections inside and out who had the strength to stand up for this. This was not a popular movement." For all of these reasons, and also out of long habit, political conversations among ordinary people, though they do happen, are circumscribed and take place only with select people, inside homes, or when there is little chance of being overheard.

In these private conversations, one will hear that Cubans do not fully accept that the long-standing U.S. trade embargo, global imperialism, or their own weak and immoral materialism (the only explanations provided in the state-controlled news organs and scholarly publications) are the root causes of their problems. They see the Castros, and the laws of their regime, as what keeps them poor and dependent, and also what keeps Cuba, despite all of the potential of its educated and talented population, sadly *atrasado* (backwards, kept behind). At the same time they see their own desires as normal and as keeping pace with the rest of the developed world; their own tastes are much more like those of family in Miami and other U.S. cities than of their Caribbean or Central American neighbors.

To trump the system, and to satisfy their tastes, many citizens have come to depend almost entirely on a mixture of dollar remittances from family abroad, pilfering or stealing from the government workplace, and income earned from black-market enterprises. Others take advantage of the increasing tourist presence to rent *casas particulares* (private homes) to vacationers for dollars (a practice legalized in 1998, but practiced illegally and at high risk both before and after that date); to run *paladares* (home-based restaurants), technically seating twelve or fewer guests (see Henken 2002b); or to engage in *jineterismo* (hustling/prostitution)[14]—income-generating strategies that allow ordinary citizens to earn more in a week, a workday, or just one night than they would in a year or more at state wages. One of the most widely circulating testaments to Cuba's changing values and loss of socialist prowess—one which appears ubiquitously in the international press and travel guides, as well as in popular discourse—is that a *jinetero/a* can earn more in one night (approximately US$370) than a medical doctor can in one year (US$120) (calculations from author's interviews and an extrapolation in Mesa-Lago 2000).

Still, income does not solve the problem of obtaining goods unavailable in the seriously limited and unpredictable Cuban market. To counter this, Cubans with wide social and family networks also receive gifts hand-delivered from families, friends, and visitors from the United States in order to obtain direct access to higher-quality products (particularly electronics, clothing, medicine, nonperishable foods, and baby care and beauty products). The presence of these products provides a veneer of relative wealth and consumer access in some homes that belies low salaries and market caprice, even making it seem to outsiders as though Cuba's national system of distribution is working.

In reality, the Cuban socialist distribution system is weak, and continues to grow weaker in the face of informal and underground operations, abounding police corruption, payoffs to officials, and growing disparities and jealousies between what were once comrades (*compañeros*). Nevertheless, a public safety net continues to serve as something of a national equalizer. Against the fiscal odds, the Cuban government has continued to provide universal education, health care, and modest rations to its citizens. Cubans still hold a degree of pride in the history and achievements of Cuba's socialist system, particularly in health care.[15] Yet, as citizens will explain, these public goods, the "jewels in the crown" of the revolution, are not truly "free" in any sense of the word.

Payoffs are built into nearly every supposedly free service, but more than that, the cost of being a Cuban is too much to bear for a lifetime.

Cuba has been a land of shortages for years now, citizens explain, where not only ubiquitous state ownership but also the perpetual threat of state surveillance makes nothing private by any stretch of the imagination, and most gravely, where there is no future for themselves or their families. Cuba is a place to leave, to flee. They have visions of a much-referenced *allá* (literally way over there, far, and beyond—evoking elsewhere, but mainly synonymous with America), full of creature comforts, conveniences, and desirable goods sold for reasonable prices—all this as well civic freedoms, which are sometimes mentioned, but are not elaborated on with the same detail or intensity.

What Cuban public space lacks in overt commerciality and expression of public opinion, it compensates for in the charm of outdoor living and communal street space where children run, shout, and play stickball freely in the road. In most neighborhoods, music, noise, cooking smells, and voices drift easily, laundry flaps openly, and neighbors hang out on stoops and porches of Havana's often-deteriorating prerevolutionary mansions and tenements, and in their passageways and courtyards, where Cubans share in parallel struggles to get by. But despite this apparent neighborhood cohesiveness (and sometimes because of the suffocating nature of it), Cubans also feel desperately trapped as citizens and as consumers in the face of official neighborhood surveillance organs, lack of options, and stagnation.[16] As an informant wrote to me in April 2006, referring to my visit to Cuba three years earlier, "If at this very moment you crossed our doorstep, you would see that all remains the same as when you left. There are few chances for change."

Cubans cite economic traps, more than anything else, as their motivation for endlessly hatching plans to escape. If they could just reach U.S. soil, they would magically be granted asylum under the 1996 Cuban Adjustment Act and become U.S. citizens within one year of their arrival, simply by proving their Cuban identity. Many Cubans have friends and family who live abroad, simultaneously linking Cuba directly to somewhere else and giving citizen-consumers more intense feelings of isolation and lack of progress through their inability to purchase, own, or experience what their kin in exile have, let alone to join them.

While in reality most cannot physically break free because of the remarkably tight government restrictions over citizens' ability to travel outside the island, I argue that any access to and control over dollars and foreign goods nevertheless precipitates some freedom from the state. Such decreased economic dependence—and therefore reduced overall interaction with the state as a restrictive entity—opens unexpected avenues for a particular form of civil liberty and social change while people bide their time waiting for the Castros to lose power. This development of an extrapolitical and extralegal "private" market paradoxically allows for a form of public sphere that I will illustrate in my discussion of Cuban unsatisfied citizen-consumers and the development of the Cuban shadow public.

Cuba as Welfare State

The welfare state in this project is a key macro-institutional structure. I define a welfare state government as one that provides or directly subsidizes the basic social security and "consumption needs" of its citizens, most notably health care, education, unemployment insurance, old-age pensions, and housing, and, as I emphasize, creates an uneasy intimacy between citizens and the state as the paternalistic provider.[17] Furthermore, the expectations of these provisions shape a particular notion of "rights-bearing citizens" in the collective public consciousness.

Cuba's welfare state provides the most universal coverage of any Latin American welfare state, which makes it regionally exceptional. Yet despite Cuba's regional exceptionalism, it shares features with other Latin American welfare states. The expansion of the role of government in the social welfare arena was a defining feature of many nations from immediately post–World War II until the 1970s, and most modern nation-states still provide at least some welfare benefits to their populations. Nevertheless, to both earn an international reputation and be locally understood as a welfare state, comprehensive social provisions and a national distribution system must not only be guaranteed in the national constitution, but state leadership must also reinforce that guarantee in legislation and political rhetoric. Yet, most important for the central argument of this book are the cultural elements of welfare-state membership and the uneasiness of the relationship. The tension between the "experience-distant" (Geertz 1983) state ideology and policy of socialism versus the lived experience of receiving state welfare is expressed primarily through instances of citizen discourse occurring within households.

Welfare states "are compelled by their logic to be closed systems that seek to insulate themselves from external pressures that restrict rights and benefits to members. They nonetheless fail to be perfectly bounded in a global economy marked by competition, interdependence, and extreme inequality" (Freeman 1986). This is certainly true in the case of Latin America's welfare model, which has been characterized as being in prolonged crisis. Under the intense pressure to continue making social provisions in the context of political and economic strain and, in most countries in the region (though not Cuba), within the context of a growing population, Latin America has experienced ongoing adversity, peaking in what has been dubbed the "lost decade" of the 1980s and Cuba's Special Period of the 1990s. Overall, as with other welfare states in decline, the result has been uneven development, low coverage of the population, increasing privatization (Sherraden, Page-Adams, and Yadama 1995), and as I have mentioned, the growth of "informal security regimes" (Gough and Wood 2004).

Like the rest of Latin America, Cuba has been managing intense fiscal crises over the last three decades, and although it has made a firm commitment to keep its social, health, and educational services free and its coverage universal (see Feinsilver 1993), the system is suffering from shortages and riddled with corruption at all levels (see Crabb 2001; Díaz-Briquets and Pérez-López 2006). The result is that unsatisfied citizen-consumers have turned to informal security regimes, since, when "people assume that they cannot meet their security needs via services from the state or via participation in an open labour market," they rely to a greater extent on community and family relationships (Gough and Wood 2004: 50). In other words, there is an increasing reliance on forms of private and unofficial support that predate the revolution and are also the primary mechanisms for social support in countries with no public safety net whatsoever.

In any analysis of contemporary Cuba, it has become requisite to mention some of the hardships that ordinary Cubans have undergone during the Special Period, but few projects have shed light on how official state ideology, official national narratives, and the art of welfare government usually stand in contrast to the lived experience of dissatisfaction in late-socialist Cuba. This is my aim: to provide a thick description of late-socialist reform, and in the process, to illuminate citizen-consumer–produced meanings of the era.

Cuba as Late-Socialist State

Since the dawn of the Special Period, there has been a growing consensus that Cuba is undeniably in transition. Recently, some scholars have begun to locate Cuba in a historical moment with characteristics of late socialism (see Hernandez-Reguant 2004, 2009; Fernandes 2006; Gordy 2006: M. Hill 2007; Whitfield 2008; Venegas 2009). Late socialism is variously defined in the Cuban context, but consistently emphasizes the collision, blending, hybridization, and above all, the *paradoxes* of "Cuba's venture into a sort of never-never land between communism and capitalism . . . [as] the island has drifted between two opposing economic systems" (Chávez 2005: 1) (figure 1.2). Differently stated, "Cuba is a laboratory of pre-post-communism and an ideal environment to study the dying beast while it is still (barely) breathing" (Codrescu 1999: 2).

Figure 1.2. A poster advertising forty-four years of socialist revolution hangs in the window of a modern car showroom—an ironic late-socialist palimpsest.

In her relevant discussion of recent societal transformation in China, Zhang (2001) uses *late socialism* to avoid implying that current transformations will necessarily lead to the complete demise of the socialist regime, thus leaving it in a contradictory "pre-post" state:

Rather than conveying a sense of breakdown, rupture, and death of the existing system, late refers to a condition characterized by some fundamentally new developments mixed with the legacies of the old system. Hence, the notion of "late socialism" is similar to Jameson's conception of "late capitalism" in that "what 'late' generally conveys is the sense that something has changed, that things are different, that we have gone through a transformation of the life world which is somehow decisive but incomparable with the older" (Jameson 1997: xxi). (Zhang 2001: 196–97)

Irony in Late Socialism

Perhaps the way that late-socialist change, and the friction caused by that change, is felt most is through ironies. Hernandez-Reguant (2004) captures an ultimate late-socialist irony at the commercial level in tracing the trajectory of how the famous portrait of Che, icon of revolutionary sacrifice and socialist ideals of collectivization and selflessness, has been copyrighted. Any time his image is used, it reaps a profit for the Cuban photographer known as "Korda," on top of the US$75,000 he won in damages for copyright infringement. "Korda had clearly triumphed," she writes, but highlighting the ambiguity of the victory she continues, "so had all of Cuba, for he donated this substantial sum of hard currency to the cash-starved coffers of the country's welfare system. However, at the end of the affair, it was still unclear whether the now copyrighted Che—and his legacy to Cuban late socialism—had really beaten the forces of capitalism or rather surreptitiously joined them" (Hernandez-Reguant 2004: 4).

Late socialism in Cuba is also reflected in a spate of new state slogans that "have been invented to try to link current developments to revolutionary traditions" (Gordy 2006: 383). At the Carlos Tercero Mall in Havana one sign reads, "In the New Millennium, Sales + Economy + Efficiency = Revolution" (Gordy 2006). The collision of systems also creates contempt among citizens: "Official socialist rhetoric in Cuba often appears to be mocked by daily life. Street hustlers wear T-shirts condemning the blockade or urging the return of Elián while they work in the illegal economy and hope to meet a foreigner who will take them out of the country" (384).

Late Socialism in the Global Context

Despite the lack of regime change and some of its unique anachronisms (vintage cars, crumbling colonial architecture, and the same commander in chief for nearly a half-century), Cuba does not exist in a global vacuum. The "myth of isolation" and the efforts to present Cuba as disconnected from the world have both served to promote Cuba as an exotic destination and allowed Cuba to carry out its "idiosyncratic national policy" with regard to national security and sovereignty (see D. Fernández 2005). One way that Cuba has been informally connected to the world is through its comparison to communist (or formerly communist) settings, with communist symbols and realities, albeit superimposed onto a sunny, Caribbean milieu:

It's Moscow, but instead of grim-looking white people walking down the road, you have happier-looking white and black and brown people walking down the road.... It's China, too, with the bicycles, whole families packed on some. (Tattlin 2002: 7–8)

I remember being a contented Pioneer, safe in the cocoon of the state, protected from the nasty news of the real world, warm in the embrace of Stalin, my true father. Stalin's moustache, like Castro's beard, watched over my childhood, a horizon of security. Socialism had made it similarly safe for children in places as dissimilar as Romania and Cuba." (Codrescu 1999: 92)

Other examples include, "A tropical version of Stalin, even behind beards, could be tropically lethal" (Cabrera Infante 1992), or references to the regime as "Still Isolated Behind the Palm Curtain" (Corbett 2002: chap. 14).

Opening up "alternative geographies" and analytic frames for Cuba, and even arguing for Cuba's possible inclusion in post-Soviet studies, is a crucial step for understanding Cuba's place in the world (see Hernandez-Reguant 2005). Part of the larger late-socialist scholarly project is concerned with local socialist transitions and can be mapped onto a larger topography of economic and cultural globalization. This is particularly necessary since there are undeniably "shrinking horizons of international communism" (Hernandez-Reguant 2004: 5), which have changed the close international relationships and dependencies of countries such as Cuba and subsequently have transformed its relationship to other countries across the globe.

In a sense, the *post-Soviet* era immediately ushered in Cuba's *late-socialist* era. Instead of its economic relations being tied almost exclusively to the USSR (and the CMEA), as they were in the late 1980s, over the last fifteen years, Cuba has been forced to forge new allegiances and establish joint business and urban renewal ventures on the island. European companies and countries (especially Spain, Italy, France, and Germany) have launched a series of cooperative ventures. Cuba has also strengthened relations with Canada; formed a regional, populist brotherhood with left-leaning governments in Venezuela and Bolivia; increased trade with Mexico; and, because of loopholes in the embargo, also increased its commerce with the United States. Indeed, the United States now provides a surprising 30 percent of Cuba's food imports (CBS Broadcasting 2006). In addition, there has been significant growth in Cuba's tourist sector, with visitors arriving from all over the world (figure 1.3).[18]

These are structural changes reflecting global capital and markets, and they provide an important backdrop to changing social identifications among Cubans themselves. These include the strengthening of shared cultural networks among Cuban international diaspora communities as a consequence of both the repositioning of Cuba and the "diasporization" and de-politization

Figure 1.3. Schoolchildren in Old Havana buy snacks in pesos at the kiosk on the left while restoration efforts indicated by the scaffolding in the background hope to attract tourist dollars.

of Cuban migration away from the hot spot of Miami and into an increasing number of other cities and towns around the world. Throughout this book I emphasize the global in several ways that contribute to the conversations on Cuba's transnational identity as it undergoes a transition away from classical socialism.

Cuba's Late-Socialist Future

As part of the collective scholarly project of defining late socialism, there have been recent critiques against appealing to "binary socialism." According to Alexei Yurchak (2005: 5), a leading figure in this argument, clear-cut categories subject to dichotomization include oppression/resistance, repression/freedom, the state/the people, official economy/second economy, official culture/counterculture, totalitarian language/counter-language, public self/private self, truth/lie, reality/dissimulation, and morality/corruption. Yurchak and others propose that such binaries should not be invoked over a more nuanced "self-embedding or interweaving of these categories" (Gal and Kligman 2000: 51; see also Gal 2005, Lampland 1995), or the "range of conflicting meanings" involving public versus private (Warner 2002: 29; see also Weintraub and Kumar 1997 on the "Great Dichotomy"), all which may in the end reveal more about daily life under late socialism.

As subtle and appealing as these blended categories are intellectually, they are perhaps best suited to the retrospective analysis of the former Soviet Union and post-socialist Eastern Europe, where these ideas have been most widely applied by theorists of the "velvet" revolutions (see Lemon 2000; Boyer 2005; Monroe 2005 on Europe; see also Hagedorn 2001; Hernandez-Reguant 2004; Frederick 2005; and Fernandes 2006 for the Cuban case). I propose that in the contemporary lived experience of Cubans in general, and for unsatisfied citizen-consumers who compose the shadow public I describe in particular, many of these categories remain active cultural categories around which they must constantly navigate. I also argue that it is easier to analyze late socialism in retrospect, when it has already come and gone, than when it is in process. In an era of post-socialism one can go back and talk about what has passed and how it has been replaced by something else.

Ethnographies of post-socialism can be summarized as including transformations of social and cultural logics; power relations; and people's understandings, aspirations, and practices since the decline of socialism. The category of post-socialism allows analysts to consider the position of a given nation-state in relation to the larger map of economic and cultural globalization and transnationalism (see Grant 1995; Verdery 1996, 2000, 2003; Wanner 1998; Verdery and Buroway 1999; Hann 2002; Humphrey 2002; Mandel and Humphrey 2002; Petryna 2002; Dunn 2004). This characterization of a post-socialist ethnography also fits most goals of this book. The difference is however that in Cuba, as I have said, we do not yet have a secure retrospective view of what socialism was; we cannot speak of socialism in the past tense. What I present can therefore only be an ethnography of late-socialist transition with many binaries—even if they are paradoxical or ironic—still real, crude, and in place for the people who live them, not ready to be analyzed away. Furthermore, now, while citizen-consumers are still in the heat of daily distress, and still bearing the weight of late-socialist stagnancy, socialist dichotomies remain open wounds. Cubans know that the passage of time does not guarantee regime change. As some say, it has already been fifty years.

I

Private

Elena's Bedroom
Apartment Complex
Havana, Cuba

"Can I ask you something?" inquired Elena, a divorced, middle-aged mother of three and a practicing Catholic. It was just a few days after we had met in a leafy side street in Havana, and I was visiting her apartment. Lowering her voice, she then added, "come into the bedroom." Cubans, as I discovered first through Elena, generally know the best tactical locations to have private conversations—the spaces where they are least likely to be overheard by "those who overhear"—usually somewhere in the recesses of one's home. Or sometimes they purposefully at least allow the blare of the TV or stereo to drown out the details of what they are saying to the outside world.

"Look," she continued, "I need your help accessing e-mail, and I was wondering if I could come with you to an Internet center next time you go." It did not seem like a major request, but both her nervousness and the momentous way she framed the question made me wary.

She went on, "It is not only that using the Internet is very expensive here, and that it takes me such a long time to type, which wastes even more money, but sometimes it just looks better for a Cuban to come with a foreigner to an Internet place. And there are some messages I really need to send." She looked at me for a moment with tense, hopeful eyes, but continued before waiting for my response.

"You can type the messages that I write by hand, save them on your computer disk, and we can just bring the disk to the Internet place and send them off very fast." She tried to further sweeten the deal: "You will learn a lot about the situation in Cuba for your project through what I write." I agreed to her plan.

"But," she added, lowering her voice one more notch, and now moving her lips very little as she spoke, "what I write is private. And even that I am going to the Internet is private information. No one but you needs to know. ¿Entendiste?" (Understood?)

In the context of heavy state control, citizens' continuing economic reliance on the welfare state, and mounting consumer desires in late-socialist Cuba, that which is "private," though more common than before, is still rare and costly. Although this fact gives whatever is private a high value on a number of dimensions, the most important of these, in people's own lived experience, is related to maintaining control. For example, one can choose to conceal or display the private at will. One holds veto power over whom a given item or experience is to be shared with. In addition, the private is not associated with hidden duties to *la patria* (the fatherland) or El Partido (the Party), and thereby is less associated with close watch and regulation. Consequently, the private harbors or embodies the potential for what many see as higher quality, more authentic, and more intimate social interactions.

Emphasizing the private is, of course, premised on a prior distinction between the private and the public. As I mentioned in chapter 1, this distinction runs somewhat counter to current intellectual trends in the social sciences.

Figure I.1. *Uso particular*: a "private use vehicle" is parked alongside the pastries from a lavish first birthday party, paid for with profits from a *negocio particular* (private business).

These tend to dismantle binary categories in general, and to consider the public versus the private a false dichotomy in the analysis of citizen-state relationships in particular. Equally relevant to writings about Cuba, these also tend to critique the "neoliberal project."[1]

Although these are important trends, I argue here that there is a critical difference between non-reductionist thinking concerning binary categories of late socialism as an analytic tool versus the lived experience of late socialism. In the late-socialist Cuban population I introduce here, in particular, public and private are locally important categories. People also routinely use these categories to mark themselves as citizens or consumers who prefer and actively seek *lo particular* (that which is private) whether as an end in itself or as an alternative form of capital (figure I.1). In their citizen's-eye view, therefore, the private and public are easily distinguished, the boundaries between them apparent to all and filled with meaning.

In this section, I define what constitutes the private in Cuba and how these definitions of private blend modes of citizenship and consumption. I describe how accumulating the private and engaging in private experiences—enjoying intimate, domestic, family space; communicating by e-mail; interacting privately with written texts in limited circulation; obtaining goods and services on the private market; achieving private ownership of things—shift individuals away from the state and towards a "public" composed of citizen-consumers (even if it is a shadow public) in the late-socialist era. Specifically, chapter 2 illustrates the importance of private space in this process. Chapter 3 expands the argument to include ethnographic cases of private enterprise and private forms of communication and protest.

Private Space

In defining private space in Cuba, I must first recognize some contrasting attributes of public space, and what important private, citizen-consumer details do not register on the radar in public space and the official domain. Some official buildings are the lumbering, gray, Soviet-headquarters kind. Others are the colorful, mansion-converted-to-ministry kind that dot many residential neighborhoods in the city.[1] These buildings are pillared and majestically repainted in what I came to think of as "Caribbean socialist colors" such as canary yellow, salmon, or aquamarine—emblematic of the state's capacity to envelop lavish, formerly private homes in order to house public services.

Mansion to Ministry

I would at times seek the shade and the cool breeze of the electric fans that the lobbies of such buildings offered, but my most important task was to approach the simple, wooden, computer-less reception desks to inquire about opportunities that would allow me to stay in the country while following tight Cuban regulations concerning research visas. Sympathetic but powerless *secretarias*, ambivalent handmaidens of the state, lured me into the bureaucratic labyrinth, telling me to come back again on a certain day, since the person with whom I really needed to speak was not in. While I rarely met the important, faceless characters lurking in the recesses of such buildings, I did come to know the secretaries, and while we could rarely discuss anything substantial, we would greet each other with a kiss on the cheek, and they would recommend that I sit and rest, have a drink, nurse the baby, and keep company in the quiet inactivity of the aptly termed *sala de espera* (waiting room).

Down a side corridor of one Health Ministry building, I changed the baby's diaper on a bench next to a lolling pile of freshly minted José Martí busts that were to be distributed to other official buildings in the municipality (figure 2.1).[2] Another breezy, marbled waiting area in a research institute seemed to have a soporific effect: male professors with pens in their shirt-front pockets dozed peacefully on worn, vinyl couches.

Figure 2.1. Busts of José Martí not only mark most public buildings but here his likeness towers over the Plaza de la Revolución (Revolution Square). Leader of the Cuban independence movement, Martí is at once a Cuban state icon and a hero among dissidents, representing freedom, independence, and democracy.

These ministry images reflect the absence of bustle in public, official spaces—and also a distinct lack of productivity and meaningful interaction. It is such ministries' simultaneous ubiquity and inactivity, albeit framed within part of the bureaucratic rationale, that allows the current communist system to be maintained. These are the buildings in which citizens are officially employed as state functionaries. But nothing really gets done in them. Rather, they are subdivisions of a state that prevents anything out of the ordinary from occurring. Such institutions keep people, as David, my key informant explained, *inmovilizado* (immobilized, tied up, unable to go any farther). Some systems are maintained through changes in policy, but the stronger, more elusive systems are upheld through a constant dormancy.[3]

Public Posts

The state not only envelops buildings in order to maintain its system, it also shapes the Cuban urban and neighborhood landscape—billboards, murals, slogans, and state-sponsored, neatly stenciled "graffiti" on walls serving as a constant reminder of state presence, further marking off official, public space (see also Rosenberg 1995; Gordy 2006). Despite recent market-oriented reforms, public space still lacks a sense of overt commerciality and consumer choice or citizen opinion. Commercial billboards, banned by law since the triumph of the revolution, have been famously replaced by state-sponsored socialist messages, as if the state were "selling a new brand of cigarettes" (Brotherton 2005: 340, quoting fiction writer Cristina García). This means that the most visible messages in public space are official, are posted by the Communist Party, and fall under what I consider seven basic categories:

1. Promoting the triumphs of the revolution
2. Denouncing U.S. imperial aggression at home and abroad
3. Commemorating revolutionary events or achievements
4. Promoting tourism in Cuba
5. Advertising upcoming patriotic events
6. Promoting national public health or social service campaigns
7. Celebrating the strength and presence of the Comité de Defensa de la Revolución (CDR), the nationwide, neighborhood-level community safety and state surveillance organ

Most of these public messages are of little interest to unsatisfied citizen-consumers, and their ubiquity and consistency make them a sort of visual equivalent of white noise, unrelated to unsatisfied citizen-consumers' private desires or projects at home.

Cubans do sometimes transform the meaning of the public billboards through jokes, however, turning political messages into personal, consumer ones. A journalist describes a huge billboard at the José Martí International Airport entrance that beckons visitors to "come back soon." He describes the image of "smiling Cubans, waving, giving peace signs, and holding a single finger in the air, as if to say 'Cuba #1.' The big joke in Havana right now is that the people on the billboard are gesturing with their hands for what size shoes to bring back. 'You see, that guy wears a size five,' they say, 'and his daughter needs a size two.'" (Corbett 2002: 53). They also joke about the billboards commanding civilians "Adelante!" (Forward!), which they say should really declare "Atraso!" (Backward state!). Public messages are privately transformed with regularity, but it is hard to sense the impact or extent of collective criticism, since it is diffuse, fragmented, and selectively articulated, only with certain people and only in certain spaces.

This is a key feature of the criticism voiced by what I am calling the shadow public. There are crucial details and dissatisfactions, private thoughts and wishes, that citizens are conditioned to withhold in public types of spaces (see related discussion of the "official public" and the "hidden intimate" in Kharkhordin 1999: 357). As Warner (2002: 26) writes, "The boundary between bedroom and market, home and meetinghouse can be challenged or violated, but it is at least clear enough to be spatially distinct."

Setha Low's application of Carr and colleagues' (1992) analytic framework for defining the publicness of spaces and "spatial rights" is relevant to this conversation on space in Cuba. Low filters spatial rights the following way: "*Access*: the right to enter and remain in a place; *freedom of action*: the ability to carry on activities in the public space; *claim*: the ability to take over a space; *change*: the ability to modify the environment and *ownership*: the ultimate form of control" (Low 2000: 241). Until very recently in Cuba, each of these "spatial rights" has been limited, and some would say are increasingly so, despite some market-oriented reforms. For example, from the early 1990s until 2008, Cuban citizens were prohibited entry into state facilities such as luxury hotels and related tourist sites, to which they used to have full and free (or very low cost) access—a policy some citizens called *discriminación* and that the international press referred to as "tourist apartheid" (see the epilogue for an update). As in any nation-state, freedom of action, claim, ability to change, and ownership of all public space is limited and monitored by the state, but in Cuba the restrictions are taken to an extreme, and Cubans feel they must monitor carefully what they say and do in parks, plazas, boulevards, malls, museums, marches, meetings, queues, and so on. Because of these constraints, home and "private property" have become increasingly important and meaningful spaces in which to do things.

Moving along the surface of Cuba, absorbing the urban and institutional landscape, having conversations in public spaces, and cooling off in the marble halls of officialdom, it is hard to see the Cuba that I came to know, one composed of a shadow public. Trapped within a monitored social network, a foreigner could easily believe that most Cubans are content with the existing system of government and unambiguously committed to socialism, and that problems that they face were brought on primarily by the tightening of the U.S. embargo.

Indeed, the "real" Cuba, Cubans tell you, happens behind closed doors, inside ordinary people's homes, in their living rooms and kitchens, and on their balconies and rooftops.[4] These are the spaces of Cuba's "shadow public," where things are beneath the surface. To mobilize or gain any real sense of the activity and perspective of average citizens, one must—as anywhere, but particularly in Cuba—enter private space.

Entering Private Space: Scenes from the Neighborhood

At the end of the dinner hour, another spring evening closes in on a neighborhood near Havana. Down a narrow residential alleyway, a series of open windows reveal the interiors of Cuban homes, framing a row of live scenes, offering up fleeting glimpses into private Cuban domestic worlds. Those worlds are just inches away from anyone passing by. One window reveals a smiling mother carrying a freshly baked flan: perfectly circular, caramel on top. She leans over to present it to her husband and young son, who have finished their dinner and remain seated across from each other at the little glass dining table. The husband's mouth forms an O and the boy brings his hands together in anticipation: a moment of simple delight, a little family making it in Cuba, able to enjoy a surprise at the end of a dinner at home. All three look up to greet me and my family, and we move on.

Each time I passed the row of windows in the neighborhood, the scenes inside them would be somewhat different, but they created a familiar collage over time—the hiss of an unattended compression pot leaking the earthy smell of black beans, the only reliable staple; an extended family crowded around a TV in the semidarkness waiting for the state broadcast of the Saturday-night movie, only to find that a rebroadcast of Fidel's four-hour speech from the day before would preempt it; the vigorous sounds of women sweeping away leaves and debris after a heavy afternoon rain; a man slouched in a chair, taking a nap, home from work for the day though it is still early afternoon; three women sitting together at a dining room table with nail polish bottles and acetone as one bends over to start painting another's nails; a plump, newly retired woman wearing a summer housedress, fresh after her shower, talking with animation on her fancy Panasonic cordless phone, another gift made possible by her son in Miami, but this one shared with her eighty-year-old upstairs neighbor, who uses it to speak to her daughter in Miami but then forgets to hang it up, driving the plump woman crazy, because she might miss a call from her son. "¡Perdóname!" the older woman shouts down from her balcony, having again forgotten to hang up the phone, "¡Estoy media loca!" (I'm sorry . . . I'm half-crazy). They both worry they will only speak to their children through the phone, perhaps until they die, they explain to me on separate occasions, a sorry replacement for a real visit.

All of these people are used to living with the stress of continual entanglement in the illegality, corruption, and secrecy that allows them to make ends meet while avoiding government informers. But one of the things that bothers people like them most is the sense that few of their belongings actually belong to them. Acquiring, protecting, and maintaining any type of private property or private goods in Cuba requires time, energy, and sometimes more money for taxes or payoffs. Furthermore, what were once private goods can be con-fiscated as public property if ever-changing rules are not followed, making ownership unstable. Perhaps more than class or income, the number of private possessions you are able to maintain dictates your status in Cuba.

Private Problems, Private Guide

The person who deftly guided me through the ins and outs of Cuban poli-tics, culture, and practice was David, my key informant in Cuba, whose name appears throughout this text as a source of local knowledge. I stay in touch with him to the present day, tapping into his indigenous expertise and mak-ing sure that I "got it right" and that my information remains accurate and up-to-date.

David lived with his wife, Tatiana, and their school-aged daughter, Wendy, in a small, welcoming apartment up the road from me, and we visited each other daily. Tatiana was also an indispensable key informant, though primar-ily in the domestic sphere of child care, the Cuban kitchen, shopping, launder-ing, and how to *resolver* (resolve, a very common Cuban verb, see discussion in chapter 4) my various predicaments in the local environment. I also paid Tatiana to launder (we did not have a washing machine but she did) and oc-casionally to clean. While this income helped her family significantly, allow-ing them to indulge in a few luxuries they had not enjoyed in years, such as going out dancing or paying the entry fee to a hotel pool, our relationship was primarily social, with many shared meals, movies, and long evenings of conversation at both of our apartments.

David immediately showed interest in my project and presence, and our first conversation was several hours long. He presented himself as sensitive, knowledgeable, balanced, and observant. He thought quietly to himself, spoke in direct and explicit ways about his political concerns and observations about Cubans, and helped me interpret difficult events. David was well-read, was interested in international news and politics, had lived for years in a Central European country completing a state-sponsored degree in economics, and spoke three foreign languages fluently. He was nationalistic in the sense that he spoke of other Cubans highly, defended them in difficult times, and asked me, as an explicit favor, to do the same in my writing. David said he planned on staying in Cuba, not wanting to separate from friends and family and being curious to see "how the story ends."

Still, David was capable of being quite critical of Cuba. Whenever David and I were talking and the content heated up, he would close the door and start whispering, looking up nervously to check the identity of anyone who cast a shadow while passing by the window. In an early conversation he explained, summing up the basic problem of privacy in Cuba: "'Él' es el dueño de todo." ["He"[5] (Fidel) owns everything]. But, of course, that is not going to work. 'Here, this is yours, this is the title, but you don't own it?!' What kind of system is this?" demanded David, laughing and then describing some problems with property and control in Cuba. "Luckily, *el subterráneo* [the underground] takes care of it all. You can buy and sell *anything*," he assured me. "Out of curiosity, we've even had our apartment appraised by a private specialist." He added, "It's worth 16,000 U.S. dollars on the current market."

He continued on the topic of privacy, "Cubans have grown used to having a public and a private life, a *doble vida* or a *doble moral* [double life, double standard].[6] There is that which you do in the street, which can be seen openly. And there is that which you do with your friends, your family, which only some people know about. The ways you live, and the ways you acquire things." This double life allows Cubans to maintain public support for the revolution while their private activities undermine its values.

The CDR and the Everyday Bridge between Public and Private Space

There are, however, many unwelcome bridges between public and private space that interfere with comfortably maintaining a *doble moral*. The CDR is the most unwelcome and also most common bridge. Any discussion of any length in Cuba must include a mention of the CDR, neighborhood watchdog and the backbone of revolutionary surveillance, although it is variably defined. I asked a committed CDR president, an Afro-Cuban woman who had migrated from the east in 1959 and had maintained her position since the establishment of the CDR on September 28, 1960, to explain what, exactly, the CDR does. "Defend the Revolution! Maintain ourselves on high guard! Make sure the neighborhood is clean and hygienic! Make sure it is safe from thieves!"[7] She bellowed proudly in reply.

The formal goals and actual activities of the CDR were more diverse in the early years of its establishment. As Lewis, Lewis, and Rigdon write (1977–78: 3:xxi), CDRs "are active in a broad range of programs including public health, education, political education, urban reform, sports and recreation, local administration as well as in surveillance activities." Consequently, they recruit volunteers to work in various sectors, particularly agriculture, encourage adult education, and organize study groups.

Since the CDR was established by Castro in 1960, citizens have been organized into *barrios* (neighborhoods) of three hundred. In its ideal form, the volunteer CDR president takes note of the comings and goings of the people under his or her charge and reports to the Party any unusual or illegal behavior.

Surveillance and reporting could pertain to anything: noting new goods that residents bring into their homes, ensuring that everyone attends mandatory marches and community meetings, making certain that the neighborhood is safe and guarded at night from crime and delinquency and that neighborhood children are getting their vaccines on time, spotting suspicious sources of income, and knowing when residents leave for and return from trips. In short, the CDR makes all matters considered private in most other settings into matters of public concern, making these committees the primary mechanism that keeps ordinary citizens in line with revolutionary priorities. Any Cuban born in the last fifty years has never known life without this neighborhood-level policing.

Such is the theory. In reality, the absolute power of the CDR is flexible, depending on the personality and beliefs of the neighborhood CDR president, the historical era, the current directives from higher-ups and also, I noticed, the mood or level of insecurity of the person talking. It seemed the importance of the CDR president would shift, depending on what plan the informant was hatching.

For example, David first introduced me to the contemporary relative insignificance of the CDR, in this era of payoffs and a flourishing black market. "It's a dead body," he declared plainly, without lowering his voice, as we chatted in his kitchenette while his wife showed me how to grind garlic and fresh herbs picked off local bushes with an impressive mortar and pestle. "It exists in name only. Seriously," he continued, "our CDR president is just some fat black lady whose son is in jail."

But when David was switching jobs and becoming involved in a new underground enterprise, the importance of the CDR suddenly mushroomed in his mind. His building was located across the street from the home of the CDR president (to whom, for reasons of local politics and to make my alliances clear to my informants, I never introduced myself, and with whom I never had any direct contact). He mentioned that when someone is switching jobs, the new employer is obligated to get a report on the applicant from the applicant's CDR president.

David was really hoping to leave his dead-end managerial post at a state warehouse and land a coveted position at a Cuban-European joint-venture company. This would provide him with the rare opportunity to train and work alongside foreign professionals; have access to computers, the Internet, and his own e-mail account; and most importantly, learn technical and marketing skills that could actually matter in the world outside of contemporary Cuba, and therefore a world beyond Fidel. He now had private information to protect, and he spent a couple of nervous weeks lurking around and speaking sotto voce about anything potentially illicit, in a way that I did not associate with him and that reminded me of much more paranoid informants, who were nervously hatching escape plans all the time.

He told me, sounding anxious and down, that rumors were circulating that Fidel wanted to reinvigorate the CDRs, which seemed unbearable given his current frame of mind. But soon everything fell into place; he was offered the job (regardless of whatever might have been in his history or CDR report, David was multilingual, fluent in a language important for direct communication with European executives bringing money into Cuba, making him the most valuable candidate). Communicating his private thoughts carefully and maintaining a *doble moral* had been essential in securing the job.

E-mail Elena's Space

Elena, whom I happened upon on a quiet side street as I ran neighborhood errands, is another person who opened the door to this other, private world for me. I suspect anyone who spends any time in Cuba, and especially anyone who does fieldwork, develops a relationship with someone like Elena, someone who eagerly leads you inside and begins to tell you the unofficial story in hushed tones, as if she (or he) would have blown a gasket if she had not happened upon you that day. People like Elena approach outsiders because it is easier and safer to speak about problems quietly with foreign visitors than with other Cubans, as they are more trustworthy with information and are unlikely to report you.

Nearly any description of Cuba by travel writers or journalists (who hold the current descriptive monopoly on Cuba) contains the pivotal moment of meeting such a person, but how the relationship develops shapes the plot. In Cuba, foreigners are safe, potential links out, and since there is no real or secure public sphere in which to voice opinions and concerns, foreigners effectively serve as ephemeral nodes, composing a fragmented public sphere until something better evolves. If one compiled all the hushed conversations Cubans had with journalists, researchers, and visitors, I suspect one could capture a clear portrait of national public opinion.

At the time I met Elena, I was beginning to move fluidly from public buildings to private space, and having publicly sanctioned conversations followed by furtive ones within the course of hours threw into sharp relief the difference between public and private domains, and the monumental cultural, practical, and political importance that the distinction between public and private holds for Cubans.

Elena's tall apartment building was down a busy arterial road. The creaking, blue metal elevator that took us up to her upper-floor apartment often threatened to stall and smelled of stale urine. The dim, communally shared but ambiguously owned halls were covered in fine black soot from the road below and suffered from lack of attention. This was initially a surprise to someone like me, since I had romantically thought that Cubans took special pride in communally shared things, such as their guaranteed housing, and that revolutionary ideals such as solidarity, sacrifice, and collective action on behalf of the common good would translate into participating in the upkeep of an apartment building.

Elena's door, which stood behind slim metal bars, touted a popular sticker commemorating Pope John Paul II's historic visit to Cuba in 1998, and another pronouncing that her household had been counted in the much-publicized Cuban census of 2002. I would twist the old-fashioned doorbell that turned like a key. Elena always first slid back a peephole cover to ensure my identity, then a noisy series of clanks and jangles would issue from the inside, as she undid bolts and chains. She was protecting herself against some kind of invasion, but I was not sure at the time from what or by whom. Inexplicably, there was always someone at home guarding the fort, sometimes even her school-aged daughter in the middle of the day.

In contrast with the muskiness of the building and the barricades to her apartment, Elena marked off her own space by keeping it immaculately clean and orderly, and by making it open, sunny, and airy. Doors opened onto her balcony, and her eldest son was even in the process of repainting the kitchen walls white. This all created a pleasant ambiance that, as I came to learn, defied Elena's daily sensation of being inexorably trapped. She decorated her apartment with Catholic and Cuban curios and sepia-tone photographs of her children when they were toddlers with heads full of curls. When talking, we usually sat at a large wooden table in her living room next to her classic Singer sewing machine, which she used for mending clothes to make them last as long as possible, and for off-the-books sewing jobs.

Virtual Private Space

Just to cover her bases, and avoid arousing suspicion concerning our relationship, after I granted Elena's request to help her with her e-mail, she told me I was to be kin for the duration of my stay in Cuba, and she reinvented me as her *media prima* (half-cousin) from a town she knew of in New Jersey. "We have to do this because people here are very curious. Nosey. They want to get into your business, and it just makes more sense that we are relatives. Why else would we be spending so much time together?" My interest was piqued concerning exactly what kind of messages Elena was going to send.

In agreeing to be Elena's Internet sponsor, I was providing her with a potentially important favor, as Internet access for ordinary Cubans is both rare and prohibitively expensive.[8] Some Cuban citizens can actually obtain intranet access for free through select state workplaces, but as they explain, it is not possible to surf or compose e-mails *con calma* (calmly, and without pressure or surveillance), and few have private accounts, making it hardly worth their effort to make the attempt. Technically, to obtain a legal e-mail address or Internet account, one must apply to the national telecommunications company and a local CDR panel, as well as undergoing government review, but citizens rarely choose to go through with this process. Ideally, they prefer to find someone trustworthy who can accompany them to an Internet center, gain entrance by signing the visitors' log in their name, and preferably, write down a foreign, not a Cuban, ID number on the log.

But price is a barrier to access. Online access costs US$6–$12 per hour, or US$1 for every ten minutes, depending on the venue and regardless of the speed of the connections, which were all exasperatingly slow (none were broadband, a fact the Cuban government attributes to the embargo). For someone like Elena, who was the single head of a four-person household and whose income, through a combination of remittances and off-the books jobs, ranged between $100 and $150 a month, it was a weighty decision to spend so much money on something as fleeting as an Internet connection.

Elena, however, saw it as an invaluable investment in her future, and definitely worth the effort, especially since she had already obtained a precious individual e-mail address for free. A few weeks before, a Spanish tourist using a hotel business office had been kind enough to open an account for her through Yahoo Spain, and now all Elena needed was a way to get online and actually use the account.

Elena treated the entire e-mail ritual as sacred. She dressed nicely, not in her house clothes; showed up on time to the minute for our meetings; and had neatly scripted messages ready to go in a little blue school tablet with soft, brown, pulpy third-world pages. She was always eager to schedule the next session, although she was equally nervous, pointing out to me suspicious individuals in, near, or on the walk to the business center or hotel where we went online. These people had the difficult-to-pinpoint but telltale aura of government informers. "I know the type" she assured me when I asked her how she could tell. "They are always *looking*," she finally decided, when I pressed her for a more specific description. She provided a quick demonstration of a constant, fluid movement of the head and eyes. She, like other people whom I later walked and talked with in the streets, would suddenly tell me to stop talking or would abruptly change the topic of conversation in anticipation of a stranger passing in the road. This was just part of the taken-for-granted rhythm of private conversation while moving through Havana's public space.

As Elena's e-mail project began to grow, I began feeling frantic and resentful. I resented spending my own precious fieldwork time typing out someone else's e-mails, which initially, seemed remarkably paranoid in their vagueness and childish in their content. Perhaps I would have selfishly cut ties with Elena completely if she had not continued to speak so frankly, to provide me with practical favors, and I admit, to offer her home as a welcome sanctuary. Elena's hospitality provided a break when I was ravenous and hot and tired of trying to penetrate the elusive inner sanctum of too many ministry buildings during those early days of fieldwork. Elena's son, Federico, who was working on his bachelor's degree and studying to be a priest, generously revived me with warm midday meals: huge piles of white rice and cups of soupy black beans to pour on top, onion omelets, and bright-red Kool-Aid-like drinks.

As it turned out, although I eventually limited our e-mail sessions, they evolved in a very revealing direction. I came to the conclusion that she was not keeping me from more important fieldwork at all. On the contrary, along with helping me clarify what frustrations she had as a consumer and a citizen in Cuba, Elena was providing me with invaluable data concerning private means of communication to the outside world and the trajectory of planning necessary to accomplish it, which she was weaving together through her private and apparently un-surveilled online communication (discussed in further detail in chapter 7).

Even as our relationship developed, her desire to keep everything we did and said under tight cover did not relax. She pelted me with a perpetual litany of questions: "Did anyone see us leaving the library? Did your secretary friend mention that she saw me waiting for you outside?" "Who was in front of my apartment building when you entered? Did you speak to them?" "Have your neighbors mentioned anything to you about my coming around?" "That woman sitting alone in the empty room in the hotel was an informer. She was watching us. I'm sure of it." And her favorite and most-repeated: "Don't tell them anything they don't need to know, and remember: don't let anyone else wash your underwear!! There. Now you know everything you need to know about Cuba."

Not sharing her sense of being watched, I finally accused Elena of being overly worried and careful about her every move, unlike other people with whom I was also developing relationships and who seemed much less jittery. "What happened to you?" I finally asked in exasperation.

She explained that in the past, she had been harassed by state officials. Her mail had been obviously opened on repeated occasions, or never delivered, her water and electricity had been shut off while her neighbors continued to receive service, and there was evidence that her home had been entered and rummaged through by what she assumed were government representatives, looking for information and evidence. That was why she always had someone at home and never left the apartment unguarded. "They are trying to create psychological pressure and disturb my family peace," she concluded. Elena further explained perhaps she was the target of special surveillance not only because her former husband had worked for many years for G-2, a police branch of Cuban Intelligence, but also because she had in the past made efforts to openly criticize the government.

While she had no viable means of organizing protest, she had more motivation than the average Cuban member of the shadow public and used what venues she could. She had written a poem with double entendres and hidden messages about freedom of the press under the guise of "the beauty of truth and the value of truth-telling." It was read to the Cuban public on a national radio program by a friend. More than that, she herself had even spoken on Radio Martí,[9] denouncing state policies regarding individual liberties, violating the 88 Law (February 1999), which allows for sanctions against any individual who collaborates in any capacity with foreign media or provides information that is likely to serve U.S. policy. Finally, she had applied for refugee status and sought to open a human-rights case through the U.S. Interests Section in Havana (the equivalent of a consulate, as there are no official U.S.-Cuba relations). Elena had successfully obtained a refugee case number, which she often referred to in her e-mails, giving her a special asylum-seeking status, but she was still desperately waiting to have her case processed and approved, though she did not trust that she was not speaking to government informers when she called the Interest Section to check on her paperwork.[10] In the meantime, she continued to participate individually in mild forms of resistance.

3

Private Experience

When I first met her on a residential side street, Elena handed me a something from a short stack of photocopies she was carrying under her arm. It was a pastoral newsletter entitled "No hay patria sin virtud" (There Is No Country without Virtue), published by the Cuban Conference of Catholic Bishops. It was dedicated to Padre Félix Varela on the 150th anniversary of his death and signed by Monsignor Jaime Ortega, archbishop of Havana.[1] It criticized the government's strict control over the Catholic Church. In particular, it condemned state restrictions on religious education and lack of access to mass media, as well as the increasingly amoral and godless character of Cuban society under communism. She encouraged me to read it carefully. Scanning the title, I thanked her, folded the newsletter, and placed it discreetly in the recesses of my jumbled diaper bag, quite curious about her cause, but not sure if I wanted to be associated with the document.

In theory, no news circulates in Cuba that is not broadcast, published, or written by representatives of the regime. Therefore, openly dissident texts are nearly nonexistent in Cuba.[2] The government does, however, allow an estimated twelve to twenty independent Catholic magazines or newsletters, with small circulations, to be distributed. These are the only legally produced documents not to come from state-owned printers and distribution networks, though technically their legal distribution is restricted to church premises. Elena casually handing them out on the street was thus not technically legal.

There is, however, an unwritten rule that the state neither censors church publications nor comments on them officially. As a result, David explained, church officials may print controversial material, but they still present it *suavemente* (smoothly, softly, gently)—they maintain a respectful tone concerning the government, and their criticism is consistently indirect. He said this as he handed me a stack of a year's worth of issues of *Palabra nueva* (New Word) magazine,[3] which his parents had bought for him at their church for eight pesos an issue (about 80 U.S. cents). The articles generally hold much more resonance for readers than do those of official news organs. Therefore, the Catholic press provides an important gray space for the expression of dissenting opinion, even if journalists, not "ordinary citizens," write the articles and opinion pieces.

I write about the gray space of this alternative press not to discuss the existing "freedom of expression" or "freedom of the press" that certain publications have in Cuba. On the other hand, I do not want to underestimate this channel for expression and formation of opinion, excluded from and seemingly incompatible with official news organs and official discourse. Rather, I want to describe the private ways in which the texts that are of interest to the shadow public are handled, must be circulated, and are read by individuals. I also want to suggest, following Michael Warner's stream of thinking, that that "texts cross one's path in their endless search for a public of one kind or another" (2002: 7), suggesting that the text itself could assist in identifying the public, and assist in forming their self-understanding. But what public? Certainly a more specific public than the readers of the Communist Party organ *Granma*, which people routinely told me was best used as toilet paper and for the discreet disposal of sanitary napkins.

The editor of *Palabra nueva*, Orlando Márquez, explains, "our problem is to see that we're not confused with the opposition press. We are clearly the Church press and the Church is not allied with the government or with the opposition. But caution doesn't mean silence or complicity. Our message is for everyone, whatever their political affiliation" (Lionet 2003). So, purportedly, *Palabra nueva*'s message is perhaps directed to the "Cuban public" at large, but nevertheless at a weak public (Fraser 1992) that cannot safely be identified with the opposition; furthermore, the Catholic Church takes all the credit for the publication's sins (partly to protect citizens), which makes the actual "public" more difficult to identify. It knowingly encourages the private discussion of common concerns, and takes measured stances in opposition to existing power structures. But witnessing the actual circulation of the magazine reveals how such efforts perpetuate the existence of a shadow public.

Private Circulation, Silent Marginalia

An article in *Palabra nueva* on *renumeración salarial*, about the importance of decent and fair salaries to maintain the dignity of a people, was of particular interest. The only words exchanged between readers as they passed the magazine, whose cover bore a pencil sketch of a serious-faced Jesus breaking the chains that surrounded his body, was, "Here, and you should also read the *opiniones* section," or "very interesting article," or "it's true." Thoughts about the text are not shared or discussed at any length in groups, people assured me, though the act of reading the magazine and passing it around, even if only erratically or unpredictably, seemed to provide some release of pent-up personal frustration. I had the stack of magazines at my house, and since David had offered them to me as a gift, I had the opportunity to witness people as they leafed through them, borrowed them, returned them, asked if they could lend them to someone else, and asked where they came from (which I did not share, not wishing to "out" David as their original owner, instead saying I had picked them up at a church for my studies).

In discussing ownership and texts in Cuba, David mentioned one of the few acts of protest he had witnessed at the neighborhood level. In 1994, during the height of the Special Period, it was common to see copies of the *Communist Manifesto* and other works by Marx in the trash bins of Havana—a silent and anonymous statement made by the shadow public through discarding their belief in the socialist ideology on which the system was built.

Sometimes people marked up their texts. Elena's own copy of her pastoral newsletter, sitting on her dining room table, had underlines, sidebars, and comments written in the margins that she went over with me. David also wrote marginalia in his magazines, or wrote cryptic notes on scraps of paper if he didn't want to forget important points for discussion with me. Flipping through an issue of *Palabra nueva* at the house of an architect in private practice, I noticed that he also penciled in little stars throughout the text. Marking text is an individual, private interaction with the text. It is intimate and political, but it is distinctly not public.[4]

Reading privately is part of the activity of the shadow public in Cuba. Keeping reading materials out of sight in the living area of a home is sometimes an aesthetic choice to prevent domestic clutter, but in Cuba reading materials are stored under the mattress, circulated quietly, and never discussed in public venues or the public sphere, but rather in the privacy of one's *sala* (living room).

A Private Public?

In my overarching goal to consider the capacities of unsatisfied citizen-consumers to form a "public," it is relevant to note Warner's (2002: 50) discussion of the kind of public that comes into being "only in relation to texts and their circulation." Warner also argues that "a public" exists by virtue of its address. If these Catholic magazines such as *Palabra nueva* index an emergent public—or even if they have created a public or address a public in a way that is reassuring to readers—this still does not mean that public can organize itself. The readership, or "public," is divorced from public action because the readers have no "political confidence." Furthermore, reflections of their thinking in a magazine had, at least at that point, little effect on their actions or sense of collective agency.

All of Elena's activity and reading, for example, was independent and in the shadows, often without her name associated with it. To others, she hoped to appear to be following the rules diligently, so as not to get caught. If there were other people engaged in similar activities, she did not know about them. Collaboration could either draw the wrong kind of attention or too easily be a trap. It was just too risky. Like most unsatisfied citizen-consumers in Cuba, for all her acts of resistance and passionate discontent, Elena claimed that not once had she spoken with another Cuban specifically about her ideas or needs as a citizen, at least not beyond consumer complaints.

Part of the Cuban dance of mistrust is directly linked to the desire to maintain privacy, or perhaps better stated, part of the desire to maintain privacy is lack of trust. If one does not trust others, one must keep one's privacy from them. You want to keep what is yours to yourself. Privacy and secrecy ensure a level of personal independence to earn, spend, and live as one wishes, within the limits of the system. Giving up a little privacy by letting others hear or see what you have encroaches on personal freedoms. Privacy means preserving one's dignity by preventing one's life from being watched. In Cuba, explained my landlady, Ingrid, in a rush of anti-state emotions and ideas that took me by surprise one afternoon over *cafecitos*, "there is a fear that even *dreams* could be monitored"; nothing is truly private, nothing is truly safe, nothing truly belongs to you.

Privatization

While "nothing belongs to you" in Cuba, a private business can feel akin to ownership. The mid-1990s were boom years for self-employed workers in Cuba. While many private businesses had been operating clandestinely on the black market for years, for the first time and in tandem with the legalization of the U.S. dollar in 1993, *cuentapropistas* (the self-employed), were able to surface as operating state-recognized "private enterprises." A total of 130 trades were eligible for licensing and obligated to pay a set monthly tax, regardless of profit earned (see Henken 2002a). Among the most common and visible licensed *cuentapropistas* in Havana remain manicurists, pizza vendors, shoe repairmen, seamstresses, clowns for hire at kids' parties, tire repairmen, and piñata makers. The most lucrative businesses remain those that tap directly into the growing tourist market—operators of *paladares* (small, private restaurants seating no more than twelve guests) and *casas particulares* (private rooms for rent to tourists in one's own home; for more detail, see chapter 6).

Despite this recent liberalization, as unsatisfied Cubans are quick to explain, the nature of legality is shifty. Rules are subject to sudden change, so expecting a crackdown is part of self-employment. In other words, a private business may be truly legal for a time, but then may become dangerously illegal for those involved in its operation—threatening debilitating fines, confiscation of goods, or even imprisonment. And between 1995 and 2003, the number of legal private enterprises has dwindled.[5]

Between the lines of legal and illegal, however, is a third, gray zone: not permitted but "tolerated." It is in this zone that many, many private businesses function, with officials turning a blind eye. They are not under immediate threat of seizure, but nevertheless operate in the shadows, out of plain sight. Such micro-businesses include renting out or showing pirated videos, freelance masseurs and beauticians, in-house juice vendors or cake makers, translation services, English tutors, and gypsy cabs, to name just a few.

Countless Habaneros (residents of Havana), and definitely the majority of unsatisfied citizen-consumers, run some such small enterprise and learn to live with uncertainty, because for a time they can likely evade taxation and surveillance. This keeps them from fully enjoying the rightful earnings of the hard work of their "private business" (whether profits are a substantial sum or just a few extra dollars a month). Cubans are well aware that what is illegal for them in Cuba is perfectly legal in most other places, increasing their frustration and sense of limitations as Cuban citizens—they are criminalized for buying and selling goods and services and fall victim to stressful cycles of threatened legal penalties and personal financial loss.

Older unsatisfied citizen-consumers remember a time when private enterprise ruled the island and do not necessarily see socialist change as beneficial. Eighty-year-old Iris told me, as she tested the softness of cooked grains of rice between her fingers while teaching me to make pudding, "I remember when the Revolution triumphed. I was a cigar roller, and went from rolling cigars artfully and at my own pace from home, for a private company, to being forced to work in a big state factory with long hours with a bunch of catty bitches who'd never rolled a cigar in their life. No, not for me. I was never so impressed with that Revolution, *oíste*? [you hear?]" But Iris was not poor, and never had been.[6] She lived in a comfortable, breezy apartment, she received regular household help from a young woman, and when I opened her immaculate, brand-new refrigerator, I was met face-to-face with a whole, pink *cochinillo* (suckling pig), a rare luxury.

Iris is not the only person who links early revolutionary-era disappointments to present-day repression in a chain of continuity. Paco, a Ministry of Culture–sponsored musician who had recently been particularly down on his luck, said, "Oh, yeah, my family remembers the first week of the Revolution. That was the day we *lost* our house, and had to hand it over to the government—or else—and we got to move into a lovely new tenement packed with people."

Irritation with issues of ownership and control is also expressed through underhanded complaint in the consumer setting. For example, once I was in line at a dollar store behind a Cuban couple who demanded explanations for the extremely slow queue, broken air-conditioning, and malfunctioning cash register. The cashier mumbled, "Hey, talk to my boss. He's been in charge here for forty-five years." The boss to whom she was referring was, of course, El Comandante en Jefe (Commander in Chief) Fidel Castro. Private enterprise, private ownership, and private property are just a few areas in which privacy is valued, and privacy and privatization of business are linked.

Private Micro-Enterprise

The same week David was hired at the European joint venture and no longer feared CDR reprisal, he also reopened his black-market video library, which he had abandoned a couple of years earlier, joining forces with a new local business partner in a new location. He lent out first-run pirated films to bored neighbors in need of evening entertainment, the nerve-wracking Havana version of renting from Blockbuster. His supplier was a night guard at a state facility who had satellite access to HBO and taped films for him, happily taking a cut of his rental money. When David was out of the house taking care of tasks relating to his video business, his wife, Tatiana, would use a code, saying he was at "el banco."[7] Our CDR president permitted David's video service, along with a lot of other black and gray businesses, to go on right under her nose, allowing a network of private enterprise to flourish in a space that technically should have been free of "counterrevolutionary activity."

Other common private (and untaxed) services available in homes, in addition to video rental, included manicures, pedicures, hair salons, laundry services, massages, and indoor plumbing repair, along with unlicensed room rental and satellite TV viewing, all of which was spinning around the CDR president and any potential informers who cared to take a hint. There were also illegal sales of coffee, beans, cheese, powdered milk, fresh eggs, frozen fish and seafood, homemade candy, decorated cakes, bootleg vinegar, imported clothing, and music CDs, all going unreported to, and seemingly unnoticed by, the CDR president.[8]

The Case of Private Child Care

Similarly, two stories up from the CDR head's apartment was the black-market child-care place to which I sent my daughter, meaning that twice a day I would pass her open window for drop-off and for pickup. There was also another, competing, unlicensed *círculo infantil* (child-care center or nursery school) a stone's throw from her house, and three others within her jurisdiction (and those were only the ones I knew of from my own social network), all operating under the unlikely pretext that the child-care provider was caring exclusively, and therefore legally, for kin.

Círculos particulares ("private" or informal, non-state-run daycare "circles") are blossoming, and their presence in and around Havana appears to be driving the public *círculos* into the ground, providing an interesting example of citizen-consumer–directed privatization of a system.[9] Former state *círculo* instructors, who were making 148 pesos a month (around US$6), have quit their state jobs, finding it much more lucrative to work from their own homes and charge US$6–$15 per month *per child* enrolled. On average, most black-market *círculo* instructors are pulling in at least US$100 untaxed a month.

Minda, with whom I spent time while observing her day-care service as a potential client, explained, "Nothing, *nothing* in the schools is *particular* [privately owned, one's own]," emphasizing the growing appeal of being able to have some individual authority to tailor the day-care experience. Minda had worked for more than twenty years in the state system before "going private," sharing the same history as two of the other *círculo* owners in the area. She described a number of incentives for parents to enroll preschool children in private *círculos*: parents preferred to pack their own, nutritious lunches from home and to allow children to bring their own toys, wear their own clothes, and get more individualized attention in a smaller group. In addition, they had the freedom to pick up and drop off their children at their own convenience, rather than at strictly set hours when the gate would be open. In short, whereas state centers squelched parents' ability to take care of their kids as they wished, *círculos particulares*—at least for those who could afford them— gave parents more control over the quality of their child's care. In some social networks, as a result, it had become normative to use them.

The history of state *círculos infantiles* claims that they played the important role of planting the first seeds of revolutionary pedagogy (see Wald 1978). As yet, however, no publication has discussed their decline. I suggest that this is a significant structural change in Cuba's educational system. Although it is not publicized, the primary effect of this informal privatization of child care in Cuba is that some state *círculos* have actually closed their doors, and there are no longer enough state centers in some Havana neighborhoods to serve all the children under five years old, leaving parents who cannot pay private rates to wait for spaces to open up on over-full waiting lists.[10] This change in the structure and privatization of child care in Cuba is among the first citizen-consumer–initiated moves towards privatization of a state-provided service.

The shifts towards private enterprise in child care, as well as dining, lodging, and home repairs, are emblematic of changes in the structure of Cuban society and of an increasing move toward the market. While privatization is a state-related project, *lo particular* is a citizen-consumer project. From a citizen-consumer's view, it provides a new venue for earning and for operating in one's own space, but not everyone has access to legal or semi-legal opportunities, causing growing and visible inequality (see chapter 6). In everyday discourse, *trabajo particular* (private work) is becoming part of the Cuban lexicon, usually in terms of the types of jobs a person works (for example, "Now he has two jobs: one *normal* and one *particular*"), and successful self-employment is a symbol of status and ingenuity in unsatisfied citizen-consumer circles. The legacy of Che Guevara's *nuevo hombre* (new man)—a model individual who worked, body and soul, for the good of his people and would transcend individualism and materialism for the socialist cause—has little influence on contemporary Cuban private workers (though see Serra 2007). Still, it is hard for some Cubans to contemplate that in other places most work is not done for the state. "Mi padre," says seventeen-year-old Felina with a serious face and a hint of pride in her voice, "es un barbero particular en Miami" (is a private barber in Miami). The divided worlds of state versus private work are so entrenched in Cuba that she assumes all barbers in the world come in two categories, and that she needs to specify that her father is not a "state barber" like the low-paid ones in her Old Havana neighborhood.

Drawing Private Conclusions

In summary, there are various kinds of "private" in Cuba, all of which occur in mundane and often ephemeral contexts of space, communication, and enterprise. First, there is *su propio* (one's own), that which an individual—*el dueño* or *la dueña* (the owner), or *el propietario* or *la propietaria* (the proprietor)—*owns* and over which he or she has a relatively high degree of control. Material objects purchased or received as private gifts fit into this category of *particular*—"one's own" clothing, shampoo, and photographs, for example—at least if one did not acquire them illegally and does not place them at any special risk by trying to sell them illegally. Such material possessions and *los particulares* (privately owned things) hold particular allure in the context of Cuban authoritarian rule, where ownership is often a contested category. (I discuss private goods in greater depth in chapter 5.) Second is *lo personal* or *lo privado*, things that are socially private—those personal or private details about one's life that belong to that individual: thoughts, dreams, ideas, and plans that one holds on to dearly and tries to conceal from the state by not speaking about them out loud, or at least not speaking about them to the wrong people or in the wrong place.

Finally, and most connected to the market force, there are *negocios par-*

ticulares, "private" or individual commercial business enterprises. *Casas par-ticulares* (the ubiquitous, lucrative "private homes" for rent) have put the term *particular* in wide circulation. Some Cuban *cuentapropistas* (literally those "earning their own bill") earn an income without direct government employ-ment, although such self-employment is often referred to simply as *trabajo particular* (private work). Many citizen-provided services, cottage industries, or micro-enterprises remain illegal, however, or operate under punitively strict guidelines.

A key way that the private remains defined in everyday Cuban reality is by juxtaposition with its binary opposite, the public—that which is free, shared, exposed, communal, lower in value, and less intimate; and that holds the nega-tive guarantee of lower quality, hidden obligations, and heavy surveillance. Public health care; government posts; government-provided services; rations; public events; and state-sponsored mass organizations, meetings, and celebra-tions are commonly cited examples of things public—to be avoided when pos-sible and used only to one's strategic advantage when necessary. Because of these negative associations, that which is public is devalued, and in particular, public space is associated with the limits of socialist bureaucracy, the official domain, and the limits imposed on personal autonomy and, especially, eco-nomic self-sufficiency.

In addition to the specific types of private I summarize in this section (space, communication, and enterprise), throughout the book I also go beyond "private space" to discuss in detail the mundane and often ephemeral geog-raphies, spatialities, and landscapes of private consumption and communica-tion (underground employment or services, small parties, gatherings, family celebrations or rituals in one's own home).[11] I go beyond "private communi-cation" to discuss specific topics and themes of conversation that are private (purchases, illegal earnings, migration plans, political opinions); speakers that are private (ordinary citizens as opposed to Party affiliates); and, particularly, private styles of speaking (jokes, metaphors, or aphorisms that contain veiled critiques of the state, the Castros, or the Party; managing private conversation in public space through "urban whispers"; speaking in code or metaphor or timing conversations for moments when there are no passersby).[12] Finally, I go beyond "private enterprise" to discuss all of the income-generating strate-gies and inventions—private ways and means—by which Cubans cope in the Special Period and the profound effects this period has had on their lives (see part II, particularly chapter 6).

While the categories of private that I discuss are a common way to organize everyday speech and silence, and to conceptualize the role of state power in Cuba, they are not in line with the recent critiques against appealing to "binary socialism." In such critiques, clear-cut categories (including that of "private" versus "public") would be eschewed for more nuanced distinctions. As I have mentioned, in the lived experience of Cubans in general, and particularly for the shadow public, however, public and private remain "active cultural categories" around which they must navigate, despite (or perhaps because of) "the party-state's attempts to eliminate private property and radically restructure family life," as Gal (2005: 30) has said in reference to the communist period in Eastern Europe, a statement equally applicable to Cuba. Despite the actual embeddings and nestings of private into public and vice versa,[13] I argue that Cuban citizen-consumers in their present situation are acutely aware of private options and alternatives, and look towards the future of "the private" in Cuba's transition out of late socialism.

II
Means

Habaneando

Havana-ing
Havana-ing, guitaring, I'm on my way out
Havana-ing, negotiating, hawking
Bicycle down the street to the Belén neighborhood[1]
This is the hidden Havana that you never see
Full of special people
Humble by tradition
They carry nostalgia and resignation
Looking in every door for the solution

Chorus:
The system squeezes and doesn't want to let go
And the black market arrives to resolve just enough
Behind that very touristy façade of the Cuba you see in posters
There is a worker, every bitchin' day, giving birth and existing
You know . . . the island isn't only rum and tobacco, whores, Varadero,
Cayo Largo
It's not just that, there are people that spend the day working from sunrise to sunset
For a better future, this is how we go

"Habaneando," from the film soundtrack to *Habana Blues* (Garrido et al. 2005;
English translation by the author).

As expressed in the lyrics to this song from the locally popular film and soundtrack *Habana Blues* (2005), there is a hidden Havana, behind the tourist façade, one that "people never see." These are the neighborhoods in a fix, where people are struggling and where the black market provides the means to make ends meet. Increasingly, this is how ordinary people in and around Havana describe and define their lives. Part II of this book, "Means," explores in detail the inner mechanisms and meanings of how unsatisfied citizen-consumers

earn, cope, cheat, and obtain goods, and how they talk about their predica-
ment in the current era, as well as the broader political implications of this
daily struggle.[2]

Chapter 4 introduces the "Special Period lexicon"—the four most important and widely circulating verbs concerning means of getting things done in
Cuba during the Special Period. Chapter 5 focuses on the means of obtaining goods and information about goods in the late-socialist era. Chapter 6
discusses what the legalization of dollars means for the trajectory of Cuba's
socialist project. Specifically, it explores how the stratification of the population through differential access to dollars has spawned social changes related
to types of employment, social and discursive networks, relationship to the
state, lifestyle, and the laws or philosophies that govern earning—all which
have implications for Cuba's socialist future.

Overall, this part of the book considers the construction of the "social
imaginary" in late-socialist Cuba, and uses the social imaginary to frame
means of living in Cuba. Specifically, I describe how global media contribute
to the social imaginary of unsatisfied citizen-consumers by providing *models
of* and *models for* comfortable living and possibilities for living in the world
(see Geertz's classic statement [1973: 93]), even if these norms and models cannot be emulated under the existing conditions in Cuba. I also illustrate how a
shared social imaginary of "normal" consumption allows Cubans to express
consumer choice and to resist the state through obtaining goods, thus allowing them to express choice in a way they cannot through orthodox forms of
citizen participation.

4

Words and Means

The Special Period Lexicon

Talking about, fretting about, and figuring out means to earn income and obtain commodities have become fundamental to how Cuban citizens characterize daily life within the confines of their country when describing it to outsiders—whether tourists, journalists, or researchers. It has also become central to a shared, intimate national conversation among Cuban consumers in the late-socialist era. While shortages are not as extreme as they were in the early 1990s, where and how to obtain desired items—before they run out—is still central to everyday neighborhood talk. "No es fácil" (it's not easy) is the chronic refrain.

Ordinary Cuban citizens see themselves as distinct from ordinary citizens in other countries—whether poor or wealthy—because of their chronic lack of "normal" means to eat, own, enjoy, and save. The strategy elsewhere in the world, they are convinced, is relatively simple: generate more income by working more hours at the same job, or if possible, by adding new sources of income through a second job. In Cuba, this is not how things operate. "Legally, you can hold only one job, no matter how little it pays," people lament. As a result, as part of their popularly conceived, collective national identity, Cubans have developed the entrepreneurial capacity to *inventar* (invent) ways and means quickly, creatively, and discreetly within the constraints of their citizenship and circumventing the laws that bind them. This means that many of the most important moments of exchange and unmonitored social interaction take place *por la izquierda* ("on the left")—on a flourishing *bolsa negra* (black market), out of sight and earshot of the state-sanctioned, public domain.

Since the dawn of the Special Period, a lexicon of references to the daily strain of Cuban ways and means of living has emerged, the most important of which are *luchar,* "to struggle," the master term of the era; *conseguir,* "to find"; *resolver,* "to resolve"; and *inventar,* "to invent." This cluster of verbs has taken on new and specific meanings in this historical moment. They evoke the illicit, the contraband, and the clever manipulation of state systems. They are incorporated repeatedly into everyday speech acts, and are used emotively and referentially to describe coping, adjusting, and resourcefully obtaining income, goods, and services in the current political and economic climate (see also León 1998; D. Fernández 2000; Moses 2002).

All of these reappropriated verbs serve as proxies for deep-rooted complaint. They hint, through the use of paradox, at a crippled socialist regime, and they weave together a master narrative of the prolonged Special Period in Cuba. Finally, they allow unsatisfied citizen-consumers, as a shadow public, to speak in a veiled manner that is not immediately transparent to outside listeners.

In this chapter, using these words as an organizing principle, I describe Cuban "means," or income-generating strategies—legal, illegal, informal, and discreetly in the shadows. I introduce the everyday experiences in households as informants narrate their lives and describe dissatisfactions in the intimate and mundane contexts of domestic and consumer life, and against the backdrop of local consumer rituals and routines. I conclude with a discussion of the "lexicon," or "lexical register" (Agha 2000), of unsatisfied citizen-consumers, which both allows them to speak in a veiled manner that is not transparent to the Communist Party "out-group" and also marks them as a specific kind of citizen and consumer in the Cuban context. Finally, I consider the implications of this lexicon for the constitution of a public.

Luchar

A Father's Day dinner party was held one balmy evening in an apartment on the outskirts of Havana. Music blared from the stereo, the TV was simultaneously on, and small groups were served informally and in shifts at the dinner table, over political discussion and an abundance of rum, Bucanero and Cristal beer, and tuKola soda (all Cuban state factory brands) brought out on trays from the kitchen by the older women of the house. A fellow guest cordially told us he could pick up some salmon for us and bring it back to us in a minute, if we would prefer fish to the beef being served, both rare luxuries.

"How?" I asked in surprise, never having seen salmon in the country before. "I'm a chef at a big [state-run] hotel," he explained, and then he used the hand sign for "steal" (closing the fingers of one hand in one swift, swiping movement, signifying a fist that has just captured something). He scowled, shrugged, and shook his head, "I'm always *luchando*, so I have some on hand. But it's just because I'm in Cuba. I wouldn't be doing this—I wouldn't *have* to do this—somewhere else," he explained, placing his hands over his heart as he justified his actions.

"Robar" (to steal), explained David early on, "is a strong word, implying break-ins and hard crime. So Cubans have invented a different word that means to take from the state in order to earn an income: *luchar.*" Using *luchar* this way also plays on its conventional use in the revolutionary context, where it was first used to imply a life of struggle against imperialism, the fight for the socialist cause, or most recently, *la lucha* (the struggle), the term Fidel Castro used to describe the difficult times since the fall of the Soviet Union. In its original rendition (the source register for lexical borrowing), it presumes citizen solidarity with and service to the state.[1]

Now, in Cuban street Spanish, *la lucha* implies just the opposite. Though it still refers to daily life struggles, it evokes the illicit, the contraband, the clever manipulation of state systems, and the adjustment to shortages. It reflects a public moral reasoning in which stealing from a state that does not do their bidding is not only acceptable, but necessary for survival. A widely circulating joke that reflects this sentiment is, "Cubans have three basic rights: to health, to education, and to steal from the state."[2] When we were charged an unbelievable overweight luggage fee on exiting the country by the stern representative of the (state-owned and -operated) Cuban airline, we offered him an enticing under-the-table fee instead. "Luchando?" my husband asked him, risking this use of the word outside of our local social network. The officer relaxed on hearing the familiar use of the term, laughed, agreed enthusiastically, and comfortably pocketed the fee, wishing us a safe journey, telling us the ages of his own children at home, and letting us pass on quickly through the line.

To a certain extent, everyone is *luchando* in the current regime, whether by pilfering goods from the state warehouse, working without a license, evading taxes on income, or avoiding state services through a black market network. With time, *luchar* has also come to replace *work* itself. "Luchando?" (working?) chuckled our upstairs neighbor, looking at my husband, who was typing away seriously on his laptop at our dining room table in the middle of the day.

Part of the mundane irony of *la bolsa negra* or *el subterráneo* (the underground) that is flourishing in Cuba is that it involves illegal dealings, broadly defined as the buying and selling of contraband merchandise or providing services that are prohibited. Anything that taps into government profit, real or potential, is labeled *enriquecimiento personal* (personal enrichment) or *enriquecimiento ilícito* (illicit enrichment), and is or has the latent potential to be categorized as a crime against the state. It is also the hyperbole of what *black market* has come to mean in Cuba that annoys citizen-consumers, leading to a sense of relative deprivation of consumer rights. Whereas in other national contexts the black market might deal in firearms, jewels, drugs, or furs, in Cuba it involves anything that is not strictly controlled by the state. Thus, juice, skin creams, coffee, and so on are "controlled substances."

The reminder of state power is constant in the game of everyday survival.

If many Cubans were able to obtain and pay for a license that would legally allow them to sell the things they do, they would not be able to make a living. Selling adhesive bandages, tampons, aspirin, canned tuna, items off one's own ration card, or even used plastic bags is considered a black market activity. In fact, the following message and warning is printed on the front of a plastic bag from a popular state-run, dollars-only fast-food franchise, El Rápido:

El Rápido:
Para Ud. y su gusto siempre lo mejor.
Esta bolsa es una cortesía. Prohibida su venta.
Nuestro deber, ofrecer un servicio de óptima calidad.
Su satisfacción es lo más importante

El Rápido [Speedy]:
For you and your taste, always the best.
This bag is a courtesy. Its sale is prohibited.
Our promise is to offer service of the highest quality.
Your satisfaction is the most important
(Author translation).

The text printed on the bag presents an odd admixture, emulating capitalist-style customer service while reflecting black market reality and socialist state power. Between the lines expounding elite tastes, high-quality products, and promises of customer satisfaction is the dissonant reminder not to use the plastic bag for personal profit. But as a matter of course, Cubans do sell El Rápido plastic bags and there is a market for them. *Jabas vinyl,* as plastic bags are popularly known, are valuable, waterproof containers for many things, but they are not for sale in stores, and not everyone can pay for dollar goods that are packed in plastic bags. Such minutiae are part of *la lucha.*

Cubans have adjusted to the current system and have become used to seeing themselves as everyday outlaws. "Soy siempre contra la ley" (I am always against/running counter to the law) explained Tatiana, the inevitable response from someone who believes that in another national context she would just be earning a living, but in Cuba has repeatedly put herself in scenarios where she could be fined or even lose her home and belongings because of what she considers unreasonable laws. "Translation of [consumer] desires into efforts at attaining them turned them to illegal means, hence into legal conflict with the state," summarizes O'Dougherty (2002: 113) in her ethnography of the Brazilian middle class, a statement equally apropos of Cuba.

Unsatisfied citizen-consumers in Cuba operate in a system that equates their citizenship with lawlessness. They are members of a shadow public that is constituted partially by their breach of communist ideals and partially by their related avoidance of the communist legal and political system. In the process, communism and the state are not always faceless, of course. There are also "real communists," but among the shadow public, real communists are considered the Other (although I was often told "everyone has their needs"). Still, the Cuban shadow public is not part of the same *lucha* as Communist Party adherents.

Nor are die-hard communists considered part of the general public. Rather they are a rare, anachronistic but frightening local species who allegedly uphold the system and rules, and who could potentially "ruin it for the rest us" with their rigid ideology and standards.[3]

Tatiana came by one afternoon to warn me that *un duro* (a hard-liner) was in our midst: he is *un Comuñango* (an older slang term for a big communist), she stressed, mouthing the syllables of the word silently and with great exaggeration. "He sits on the Asamblea out East" [The People's Assembly in the eastern province. The eastern half of Cuba is historically known for having more committed Party members]. He's here, right now, eating lunch, and he's going to spend the night and everything," she added, shivering at the thought of his presence inserted into the neighborhood's daily rhythms. "So be careful," she warned me.

"No, *you* be careful!" I retorted. She laughed and assured me I shouldn't worry: she was getting out of here, going *allá* (far away) until the visit was over.

Walking up the narrow passageway, past the open door of the apartment where *el Comuñango* was staying, I peeked in to make sure I knew what to avoid, and saw a middle-aged man watching TV, rocking lightly in a rocking chair, generally benign in appearance, but with one of those moustaches that "spells police" (see Codrescu 1999: 115). It seemed incongruous that here in Cuba, people would be whispering about the presence and special visit of "a communist," when the country is supposedly communist and a large number of its citizens are listed as Party members.[4]

Resolver

Resolver has a dual meaning. As a fitting citizen-consumer signifier, it can be translated both as "to find goods and take possession of them" in the consumer context, and also "to settle an issue with the state bureaucracy" in the citizen context. I became all too familiar with both uses of the word.

Bottles of white rum, full ashtrays, and empty espresso cups littered our dining room table, as neighbors joined us for a spontaneous weekend afternoon of conversation in our apartment. My daughter Maya, sweaty, with dirt in the creases of her neck, ran around shirtless, shoeless, and to the dismay of neighbors, also earring-less, making her not recognizably *una niña cubana*. Not yet three, she spoke fluent Spanish, asking me for a *pomo de chocolate* (bottle of chocolate milk). I told her we had none and would have to wait until the stores carried some again. I filled her bottle with powdered milk; cool, boiled water; and a pinch of sugar. Not satisfied, she scampered out the front door and returned a few minutes later, panting as she sucked contentedly on a bottle full of chocolate milk. Laughter rippled through the room.

"She's already Cuban," the guests exclaimed, "¡Maya se resolvió el chocolate!" (Maya resolved the chocolate milk for herself!)

"¿Maya, cómo te resolviste el chocolate?" (Maya, how did you resolve the chocolate milk?), asked David.

Maya removed the nipple from her mouth for a moment, "Con Petra" (With Petra) she answered, understanding the question, and then she plugged herself again and continued sucking.

In a place where you cannot always buy what you want, where a shopping list is akin to a wish list, consumer practices burgeoning at the neighborhood level entail relying on *socios*. In Spanish, *socios* literally refers to members of a club or organization, but today in Cuba, it means friends in your self-defined social group, those on whom you can count. Counting on *socios* to provide for their needs demonstrates citizen-consumers' collective independence from the state. It is a truism, reflected in wordplay, that it is "*socio*ismo"—the system of depending on neighbors, friends, and social networks, as well as small twists of fate and timing—not state "*social*ismo" (socialism), that resolves material problems.

Maya had become quite used to both *resolviendo* and *consiguiendo*. While at Beatriz's small, black market *círculo infantil*, Maya would often spend time taking long, hot walks with Beatriz, as she sought and found desired items. I watched Maya processing, through monologue and play, what she experienced in the outside world during her time away from me. For example, she would approach a pretend counter and ask a houseplant about the availability of tomatoes, *malanga* (manioc root), or some other commonly sought-after item such as rice. An imaginary shopkeeper would apparently tell her there was none, she would turn to her imaginary friend and shrug, palms in the air, saying in a resigned tone, "No hay" (there isn't any), and they would move on to the next place. "What are you playing?" I asked. "I'm just going around, looking for things that we need," was how she described her Cubanized version of playing "store."

Resolviendo between Citizens and Bureaucracy

Resolver is used ubiquitously in the shrewd consumer context, but I also became quite familiar with the other meaning of *resolver* in my dealings with state functionaries. This stems from the simple fact that *resolver* is *the* key word in Cuban bureaucratic culture. Go to a government office, and you will learn to conjugate *resolver* in all of its forms.

"Te resolviste?" (Have you resolved it?)
"No. No me resolvía a nada." (No. I haven't resolved anything.)
"Vamos a resolverlo." (We're going to resolve it.)
"Estoy resolviéndola ahorita." [I'm resolving it right now.]

But the important form of *resolver* is the blessing: "Que te resuelvas." (That you resolve it.) It is uttered with the same inflection and grammatical construction as "God be with you" or "God bless you" (*que Dios acompaña, que Dios bendiga*), and it serves as a blessing when one is being given the runaround. It is a message from the powerless as they pass me on to the powers that be, with wishes for the best, indicating at some level the lack of control that resolving implies. At the very least, it passes the resolving on to the "client."

Resolver in this important bureaucratic context does not mean to solve a problem. Rather, it means to reach a decision or make a determination—about a form, about a financial situation, about a legal requirement. It hints at possibility, strings people along with hope, and has a sense of potential closure. On the other hand, it is repeated so many times that it often starts to lose its meaning and the warmth of possibility. Such was the case when I encountered a new form of the verb I had not yet heard, one that flooded me with hope: "¡Nos resolvamos!" (We resolved it!) It appeared an extended research visa had been miraculously procured for me against the odds of the gods and politics.

"Could it be true?" I asked.

"As true as anything is in Cuba!" said the foundation undersecretary. She liked her joke so much she started laughing and repeated it to her boss, who did not share in her laughter but only smiled weakly, teeny pieces of white tape marking acupuncture micro-pressure points visible in a few places on her ear. She needed acupuncture, she had confessed to me earlier, to cut her cravings for nicotine and to calm her jangled nerves, brought on by her job.

In the end, of course, nothing was resolved, since the visa was mysteriously revoked by the same "invisible hand" that had procured it. I had signed on a dotted line for my visa and was walking, with a feeling of triumph, to assemble photographs and paperwork for my *carnet de identidad* (national ID card). During those minutes, my sponsoring research center received a shadowy call from the Ministry of Culture, saying my right to a yearlong visa was being immediately revoked.[5]

I received empathic responses from neighbors and friends. "There's a name for what you have done," explained David, when I told him of my misadventures in *resolviendo* the visa, "It's called *Experimento X*. You push a certain project with the bureaucracy as far as you can go to see what will happen. X— the unknown—will be the resolution." David continued, "I want you to understand," he emphasized, leaping to the defense of his compatriots, a quality David often exhibited (perhaps because he was aware that I was documenting everything that happened to me), "the person, the individual in the office who carried out the act of revoking your visa is not a bad person. He just had to do it. It's a problem of the system which does not let him move."

Resolviendo, by its nature, is something that only ordinary people do, not people in power, explained Paco, the cash-strapped, peso-poor, state-sponsored musician. Paco is a vegetarian and practitioner of yoga who declares that in a former life, as he works his way through the Karmic cycle, he was a woman with seven children during the French Revolution. As he served us bowls of macaroni with ketchup and soy oil, he spoke of his philosophies: positive thinking can change outcomes. Pain and illness are often psychosomatic. "La gente de abajo siempre resuelven mejor que la gente de arriba." (People below are always able to resolve things better than people above are.)

"What do you think of all this?" he asked his wife—who seemed very far away, suffering from a migraine and probably from a number of other things—as she sat at the dinner table. She just looked at him blankly, totally unimpressed, and said nothing. He strummed his guitar and sang above the sound of rain hitting the corrugated tin roof of his tiny bungalow the popular state-sponsored quasi-hymn "El Comandante Che Guevara." As this nationalistic tune drifted out of his small shack, he admitted he was going to record some of his own tunes and sell them independently. He thought this might resolve some of his pressing financial concerns.

Conseguir

Conseguir (to get hold of, to find, to attain, to obtain) has come to replace *comprar* (to buy) or *ir de compras* (to go shopping). The primary options for obtaining goods are the scantily and sporadically stocked *bodegas* (neighborhood ration stations), the state-run peso outlets (figure 4.1), and the *agromercados* and *agropecuarios* (agricultural markets), heavily buffeted by seasonality and faulty distribution systems. Most infamously, there are also the overpriced dollar stores, where a box of dry cereal or a package of frozen tough, sinewy chicken legs could cost two weeks' wages, undermining the average citizen's purchasing power. Therefore, people say, "Voy a *conseguir* oregano" (I'm going to find some oregano), instead of "Voy a *comprar* oregano," because, in practice, this undertaking means checking on the availability of oregano in the

Figure 4.1. A state store touts "Offers in National Currency" (pesos), but the display window is bare and a potential customer exits empty-handed.

aisles of dollar shops; asking about the availability of a secret stash kept behind the counter; finding out which neighbor has some available to borrow, barter, or sell; finding it growing wild on a bush, or giving up until word arrives that some has become available.

With "time like people had one hundred years ago" (Tattlin 2002: 180) and relatively modern consumer desires and expectations, *consiguiendo* is people's ubiquitous pastime. Cuban consumer logic dictates walking or traveling far to save a few pesos, or continuing to look for a desired good for extended periods of time. I was reminded many times of a local proverb, "In Cuba, there is more time than life." Time is a Cuban's most bountiful resource. It is so bountiful that it sometimes is a burden, especially if people have no other resources that permit them to use or fill up the time more productively.

In accompanying women to *conseguir* nonessential but everyday household goods, I learned about the most commonly unavailable or extremely overpriced items: kitchen sponges, cloth diapers, gaskets, lighter fluid, bras, sewing needles, skin salves, adhesive bandages, painkillers, vanilla, cumin, mint, *naranjas agrias* (sour oranges), powdered milk, oil, and vinegar.[6] These products fell into an odd, hard-to-define category: neither luxury items nor essential items, but goods whose absence changed one's quality of life. The emotions that the shortages caused sometimes pushed people over the edge and were often symbolic of an inability to "live a normal life."

One case was *hoja de laurel* (bay leaf), typically used in flavoring classic black beans and a wide variety of other savory dishes, which was completely unavailable for months. Chronic shortages of foodstuffs change the national flavor—literally and figuratively—and generate consumer dissatisfaction when people are repeatedly unable to make tasty, familiar meals for their families and friends using the traditional recipes. Ironically, in light of the chronically unavailable cooking ingredients, it is easier to produce "authentic" Cuban meals outside of Cuba than it is in Cuba, which is often a mundane but symbolic trigger that starts people thinking about life outside the island.

This became particularly clear in my interactions with Cuban exiles in Costa Rica:[7] A Cuban woman living in the suburbs of San José, Costa Rica, served me *crème caramel* (a Cuban dessert made with curdled milk and fresh orange juice) and was shocked I had never tried the sweet, one she considered *comida típica* (typical food, a national dish), until she realized out loud, "Ah, there is no milk in Cuba."

A young Cuban worker at a five-star hotel in Costa Rica who had risen to the ranks of senior management of a major international hotel chain had the opportunity to sponsor a Cuban food festival on the palatial hotel grounds, the entrance fee for which was $57 a head.

"I feel quite sad right now," he admitted with an air of fatigue, shedding his crisp managerial persona for a minute as he gave me a private tour of the massive buffet and separate dessert room. We stood in silence for a moment, surrounded by the Cuban banquet he had reproduced from his memory and imagination. "Look at all this food. I've put Cuban street food on silver platters. My mom used to make that cake," he scoffed, shaking his head as he ran his fingers through his gelled, black hair and over his face. "*Bueno*. It's Cuban food, but you couldn't even make it there if you tried right now." He seemed to shake the emotion from his body and straightened up, handing me his business card and telling me he had to get back to supervising the bar.

Word-of-Mouth *Consiguiendo*

Another element of *consiguiendo* is the sociality that has developed around events when an item of unusual value or quality enters the neighborhood. A ripple of information flows among *socios*. Petra came walking towards me in the street, and we greeted each other with a kiss on the cheek. She was sweating and slightly out of breath. She dabbed her upper lip with a cloth handkerchief and stood close to me, speaking rapidly and intentionally mumbling, "Go to the corner of Calle 1 and Z, the blue house, Antolín's house, and you'll find fresh chicken. Decent quality. If you're going to go, go quickly because it could run out, and bring your own *jaba vinyl* [plastic bag]. It would be nice to pick up a little for the kids," she recommended.

This type of word-of-mouth information sharing is a more reliable means of *consiguiendo* than going to a state store is, as is finding a forming line and hopping in. For example, I happened to be outside of "el chopping" (anglicized Cuban neologism for "shop" or "shopping" market) at the moment a delivery truck arrived in the thick heat of one late afternoon. A line was already forming outside the door and wrapping around the corner. I slipped in line to find out what brought on this sudden congregation. It turned out I was not the only person in the line who was not completely sure why I was there. Others had queued up simply in order not to miss anything.

Several, but only several, cardboard boxes were being unloaded into the front door, and a guard was restricting the number of customers entering the store, so that staff could monitor what happened inside. It turned out the ice chest had just been stocked with some kind of ground meat, and long, bare arms were diving down into its depths. Body heat and respiration mingled with frosty steam. Some women had grabbed multiple packages of the mystery meat, others only one or two. There was an air of frenzy and rising pressure.

"Compañera, me da pena, pero, por favor—¡hay otras que también quieren ver a la carne!" (Comrade, it pains me to say it, but please, there are other people who also want to see the meat!) snapped one domineering shopper to another, sarcastically using the nearly defunct form of address "Comrade" to remind her fellow citizen-consumer to behave well in this tense shopping scenario.

"OK, so what do you do with this stuff?" asked one stout, middle-aged woman in spandex shorts to another as she stood in the checkout line, turning over the unfamiliar little package of shrink-wrapped ground turkey on a polystyrene tray and tilting her head to read the label, which to my surprise, was in English.

"It's just like ground beef, only it's *pavo* [turkey]," answered the other, with a tone of mild superiority, "You can make meatballs with spaghetti, or *picadillo* [spiced mincemeat]. It's lower in fat. Americans use it all the time now, I've heard." The other nodded with interest and seemed satisfied with the purchase she was about to make. "I'll cook it tonight for dinner," she decided out loud.

In less than fifteen minutes, the stock of turkey packages was depleted (many to be resold throughout the neighborhood at higher prices), and only a rumpled stack of cardboard boxes with USDA (U.S. Department of Agriculture) stamps on them remained in the wake of the "distribution."[8] A dejected crowd of those who never made it inside the store dispersed, growling, "Why so few?" Quieter speculation ensued about who made it inside to take advantage of the ground turkey distribution event, who did not, how much people might resell the turkey for, and of course, where it might be possible to *conseguir* it now.

Inventar

Our toilet is clogged; we have no plunger, and neither does anyone else. Our neighbor takes a large wooden stick, wraps a bunch of old rags he has collected to the end of it, and fastens them with twine and a fat rubber band. "Hay que inventar" (You have to invent), he narrates, repeating a mantra among unsatisfied citizen-consumers. What you cannot resolve or find, you invent. Daily life in Cuba is often cobbled together out of improvised and provisional inventions. Inventing, like resolving, has two meanings. Sometimes it refers to devising material implements, but more generally, it is an all-encompassing word of Special Period survival that means to find or create ways around adversity—from citizens battling shortages to engaging in discreet but serious infractions of the law.

Consumers Inventing Implements

So many things in Cuba are makeshift, rudimentary, substituted, converted, built on, improvised, one-thing-serving-as-another, wiggled, or modified to get them working again. The city streets and the insides of homes are covered in publicly accessible symbols of *inventando*: windows sawed out of pieces of wood, kids flying down the street on discarded two-by-fours turned into seats with wheels (*chivichanas*), little structures erected on top of multifamily buildings (*casetas en azoteas,* literally "shacks on roofs"; see Coyula and Hamberg 2003 for the urban housing context), and especially the iconic American vintage cars of the 1950s (affectionately known as *almendrones,* or "big almonds," for their smooth, rounded shape). The classic cars are not only physically preserved but still running and providing transport along fixed routes for a standard fare (figure 4.2). Often powered by belching Soviet-era diesel motors, they lure nostalgic tourists to the island and, as taxis, have become a key image of tourism promotion while filling in for a failing public transport system. As one typical report states, highlighting *inventando* bricolage: "Carlos Castellanos owns an impeccable 1952 Buick Special. But raise the hood, and you are in for a surprise. The engine is Romanian, the steering is from a Citroen, the gear box is Toyota, the pistons are Mercedes, the fuel pump Mitsubishi and the starter motor borrowed from a KIA" (Acosta 2006).

Inventando is not only material wizardry, it is also a mental process and a state of mind. When a woman is cooking, explained Fredrich, a young father, "you might look at her face and think that she is actually thinking about the cooking in front of her, but really she is already *inventando* how she is going to get the next meal on the table, and what that meal is going to consist of." There are all kinds of "making do." Ulanda, a professor of anatomy, explained that while she was pregnant, she was too busy and tired to think about managing

Figure 4.2. A vintage American car, imported to the island before the revolution, rolls by. Many such vehicles have kept running for forty years or more through a combination of borrowed, preserved, and invented parts.

the lines to ensure she got the protein she needed. So she decided to "acquire" a live hen, raising it in her Old Havana living room and collecting the fresh eggs. There are, of course, jokes about *inventando*: What is a Cuban steak? A grilled grapefruit skin. What is Cuban melted cheese? The free condoms distributed by international organizations.

Citizens Inventing Loopholes

Even relatively wealthy citizens with access to dollars have to *inventar,* in the sense of finding ways and means around quickly changing laws. For example, despite the recent legalization of certain types of micro-enterprises, Cubans are quick to explain that the nature of legality is constantly shifting "as the government has alternately encouraged and repressed the [self-employed] sector" (B. Smith 1999: 49). The most common way of preventing financial loss is a system whereby rumors concerning regulations that are on the brink of change circulate quickly within business networks. The chain of information usually begins with someone with a connection to El Partido, who then leaks the details of an upcoming crackdown to a friend, who then passes it on, behind closed doors, to other friends and neighbors whom they would not want to be burned. When feasible, those in the know concerning the forthcoming regulations invent the necessary adjustments to their businesses before inspection.

For example, the law on the books for *casa particular* owners stipulates that the owner must actually reside on the premises being rented (the ostensible reason being in order to monitor the activities of the guests). One way to enforce this regulation was suddenly to require *two* toilets on any rented premises: one for the owners and one private toilet for renters. The costs of rapid replumbing and remodeling were prohibitive to many owners who had been enjoying legal status. Ingrid, the landlady of our one-toilet *casa particular*, had been bending the rule, coming by for visits or a cup of coffee, making her presence visible in the neighborhood of her rental apartment so as not to arouse suspicion, but otherwise allowing us full privacy in her space. Within two hours of the leaked information about the new two-toilet rule, we sat visiting with Ingrid and her husband in the *sala* of the rental.

"Hecho es la ley, inventado es el engaño. [Once a law is made, the loophole is invented.] And as fast as they change it on us is as fast as we change it on them," declared Humberto, scoffing and puffing on yet another Popular (*bodega*-issued) cigarette as he stood in the *sala*. "We'll put the new toilet right here, where that closet is. I have friends who are plumbers. I can have it done by next week, or three days," he said, caught up for the moment not only in the act of inventing and outwitting, but also in the race against time.

Ingrid, on the other hand, who had been a little girl when she watched Fidel march into Havana on New Year's Day, following the 1959 triumph, sat on the sofa, her face still as she listened, but her eyes moist with anger. "It's just a matter of time," she stated matter-of-factly. "Eventually, they will shut me down. I'm sure of it. They start to see you living just a *little* bit better, and they can't stand it. They will take it away." In circles like these, the socialist welfare state is not a protector and provider, but a totalitarian competitor and a bully, robbing regular people of the good life and means of living for which they have worked hard. Ingrid was tired of inventing ways around the system.

Inventing and Home "Inventory"

Fredrich, in particular, embodied *inventando*. At age twenty-three he, unlike Ingrid, had never known life under any regime other than the Castros'. Coming into adulthood he had invented his work, invented his wealth, and invented his home, and he was inventing his future outside of Cuba. I think of him as a man of means, Cuban style. Fredrich and Felina's home is nestled on the second floor of an Old Havana *solar* (tenement) that is literally decaying. Tangles of exposed, colored electrical wires stick out of the crumbling cement walls, rusting wrought-iron railings wobble on the edges of high balconies, and packs of scruffy children, with skin ranging from milky white to espresso, run and play together in the courtyard under an open sky. Miraculously, not one soul was injured or killed in the *derrumbe* (building collapse) of one entire apartment into the courtyard. But amidst the urban colonial decay, Fredrich has invented an island of middle-class consumer paradise for himself, his seventeen- year-old *marinovia* (a common word combining "spouse" and "girlfriend" that can also mean common-law wife), and their brand-new baby son, Fredrich Jr.

Several years ago, on the flourishing underground housing market, Fredrich purchased the deed to the one-room unit. Since then, he has miraculously transformed a tiny, ninety-square-foot single room with a high ceiling into a cramped, magical storehouse with an inventory of "invented" furniture and appliances. He built a *barbacoa*—a makeshift mezzanine or loft in Cuban Spanish—that created an extra floor and nearly doubled the floor space, to make it all fit.

He also mounted a small color TV on the wall, and hooked up a stereo system with woofing bass speakers that made the walls tremble and my body vibrate. There was a red velveteen couch and a matching love seat, a glass dining table and a set of chairs, and a full-sized 1950s Frigidaire with rounded corners and a mint green interior that he had gotten to work again. Wall-to-wall carpet covered the floor, on which there were so many things it was difficult to weave my way around. A large, psychedelic tapestry with mushrooms and skulls hung on the wall. He had built a winding metal staircase up to the second floor, where there was a double bed with a mirror on the headboard, a skillfully handcrafted wooden crib protected by mosquito netting, and a heavy wooden chest of drawers (made by a private carpenter). Whereas other families in the *solar* shared bathing facilities, he had created his own. A tiny porcelain flush toilet and sink stood inside, next to a tiny, newly tiled shower stall, all expertly hooked up to the tenement plumbing system.

He also carried his handsome, titanium-framed mountain bike and a high-end baby stroller up and down the crumbling cement steps as he took calls on his cell phone. He painted the external wall of his makeshift balcony unit bubblegum pink, in honor of his *marinovia*. Any time I visited he treated me—to food, to drink, to a taxi ride, to a celebration. He wanted to give and be generous. He came across as a man of means.

Enjoying a Father's Day celebration with his new in-laws, this year for the first time as a proud father himself, Fredrich made an ardent declaration, leaning forward to address the group of male relatives and me: "I know," he said, balling his strong, café-con-leche hands into fists and shaking them, "I just know that if I were in America, I would be a millionaire, and I would be able to do it clean. I know it." His black eyes glowed with a mixture of rum-drenched fury and hope. Feeling a bit rum-drenched myself, I was inclined to believe that Fredrich, who had magically squeezed a middle-class suburban home into a walk-in box, also held the power to transform himself into an American millionaire.

But in the meantime, his booty and largesse did not come from the legal salary he earned in the packaging department of a state-run cigar factory. Rather, it came from *luchando*—in this case, pilfering a box a day into his backpack (though he claims there had been days when he was lucky enough to pack away several boxes), which he then sold, to both regular and new clients, on the black market. Because of his good relationship with the factory guards, his discreet salesmanship, and his good luck during recent raids on the bus, he had yet to get caught. I wondered if the considerable weight of durable goods in his invented home, as well as the considerable wait for his migration, would cause his invented ninety-square-foot consumer paradise to crash.

Concluding Words

The common uses of the four words I have featured in this chapter—*luchar, resolver, conseguir,* and *inventar*—lie at the heart of the "Special Period lexicon." Although they are locally associated with the Special Period, I believe that in retrospect, they will come to signify the dawn of the late-socialist period, since each captures some key attribute of lived experience in the late-socialist milieu. In summary, *inventar* signifies the need to invent things that do not exist or to invent one's way around repressive systems; *resolver* signifies irritations with consumer limitations and also the possibilities inherent in navigating around bureaucratic rationality; *conseguir* signifies the need to spend tremendous amounts of time finding desired items that cannot be simply bought. Finally, *luchar* contains the most local meaning and is the least directly translatable. It can be roughly glossed as "pilfer," but is imbued with a public moral reasoning that renders stealing from the state normative and broadly equivalent to work. As Damián Fernández (2000: 109) suggests, "the new language attempts to hide from the authorities the practices that are at the margins of legality . . . it indicates the limits of state socialization and the power of society to resist governmental norms."

The Special Period lexicon suggests both modes of and models for living in the existing system (Geertz 1973: 93), as well as a practical model for coping within a system that is unlikely to change in the foreseeable future. It reflects classic thinking on the importance of language users and language use in understanding culture and language as a "social semiotic" (Halliday 1964, 1978).

As a lexical register, the use of these words is socially indexed. In other words, they represent a "linguistic repertoire that is associated, culture-internally, with particular social practices and with persons who engage in such practices" (Agha 2000: 216). This lexical register is becoming institutionalized. It marks the people who use these words as a particular kind of consumer (frustrated, seeking better, inventive) and as a particular kind of citizen (noncompliant, evasive, light-fingered with state resources).

In creating contested meanings for existing words, Cuban unsatisfied citizen-consumers *describe* how to acquire goods and *evaluate,* in situ, a historical moment in which not enough is available, restrictions are too tight, and the structure provides too little room for consumer or citizen agency. These words not only provide a means for them to communicate with one another in a relatively disguised way, they also manipulate words that are lexically the same as, but denominationally different from, Cuban revolutionary or Party argot. Sharing a language but not the values ascribed to its vocabulary provides unsatisfied citizen-consumers with a way to evaluate their situation that is not immediately transparent to the communist "out-group."

The linguistic register serves as a critical metadiscourse about goods and bureaucracy that allows, at least for the time being, for the emergence of a critical metaculture without any need to be explicit (see Urban's [2001: 244] discussion of Habermas). This metaculture may be, as I suggest, a "shadow public" rather than a "public," since it believes itself unable to change the existing system; finds some freedom and flexibility to criticize politics, policy, and hardship through the use of its own linguistic register; and thinks that there are benefits to remaining underground in word and in deed.

The discourse I have described permits unsatisfied citizen-consumers in the late-socialist era to verbalize criticisms of the state semipublicly and indexes a specific constellation of discontent with reference to means and goods. It does not, however, allow them to inhabit a "public sphere," in Charles Taylor's (2004: 83) definition of "a common space in which the members of society are deemed to meet through a variety of media: print, electronic, and also face-to-face encounters; to discuss matters of public interests; and thus be able to form a common mind about these." If, however, one considers the public sphere to be the realm of social life in which something approaching public opinion is formed, perhaps the deployment of this register furthers such public opinion, even if the realm in which the register is used is still quite limited. In summary, the circulation of the "Special Period lexicon" at the very least allows opinions to be expressed implicitly and understood by a group of private individuals who cannot—or choose not to—assemble into a public body. Yet members of this shadow public can nevertheless communicate with one another about the difficulty of their situation, without direct threat from state power and without directly threatening it in turn.

5

What Goods Mean in Cuba

I have spoken of Cuban "means" and the words that signify such means, but it is often the phenomenological, concrete, material goods themselves that hold special significance for Cubans in the late-socialist era. Material frustrations and shortages add consumer insult to citizen injury, but unlike political problems, consumer frustrations are something that Cubans feel comfortable talking about. Goods and their value are thus a common and acceptable topic of conversation in the absence of explicitly political discourse. In this chapter I discuss what goods mean to Cuban citizen-consumers and what they tell themselves and others about goods: what constitutes luxury versus necessity; the cultural importance of brand names, quality, and pricing; and the global flows and interpersonal exchanges that allow Cubans to have intimate knowledge of and firsthand experience with foreign products and lifestyles. Finally, I consider Cuba's placement in global "millennial capitalism," and the importance of goods in the development of citizen-consumers' shared social imaginary, as well as the regime's shift away from state socialism, which is driven by citizen-consumer desire.

Personal Consumer Frustrations

One month, after waiting in line at her ration station, Elena received her monthly allotment of fourteen eggs.[1] Upon her return home, she cracked them open to make omelets and discovered that half smelled foul, having gone bad after improper storage. Elena decided take them back to the *bodega* and make her dissatisfaction known, partly for dramatic effect, but also hoping to exchange them, since she is ostensibly guaranteed a certain number per month. Not surprisingly, she found that all the eggs had already been distributed, and the woman managing the *bodega* said her hands were tied: there would be no more eggs until next month. Elena would just have to cope with her bad luck and more shortages. What was once a gift from the state had become a scant supplement, and now a rotten assault. She was disgusted.

As Elena enjoyed soda crackers spread with butter at my house one afternoon, she talked about how, since no one in particular owned the hallways of her building and no one was paid to clean them, she'd taken it upon herself to do so. Interrupting herself in the middle of her story, she ruminated, "Butter is something I miss these days," in a tone that sounded as if she were talking about an old friend. Since butter had been elevated by circumstances to a rare luxury item on her grocery list, she had not seen it on her table in many months. "Butter keeps the intestines lubricated," she asserted, attributing her recent constipation to lack of foods like butter. She squeezed some honey onto her palm when I left to go into the kitchen, furtively licking it off before I returned. Honey is a luxury item, too, she told me glumly. "I guess this isn't the land of milk and honey," she joked.

She commented on the mass-produced art hanging on the walls of our furnished rental apartment. She identified the schmaltzy double-heart-shaped clock with artificial flowers encased inside as a Mother's Day special in *el chopping* a couple of years earlier. "A lot people have that one," she reported. (I, too, had spotted it in an extraordinary number of homes.) "And I've got that one," she said, identifying what she considered another mass-produced piece: a plastic tray with a fruit motif mounted on our dining room wall. She, herself, had been given an identical one as a gift.

She shook her head in disdain. She avoids such pieces when she can. "Everyone has the same things here; it's hard to maintain a sense of individuality or style in the way you decorate your home when there are only certain things available in *el chopping*," she said, referring to what seemed to be the state-promoted and -enforced bad taste. Not only did Elena seek to prevent her privacy from being violated and her personal liberties from being threatened (see chapter 2); she also had unabating material frustrations, blending her status of unsatisfied citizen with that of unsatisfied consumer.

Petra sat on our shared patio, munching on a dry cracker and taking what she told me was an antianxiety pill as she looked down to inspect the chafing on her plump inner thigh. She had returned from her nephew's wedding inflicted with what she considered this unnecessary wound. In all of Cuba, she explained, there are no pantyhose made for fuller-figured women like her, and having no other choice, she had stuffed herself into cheaply made, ill-fitting Cuban nylon stockings. Inevitably, they had ripped and tugged, causing an injury during what should have been a night of easy dancing and celebration. "No me sirve [they won't do, they don't work]. I know *allá*, where you are from, they have pantyhose for *las gorditas* [affectionate term meaning 'little fatties'], but not here," she sighed. "Los queen-size," she added in heavily accented English, suddenly remembering the U.S. trade name of the product. Petra had wanted to go visit her daughter's family on the other side of the city that day, but couldn't walk the distance with the discomfort and the threat of further chafing. She did not have any balm to soothe her pain (hard to find in Cuba), and this week did not have the money, after the wedding expenses, to catch a cab. So she ended up spending the day at home alone, bringing on a sense of melancholy.

The lack of eggs, butter, choice of artwork, and queen-sized pantyhose do not, of course, constitute human-rights violations. They do, however, embody irritation with the lack of consumer options, fueling anger against a state that controls goods and commerce, and dictates which items are important or necessary for consumers and which are not. Moreover, consumer problems are one of the few things that citizens can complain about openly to other citizens (or visitors) without fear of state reprisal, making them part of a common and acceptable form of conversation in the repression of explicitly political discourse. The constant circulation of consumer complaints is not necessarily symbolic of greater political problems, but it at least hints at deeper dissatisfactions, or sometimes triggers latent, unspoken emotions. Consumer dissatisfaction and specifically articulated complaints serve as a vehicle for critical metadiscourse about local problems of politics and consumption in the late-socialist era.

Brand Names and Means of Transnational Comparison Shopping

Tatiana served as my personal tutor in the subject of local consumption, and thus was the person with whom I had the most conversations about specific goods and brand names. She provided a vivid picture of how important the umbilical cord from Miami to Havana was in terms developing a sense of want and deprivation at home, and illustrated how transnational circuits become personally embedded. The specificity of her knowledge about certain U.S. or foreign brand-name goods, including their costs, was dazzling. Often it equaled—and sometimes even surpassed—my own. Either way, she often seamlessly wove bits of specific North American consumer information into stories, presuming my familiarity with them.

"I don't like delinquency and petty crime. One time I had a bottle of Tri-Vi-Sol kid's vitamins . . . or wait, wait," she corrected herself, "it was Poly-Vi-Sol.[2] Anyway, you know—the one with the cartoon characters—it was sitting on the bathroom shelf when I rented out the apartment for a couple of nights to some Spanish guy and his *jinetera*. I didn't notice right away, but guess what went missing? The Poly-Vi-Sol! She swiped it!"

Comparison shopping was Tatiana's specialty, and brand names served as meaningful signifiers for quality and worth: "Wella hair-care products are a good value, but two-in-one shampoo and conditioner *no me sirve* [don't work for me]; Adidas swimming trunks, given the material from which they are made, really should not cost more than US$11; Palmolive is a very high-quality brand," she instructed. She also bought me a clear green bar of soap made with chamomile as a modern alternative to *remedios caseros,* the home remedies that involved boiling steaming cauldrons of herbs, daily, on the stovetop, to treat the baby's skin problem. Diaper rash? There are two types of Desitin she explained to me, bringing out both the "original" and "aloe *ploos*" (plus), and personally applied a coating to my son every day, after his bath, generously using her own supply. Why had I not brought Johnson's Baby Shampoo with me? Was my brand sufficiently "No More Tears" to use comfortably when bathing the baby? It would be a shame to get shampoo in his eyes. Hadn't I ever heard of Pampers disposable crib liners? She was surprised that I had not. They are very convenient and sanitary if you are using cloth diapers, which often leak at night.

Tatiana had vast knowledge not only of North American products and their uses, but also their cost, quality, and where they might be purchased. Tatiana had been charting my path as I tried to track down balloons for my daughter's birthday party, and empathetically inquired about the outcome of my various and exasperating balloon ventures, to which I was becoming shamefully emotionally committed despite the obvious shortages. I was surprised that I was refusing to throw the little party without balloons. I seemed to be absorbing and reflecting the standards and worked-up emotions of my neighbors, developing a new "complicity" with my informants (as spelled out in Marcus 1998b), in that we now had a shared relationship to "a third party"—in this case, a state blocking the fulfillment of mundane consumer desires. I had never been so determined to get balloons in my life.

After traveling around Havana, I was eventually successful, finding four balloons at the fifth location I checked. They were US$0.75 each at an elite dollar boutique. I hesitated for a moment at the counter with my purchases, which also included what seemed to be the only toy available for purchase in the country: a US$35 miniature plastic dollhouse. I commented with some distress on the inflated prices of my purchases to the young, well-groomed boutique saleswoman, attired in her state-issued navy blue uniform and bow tie, a sign that she had been granted a dollar-store retail position by the state for perceived good behavior.

"Yes. The salaries don't match the prices here," she explained matter-of-factly, "and that's why we're depressed." And then she added quickly, "pero, bueno"[3] (well, all right) and began to ring up my goods on the register, letting me know, though I hadn't considered asking, that there was no wrapping paper, here or anywhere else in the country.

When I told Tatiana the price of the balloons she cried indignantly, "That's ridiculous! But you can get a pack of one hundred balloons for $1.00 at El Wal-Mart! I had some but, unfortunately, now they're all gone."

"El Wal-Mart?" I laughed in confusion.

"Not here, in Miami," she specified. She then listed the prices of various birthday party items in the United States, able to do transnational comparison shopping without ever having set her foot outside the island.

Global Media, Intimate Sources of Influence

Most of Tatiana's intimate knowledge and evaluation of products came directly from phone conversations with her aunt in Miami (what else, I wondered, can you talk about on the phone without fear of being monitored on tapped phone lines), and from personal experience with gifts brought over by Tatiana's cousin, who was a business administrator in Miami. But some of the information came from being riveted to the black-market satellite TV at her neighbor's apartment. David, Tatiana's husband, was a great fan of satellite TV—"More than one hundred channels!" he enthusiastically announced more than once. He watched a movie most nights. The first person he knew with satellite TV got it in 1996 when the equipment was $1,200, but that price was coming down—to US$700 to buy satellite equipment and then $100 for six months' service. Obviously, that was very expensive by Cuban standards, but he said that thanks to satellite TV, he had been able to view the sports channels, Major League Baseball, the NBA, movie channels, Fox, and "I really love Discovery Channel," he added. And the best for news? "CNN." He also declared an interest in watching American commercials, especially since Cuban TV had no commercials other than public announcements.

Suddenly, I understood why David had been able to say with confidence that Cuban sports stadiums paled in comparison to the all-weather domed stadiums in the United States. It was also now clearer to me why, when we were eating cheese pizza from our local stand and I commented with genuine enthusiasm on how delicious it was, David seemed pleased and confused. "Really?" he asked, then reflected on his own response: "I guess we Cubans are *muy exigente* [really demanding/exacting]. We have low esteem for the things that are ours, and can't believe what we have could be good. We see a hot McDonald's burger dripping with cheese, or a Domino's pizza, and we assume our own pizza is worse. That what we have couldn't be good because it's Cuban. And we can't travel in order to see for ourselves."

There are other ways of receiving firsthand accounts of U.S. lifestyles besides illegal satellite, including gleaning information from an unrelated foreigner such as myself. I spent three long, hot mornings with Frances, who ran an underground *círculo* in a different Havana district and was expecting a second child of her own in several months. At the time, I still had the last of a supply of disposable baby wipes, a ubiquitous hygiene and convenience item in the developed world. "Can I hold one of those?" she asked shyly. She took the moistened, lightly perfumed towelette in her hand, feeling it between her fingers and sniffing it. "And when you're done, you just . . . throw it away in the trash?" she asked. I assented. "Well, when you run out of those things," she warned me accurately, "you're just going to have to use *caca* [poop] rags, and wash them like we do."

Frances did not have family abroad, making baby wipes quite an exotic item to her, but Beatriz, my daughter's child-care provider, was a woman in her early fifties who received generous support in the form of remittances and gifts from her North American kin. In addition to that support, Beatriz had worked quite hard for the last two years or so, running a small, illegal *círculo* from her home. She also quietly generated income by cutting and coloring hair, selling black-market children's apparel, and providing Swedish massage. While the liveliness of the children and her involvement in her other small businesses served as a distraction, she grieved over her inability to take care of her elderly mother or meet her new baby granddaughter, both of whom lived in "Virginia del Oeste" (West Virginia). Beatriz had been repeatedly unsuccessful in obtaining a visa from the Cuban government to go visit them (even though she actually had the cash to fund the trip), and was beginning to feel desperate and hopeless, as her mother aged and as she missed the milestones of her granddaughter's first year.

Besides phone calls (Beatriz did not have a phone, but her downstairs neighbor did and allowed her to receive calls from abroad on it), the West Virginia family kept in touch by videotaping themselves in their homes, giving Beatriz guided tours of their daily lives, showing her their things, and allowing her to see them in action. The videotapes had been discreetly hand-delivered (to avoid censorship) by a trusted West Virginian visitor. Beatriz watched the videotapes an extraordinary amount, because it was a way to feel close to her family, she explained. She also showed them to guests and other people who came by her apartment. When I came to pick up or drop off Maya, the tapes were often playing in the background, and I had the opportunity to watch them several times myself.

On one tape, Beatriz's tall, muscular, fair son, wearing a baseball cap, walked around his comfortable, suburban two-story home (which they owned), with Beatriz's granddaughter, baby Rosario, in his arms. He pointed out various features of décor in matching warm beiges and light blues. The camera panned to the wall-to-wall carpet, the wallpaper, a den with an enormous TV set, a full dining room set, a picture window displaying a green backyard. Later baby Rosario, wearing a headband and matching earrings and sundress, was filmed in the yard, swinging on her very own infant swing set while she gurgled into the camera. The jiggly camera also panned through a well-equipped kitchen with large cabinets and spacious Formica counters, where Beatriz's daughter-in-law was preparing food, with the whir of a garbage disposal in the background. A wooden staircase with a carved banister led to the second floor. The family spoke into the camera, telling her how much they loved her and missed her, but the guided tour of their home and its interior was the most prominent feature of the film.

"What does your son do in America?" I asked Beatriz with interest.

"He's a long-haul trucker and his wife is a schoolteacher. . . . They're middle class," she volunteered, trying to define their relative wealth in American terms.

The video footage of her aging mother was shot at a luxurious assisted-living facility for the elderly, just a short drive a way from her son's home. The rooms were spacious and clean, and she had a view of a rolling green park from her small balcony. There was also a long scene shot in the basement of the old folks' home, showing a laundry room full of white, Maytag industrial-size washers and dryers. Grandma demonstrated how to use the machine, the size of the tub inside, and the various options on the dials. "*Imagínate!*" (Imagine that!), exclaimed Beatriz, who had recently been hand-laundering, unable to repair her own Russian machine for lack of parts. Her mother assured her she was comfortable and getting good care; she only hoped to see her beloved daughter again soon.

This view of America that Beatriz soaked up through videos was more intimate, explicit, and firsthand than watching the wealth evident on "Beverly Hills 90210" or "Sábado Gigante"[4] by illegal satellite, or even talking with relatives over the phone. She was able to see, co-narrate, and share with friends, local family, neighbors, and clients images of the life that her very own American family enjoyed, to show them the things they used, how they had built their life, and the deep love they still had for her. She was able to broadcast these images and messages at will, again and again, providing an "advertisement" of the American dream that was personalized, vivid, and recurrent. Ostensibly, neighbors and friends came to view the videos because they had known the mother and the son, who had lived right in the very *barrio* where Beatriz had been left behind, but there was no denying that the material aspects of the images also held some allure.

Historic U.S.-Cuba Consumer Connections

No matter in what form it is packaged, displayed, or broadcast, the relationship between North American consumer culture and Cuban taste for commodities has a prerevolutionary history (see L. Pérez 1999). As Skidmore and Smith write in their section titled "Americanization in Pre-Revolutionary Cuba":

By the 1950s, a North American–style consumer culture had taken hold in Havana and the larger provincial cities. Cuban elites bought U.S. automobiles and went on lavish shopping trips to Miami and New York, bringing the latest fashions and consumer durables. While their social betters lived in the style of the North American rich, middle-income Cubans struggled within a dependent economy to obtain the U.S. consumer goods demanded by their precarious social position . . . working-class Cubans also held higher expectations than their Latin American neighbors, measuring their standard of living against North American workers. These unfulfilled expectations further contributed to a sense of decline and disenchantment by the late 1950s. This dilemma was compounded for Cubans employed at a U.S. firm: these Cubans were paid better than their countrymen, but worse than their North American coworkers. (Skidmore and Smith 2004: 268–69)

Falcoff (2003: 25) also argues that Cuba is, despite the political differences between the two countries since 1959, the Latin American country most strongly influenced by the United States, as measured by, for example, consumer preferences, entertainment, or tourism. Moreover, in 1958, more Cubans visited the United States than Americans visited Cuba.

Ojito also links the significance of goods to a prerevolutionary time in her personal memoir of her Cuban childhood in Havana in the 1970s:

I was reminded daily of the life my parents used to have before the revolution, of the life they claimed I should have had. My parents often talked of bathing with fragrant soaps, of using shampoos that actually cleaned long hair like mine, of American-made appliances that lasted for years, and of a sticky magical concoction, called Vicks VapoRub, that cured all coughs and unclogged stuffy noses. The cobalt blue glass bottle of one, the last one my parents bought before American products disappeared from pharmacies, still sat in the middle of our medicine cabinet. All the possibilities of capitalism, of life in pre-Castro Cuba, were encapsulated for me in that squat little container of a salve so old that it had lost its scent. (Ojito 2005: 16)

Most of these material details, and the emotions and associations they provoke, remain true today, fifty years after the revolution: the desire for fashions, health products and consumer durables; the high expectations of "working class" or lower-income Cubans; the measurement of the Cuban standard of living against that of North American workers; the salary discrepancies between Cubans working at Cuban companies and those working at foreign firms (now joint ventures with European rather than U.S. companies).[5] All these reflect the same inequalities and sense of second-class citizenship.

Most of all, the result—unfulfilled expectations and sense of decline and disenchantment—remains strikingly unchanged. Some of these emotions have deepened with time, and some unsatisfied citizen-consumers question whether the revolution has come full circle, bringing ordinary Cubans back in time. In reality, some of the inequalities have taken on new forms and intensified. "Two entire generations of Cubans," writes Falcoff, "have been brought up to expect—as a matter of right—a standard of living that the island cannot possibly produce without massive and continuous outside assistance or a radical reordering of its economic system, or quite possibly both" (2003: 40).

Many residents of middle-income neighborhoods such as Los Árboles have relatives who live abroad, linking Cuba directly to somewhere else. This intensifies citizen-consumers' feelings of isolation and restrained movement because they cannot purchase, own, or experience what their kin in exile do, let alone join those friends and relatives who supply, along with their remittances, the details that fuel consumer dissatisfaction.[6] Unlike on the other side of the Florida Straits, the promised land in their collective imagination, in Cuba there are no discount mega-stores, affordable family restaurant franchises, or even "mom-and-pop" stores offering credit to help them stretch their income (which they know operate openly even in the poorest and least-developed Latin American towns). Glumness follows from the knowledge of things to be had in the wider world. It colors the neighborhood mood. It shapes the contours of a common and socially acceptable public discourse of complaint.

Campesino Consumption and Desire

How far does the discourse of complaint radiate? While I would not argue that the unsatisfied citizen-consumer type exists in the same form throughout the country, I would argue that it is important to look beyond Havana, which is considered to be the bastion of both economic possibilities and political discontent.

In a semirural area outside of Havana, a long, bumpy ride away in a large passenger *camion* (truck), lived Stan and his wife, Jinori. Their house, like those of their neighbors, was a short, squat, one-story micro-brigade building, made of cinder block and painted white.[7] Like most of their neighbors' houses it was also in good repair. I had met Stan and Jinori at a clinic in the city, and we decided to continue our conversation over a visit.

Stan was a hospitable, second-generation dairy farmer who welcomed us into his home a few times, generously serving us meals. Stan didn't like or trust city folk, in particular *los Habaneros* (natives of Havana). He contrasted them with *gente del pueblo* (townspeople or villagers) and particularly with campesinos (farmers or peasants). He had a number of reasons for his dislike: neighbors don't know each other; people aren't as sincere; and in Havana in particular there was a *"psicosis del dólar"* (a dollar psychosis), where people had become obsessed with obtaining dollars, thinking they needed things like fashionable sunglasses to survive.

Stan did project an overall sentiment of contentment, pride of place, and quality of life. There was no talk of leaving in his house; there was a sense of bounty rather than dearth; and he and his wife did little or no complaining. These qualities contrasted with my overall impressions of Havana. "Look at what we have," Stan said a couple of times, pointing to livestock feeding outside in the back, bananas growing on trees, piles of even more bananas and other ripening fruit sitting outdoors on the washbasin, and creamy milk poured from a brown glass bottle—the first fresh, liquid milk I had ever seen in the country. He and his wife, after many years, were even expecting a second child.

He offered us a tour of the bungalow, and immediately started pointing out some new equipment he had obtained. He had originally had twelve dairy cows, but now he had just five. Despite his convictions and self-identification as a campesino, he had just sold seven cows that year in order to update and modernize his country home. Although he was confident that he was not afflicted with the so-called *psicosis del dólar,* he was, nevertheless, proud to point out the following details on his unself-conscious tour:

· Dark wood, multipurpose (*multiusado*) entertainment shelf made by a private carpenter: 1,000 pesos, 80 pesos more to refurbish, made possible by the sale of two cows
· LG brand Korean TV ($279) and new VCR ($300)—"that was also two cows"
· 3 CD/2 cassette player ($179)—Spanish in-law chipped in $100, Stan paid for the rest
· Medium-sized LG brand fridge/freezer on legs—1 cow
· Standard washing machine in bedroom—gift from his father-in-law, who worked as a metal welder in Spain
· Decorative bowl of non-standard-issue plastic fruit, gift also purchased in Spain by his father-in-law.

On a later visit, he popped a videotape, brought from abroad, into his one-cow VCR. "I love Mexican music," Stan explained. It was as we watched his concert selection together—first, a Mexican rap band, and then a sombrero-and cape-wearing Mexican macho, singing traditional love songs for a swooning Mexican audience—that the first cracks appeared. "I would actually love to go to Mexico," Stan mused. "If I went, you know what I would do? I would buy all the videos of my favorite singers, and go to a bunch of concerts. But, of course, I can't go," he reminded himself practically. "You can't leave Cuba without an invitation from the host country. And even then . . . pero, bueno," he drifted off, going back to enjoying his Mexican concert on tape. Even this self-identified, locally proud, noble campesino was *inventando* ways to get more things, whether through familial financial connections to Spain or through dreaming about Mexico.[8]

Conclusion: What Goods and Value Mean

There is no inherent value in a baby wipe or a bay leaf, a plastic bag or pantyhose, but "we call those objects valuable that resist our desire to possess them" (Simmel 1978 in Appadurai 1986: 3). Simmel's perceptions on the value of goods, as filtered by Appadurai, are relevant to the Cuban context I have presented (see also Urban's [2001: 61–66] discussion of trade, value, and demand). Cuban unsatisfied consumers' endless attempts at finding, seeking, hoarding, trading, and inventing alternatives to goods, a sample of which I have described in this chapter, make clear the desired goods' "resistance to being possessed" and, of course, unsatisfied citizen-consumers' drive to possess them. However, the subjective perception of the value of goods does not exist in a vacuum, but rather in a locally governed and globally situated "regime of value," driven, in the Cuban case, by the twin forces of foreign *origin* and local *scarcity*.

Despite the U.S. embargo against Cuba and Cuba's subsequent relative macroeconomic isolation, changes in Cuban society are undeniably happening in a global world, among citizens who want to be part of a modernizing country. The less access citizens have to globally circulating goods and information, the more precious and desired those goods and information become—and the more value they accrue. Socialities and micro-interactions surrounding goods come to reflect the most basic of economic principles: as the supply goes down, the price rises. This presents a strange but logical irony: citizen-consumers' lack of access actually spurs a hyper-intimacy with and knowledge of foreign goods, and creates unusual and socially rich paths toward their acquisition.

Simmel offers an illumination of goods or economic objects, particularly that they "exist in the space between pure desire and immediate enjoyment, with some distance between them and the person who desires them, which is a distance that can be overcome" (as summarized in Appadurai 1986: 3). But what distance? Who creates the distance? How can it be overcome? What if everything becomes an economic object, even if that was not the intent of the people or their socialist state? The heightened value of certain ordinary goods makes those goods grow in importance beyond their phenomenological materiality. In many settings this process, originating from Marxist principles, has been called "commodity fetishization" (a process by which goods have been imbued with a spiritual or magical quality; see, for an ethnographic example, Taussig 1983). It could easily be argued that a similar process has occurred here, and that goods in Cuba are fetishes.

Expanding on goods as fetishes, in this concluding section of the chapter, I consider the role of goods in a local milieu of late socialism and a global world of neoliberalism and millennial capitalism; the symbolic quality of the goods in a classical Geertzian sense; and finally, consumption as an act of resistance in the Cuban context. I will frame what Cuban goods mean in each of these contexts in turn.

Global, Millennial Capitalism and the Intimacy of Goods in Cuba

In the Comaroffs' account of millennial capitalism,[9] and specifically in their interpretation of the culture of neoliberalism in the era of millennial capitalism, they claim that such a culture "re-visions persons not as producers from a particular community, but as consumers in a planetary marketplace" (2001: 13), making the role of citizen-consumers in a neoliberal world surpass the importance of citizen-producers in an old "world systems" world (à la Wallerstein 1974). They also argue that the identity of consumers in a planetary marketplace is superseding national ideologies, as global media provoke further consumer desire for material accumulation:

> In the vacuum left by retreating national ideologies . . . people in these societies are washed over by a flood of mass media from across the earth; media depicting a cargo of animated objects and lifestyles that affirm the neoliberal message of freedom and self-realization through consumption. Under such conditions . . . images of desire are as pervasive as they are inaccessible. (Comaroff and Comaroff 1999: 20).

To what degree is late-socialist Cuba part of the millennial capitalist project? To what degree are Cuban citizen-consumers neoliberal subjects? If dissatisfaction is part of the game of neoliberalism, and desire part of millennial capitalism, it would appear Cubans are quite involved in this project.Yet it seems equally true that in the painful disjuncture between global diasporic trends in consumption and Cubans' individual hopes and expectations, they are brought into conflict with the state. This disjuncture also promotes citizens' preoccupation with material things and coping strategies, one of which is the shadow economy.

Furthermore, Cubans themselves do not frame their concerns as neoliberal concerns, but rather as ordinary human and universal concerns—what anyone would want to have for a sense of well-being. Like most Latin Americans, Cubans share "pressing economic issues" that are immediate and family-oriented, questions centering on "who works, where, and with what remuneration?" (Colburn 2002: 82). Notwithstanding Cuba's relative isolation as a state, these concerns are in fact coming from a metacultural discourse formed by neoliberalism and transmitted, at least at one important level, by global media. In this prolonged late-socialist historical moment, Cubans are comparing in explicit, vivid, and personalized ways how their daily lives and the things that fill them are different from the lives that are broadcast to them. Illegally viewed "mediascapes" (Appadurai 1996) and personal conversations are changing what Cubans imagine possible. This absorption of media is grounded in the private domestic sphere of home and family and fuels the production of hope, sometimes masking its origin. Media representations serve as models of and models for (Geertz 1973: 93) comfortable living—and even if they cannot be emulated under existing conditions, they are nevertheless incorporated into the collective social imaginary of possibilities in the world.

Goods as Local Symbols

While lifestyles and their representations can be somewhat abstract, usually viewed at a distance, goods themselves are mobile, they can be viewed at close quarters and, when obtained, they are palpable. Among unsatisfied citizen-consumers, goods are not merely ends unto themselves. Rather, they profoundly affect how social actors see themselves, what they are able to imagine at home, and how they imagine a life away from home. Goods, in other words, are also palpable harbingers of an imagined future: "A bottle of Advil, here in my hand! Imagine if only I could buy Advil for my aches, pains, and fevers whenever I liked . . . well, it's not so hard to imagine, there are places you can do that. This bottle has come from that place." Understanding and immersing oneself in the tangibility of goods and the lexicon surrounding means allows the "experience-distant"—that is, constructions of "neoliberal subject," "millennial capitalism," and the "lived effects of economy"—to become "experience-near" in the late-socialist context.

Goods, in other words, are signifiers, as evidenced by the discourse surrounding and describing them: their availability, their dearth, their quality, their desirability, and their value. Goods also signify unsatisfied citizen-consumer culture in the classical Geertzian sense of the word. That is to say, unsatisfied Cubans are suspended in "webs" of significance about goods and their value that they themselves have spun (Geertz 1973: 5). They have woven the meaning of goods into their relationships with each other, with the state, and with the outside world.

Goods are also coded for communication (Douglas and Isherwood 1996: xxi), the perfect vehicle for "publicly shared" meaning. They are "messages in bottles"—of Poly-Vi-Sol vitamins, Paul Mitchell hair conditioner, or Heinz ketchup—that diffuse from one place to another, both concretizing citizen-consumers' ideas about themselves and allowing them to project messages about themselves. Johnson's Baby Shampoo comes to signify the ability to care for one's child in a gentle, modern way; vanilla signifies one's ability to flavor rice pudding in the way that is tasty, familiar, and expected; queen-sized pantyhose signifies adorning oneself comfortably for celebration. In Cuba, the list could go on and on, and it does.

While citizen-consumers might not be able to ensure that they directly experience modernity and comfort, quality and choice, ease and ability, convenience and hygiene, goods can serve as a temporary proxy for this lifestyle. In a country where the state defines and delimits an individual's life path on so many parameters, bottles can be successfully obtained through *luchando, resolviendo, consiguiendo, inventando* (struggling, resolving, finding, and inventing) and, unlike citizens themselves, bottles are mobile. They cross national boundaries. They might once have been on a shelf in Miami or Virginia del Oeste, Spain, or Mexico. But a trick of fate or commerce brought them to Cuba.

"One means of bypassing or surpassing national blockages has been through the informal attainment of international goods," writes O'Dougherty (2002: 131) of the Brazilian case. A degree of individual agency is expressed through obtaining desired goods. *Agency,* as I use it here, is based on Anthony Giddens's (1984: 14) definition: "to be able to 'act otherwise' means being able to intervene in the world or to refrain from such intervention with the effect of influencing a process or state of affairs." In late-socialist Cuba, where a centrally planned market continues to control so much, the black, gray, underground, and transnational markets take on special allure—linking Cuba to the outside world (but most often to Miami), creating not only an alternative market, but also an alternative semiotic field where goods flow and change hands, manipulated by private citizens rather than the state. An opening up of these market and consumer options signifies a taste of freedom and a possibility for control.

García Canclini, who has also written on citizen-consumers, bears repeating in this context: "to consume is to participate in a field of disputes over goods that a society produces and over the ways of using them" (2001: 45). And what if the society does not produce the goods? Equally, then, there is a "field of dispute concerning the goods the society does not produce, or does not have access to" (O'Dougherty 2002: 131). With so few arenas for "dispute," it is no wonder that unsatisfied Cubans are so preoccupied with goods. These statements hint at creativity and agency in the use of goods, and at the role of local consumption in a global setting. Other authors also explicitly address these themes.

Deborah Thomas (2004: 250), in her exploration of what she calls the "local-global" in Jamaica (her term for the dialectical interpretation of local cultural practice/capitalist globalization and creative consumerism/cultural imperialism), critiques scholarly assertions that global capitalism destroys cultural diversity or is non-negotiable in its imperialism. She asserts that consumption is a "creative and potentially liberatory process," publicly important in that it not only reflects, but also influences global style[10]—a practice most closely associated with creolization and hybridization (Bhabha 1994, 2001; Barber and Waterman 1995; Howes 1996).

While ordinary Cubans do not generally have the liberty or the capital to use consumption as a means of creative self-expression outside of their own neighborhoods,[11] consuming does have a productive purpose: it allows a Cuban shadow public to start its own modernization process, independent of the policies of the state. It also enables them to develop their tastes, networks, and patterns of consumption, albeit according to a morality that runs counter to revolutionary ideals. In other words, through consumption practices and an occasional ability to indulge in transnational tastes, they are enabled to classify and distinguish themselves (Bourdieu 1984).[12] It allows Cubans to deploy their own social imaginary, not in the sense of a set of ideas but, as Charles Taylor (2004: 2) states, as an imaginary "which enables, through making sense of the practices of society." In other words, the diffusion of goods allows Cubans to modernize themselves and their practices, to be a part of something bigger, even if they live in a state that they deem desolately *atrasado* (held back). It allows them to reinscribe what it means to live well.

As I have said many times, unsatisfied citizen-consumers are by definition not activists, nor do they feel they have the means to organize as a group. For unsatisfied citizen-consumers, obtaining desired goods represents an important example of the limited repertoire of collective action at their disposal (Taylor 2004: 24)—even if their actions are dispersed and fragmentary (p. 85). Nevertheless, prioritizing goods in daily life is not only a coping strategy, but also a quiet, popularly led transformation of orthodox revolutionary priorities.

"Who needs balloons, Comrade?" asks an imagined State. The unsatisfied citizen-consumer responds, "Who in the hell are you to say? Why can't we decide? If we can't decide for ourselves here, perhaps we will shop elsewhere! Perhaps we will *live* elsewhere. Perhaps we will discover what freedom is elsewhere!"[13] This exchange is a private, critical metadiscourse, but one that is made partially public by critical consumer metadiscourse about goods in the late-socialist moment.

Dollars, Means, and
the New Cuban Class System

Offering me a parting gift, a dusty little *tacita* (espresso demitasse) from her own kitchen set, the elderly mother of my landlady, a pensioner, apologized for what she considered too small a gesture, "But I can't offer you something nicer, because I don't have access to dollars." No longer do people describe themselves as poor, or of humble origins, but in relation to their ability to access dollars. Since the delegalization of the dollar (popularly known as *fula* or *divisa*) in 2004, the only legal currency in circulation has been the Cuban convertible peso (CUC; see chapter 1, note 11). But, as citizen-consumers say, in the end it's all dollars, and they serve the same purpose. Dollars by any name are equated not only with wealth, but among citizen-consumers, are also tied tightly to happiness, ease of living, and a countenance that allows families to tolerate tough times. Dollars have arguably become the defining element of social life in late-socialist Cuba. For the first time since the revolution (although no such statistics are officially kept), income distribution among Cubans has become significantly unequal, and there is stratification based on dollar earnings.[1] The predictable consequences of this division can also be seen. In particular, ill-will arises between neighbors, friends, and acquaintances related to the various means and modes of acquisition to dollars, and a new Cuban class system has emerged.

While this evolving stratification is fairly well documented, the social interactions between members of the new social classes is not, and is something I begin to explore in this chapter. I describe moments of new tension between Cubans with and without access to dollars to illustrate the boundaries between citizens, and to better understand the placement of unsatisfied citizen-consumers in the spectrum of poverty and wealth in Cuba. I place names on new "classes," or social-economic networks, of Cubans that have taken shape since the legalization of the dollar in 1993 (replaced by the CUC in 2004), discuss the conundrum of race and poverty, and attempt to capture the lived experience and political potential of Cuban monetary dualism.

Legal Means and Dollar Dogs

Traveling almost exclusively in unsatisfied citizen-consumer networks, I sometimes got the impression that all Cubans operate private businesses in the shadows and, in truth, there is usually some element of any legal enterprise that is not fully aboveboard by orthodox socialist standards. Nevertheless, state-sanctioned moves toward the market in the late-socialist era have also changed the topography of Cuban society, making possibilities for legally earning dollars part of the new social and economic reality as well. Ironically, the Cuban state has had a direct hand in both attempting to maintain equality and simultaneously exacerbating inequality among its citizens through the legalization of the dollar and of select private enterprises during the Special Period.

The presence of *casas particulares* changes citizens' relationships to the state and also their discernment of each other.[2] For example, when I first developed my relationship with E-mail Elena, my family was renting a room at Stuart's while we looked for a suitable place to live more permanently. Stuart was a different kind of Cuban, a different kind of citizen, and a different kind of consumer, important for understanding the private enterprise continuum.

The four rooms for rent inside Stuart's spacious *casa particular* were freshly coated in cool, pastel shades. A crystal chandelier hung from the salon ceiling, framed oil paintings decorated the walls, china knickknacks were on display, a heavy wooden table sat in the center of the living room for meals, and a wide veranda overlooked the quiet city streets. The veranda had lawn furniture, a glass table where guests could enjoy drinks, and free weights and a wooden sit-up board that Stuart occasionally used to keep his potbelly in check. Stuart was an *arrendador inscrito* (a state-registered lessor) in the strict sense of the term. He paid his bed-and-breakfast *impuestos* (taxes) promptly and got *permisos* (permits) for anything he did within the business. He paid a $50 monthly advertising fee to have a large blue-and-white sticker placed on his door, denoting him as an official member of the state-sanctioned earning club. Stuart played by the rules (as far as the state could see), was slick and professional with his clients and, unlike most Cubans, was up-front about money, though he kept his opinions about Cuban politics to himself when mingling with guests.

Because Stuart played by the rules, he was allowed to advertise his room-and-board service on the Internet. This helped keep his rooms filled with North American and European guests, whom he charged and overcharged for anything he could think of. Like a Western hotelkeeper, he would present a final bill to the guests at the end of their stay. In the eyes of the state, Stuart was a perfect gatekeeper for tourists visiting Cuba. He kept them happy and directed them toward sanctioned tourist activities that would not penetrate the veneer of socialist Cuba.

Yet Stuart and people like him are not just part of a two-tiered economy. They are part of a two-tiered lifestyle. In my field notes, I identify Stuart and people like him as "Dollar Dogs," because they bark and bound after dollars, to which they have seemingly unlimited access. *Arrendadores inscritos* and other members of the new Cuban legal business elite of the late-socialist period, people like Stuart and his outwardly clean-living social network, are often Party members. The gross salary they earn for renting just one room for a night is much greater than what state workers in the hotel industry would earn in an entire month. If you have access to dollars, you can quit your government job and live in your own country almost like a tourist: taking nice taxis, eating in restaurants, going to the pool, and going out dancing. Dollars allow you some freedom to choose what you want to buy and where you want to buy it. Part of what being a Dollar Dog is all about is surrounding yourself with other Dogs who are able to do those things along with you, forming a pocket of wealth and an identifiable consuming sector. You can purchase an array of goods that the average Cuban cannot: self-employed Cubans patronize other self-employed shoemakers, artisans, restaurateurs, repairmen, and so on, because their goods and services are of higher quality, though more expensive, than state-produced goods (B. Smith 1999: 51). In short, private earning begets private spending.

"Other" Cubans, those outside of close cronies and the family members Stuart legally hires to help with cooking and cleaning, would rarely see the inside of his home—there would just be no logical social reason for them to. I invited E-mail Elena over one afternoon after an e-mail session, placing the two Cubans—Stuart and Elena—in an unusual position: Elena got to see the inside of a lucrative *casa particular*, and Stuart had to accept another Cuban seeing it. Stuart approached me that evening.

"Look," he said, sitting down, leaning forward on his lawn chair, and lacing his fingers, "I don't know who that woman was, but let me give you a piece of advice: be careful who you socialize with in Cuba." I explained that she was a friend, and that she was also helping me with some editing and laundry. "I saw her looking." He pointed to his own eyes and then jabbed his index finger around the room, "looking at your stuff, looking at my stuff. You can't just trust Cubans. I don't mind if you bring friends by to entertain them. But, please, keep it on the patio. And it's better that you get your laundry done through me. It's more secure that way," he said, implicitly encouraging me to keep my dollars safely in his profit and commission network. He also wanted to keep the interior of his home business private and safe from curious or lascivious gazes.

Undeniably, Elena had been looking. Even gaping. "Wow," she commented when we were alone again later. "I can't believe that place. How does he do it? I was looking at some of the details in there. Incredible. They look like Batista folks. We're back to where we were before the Revolution. You have to be careful with him. You can't trust other Cubans. He seems like the type who would try to milk you for your money without thinking about if it is fair. And there are employees in there who see a lot of tourists, and they might not think of you as an individual or a nice family, and so not respect you or your things. I saw him, the owner, watching me. He doesn't trust me."

Quincy

Quincy was the weathered, furious cook and cleaner at Stuart's. He shuffled around in trousers that had ripped down the back seam but had been thriftily restitched. His skin was brownish red from more than twenty years of work in the agricultural sector. When we met him, he had been legally employed by Stuart as a family member for four years, sharing the position part-time with his equally disgruntled sister, who used to be the personal secretary to a judge. Quincy was just one of many poorer Cubans in the new, two-tiered economy who was working for a Cuban of greater means, a phenomenon that harkens back to the prerevolutionary era.

When Quincy was not serving guests breakfast platters heavy with banana, guava, pineapple, and watermelon; or pouring strong coffee accompanied by hot milk and cane sugar in a matching turquoise china tea set; or mopping and remopping the tile floors to clear them of dust and footprints left by tourists, he was complaining bitterly to me. He was relatively vocal about his distaste for the eroding socialist system, but like other unsatisfied citizen-consumers, he made sure his complaints took place out of the earshot of his boss, in hushed tones. When I asked, he assured me he had no formal venues where he could safely air his complaints.

Quincy was not doing this kind of work by choice, he made clear. "I hate it," he quickly admitted. But he did so out of the pure necessity of functioning in a dollar economy, taking a crowded, two-hour bus ride to work each way. Like his sister, he felt he had shed more interesting, important work, better suited to his skills, to chase dollars. It was not that the work itself was terribly hard, but rather that the nature of Cuba was changing that made him hate it.

Quincy had no problem whispering and hissing accusations about his cousin Stuart, and about the government, behind Stuart's back. At every opportunity, he expressed his disapproval of Stuart's hunger for dollars by rolling his eyes and shaking his head in scorn as Stuart showed rooms to potential guests, spontaneously bumping up prices as he saw fit, depending on the gullibility of the tourists. Quincy caught my eye at such moments, rubbing his thumb and forefingers together to index money-grubbing greed and scowling with great drama.

I appeared to serve as a repository of sorts for Quincy, as he apparently cornered me with a fount of information and opinions at every opportunity: "Did you know there is private medicine in this country?" he challenged me. "Yes, that's right, there are now a few private doctors, dentists, and specialists who accept dollars for service, completely outside of the system. And in the public system, the regular system—it's very corrupt—people who have connections and money are the ones who get seen, get operations, get good service. That's private medicine, too. Am I right? Dentists, for example, charge US$3.00 for an extraction, $3.00 for a cleaning, and $4.00 for a filling, placing such services out of some people's reach. It's a known thing. People are hungry in this country, but all anyone talks about is *dólares, dólares, dólares!*"

We watched an un-narrated bombing of Baghdad live on a small TV with Quincy in March 2003, in one of the guest rooms he was preparing for the next round of visitors. Quincy stroked an imaginary beard (the most common way to silently index Fidel Castro): "He is worse than Saddam Hussein!" Quincy growled. He shook his head at the solemnity of a city in flames, but with subdued invigoration at the prospect of U.S. power intervening against a tyrant. He liked George W. Bush very much, he told me. "I'm ready for him to take care of things here!" he added, waving his thick fingers towards an imaginary Cuba, bidding welcome to radical—even violent—change, expressing a sentiment I heard echoed again later.

How the Other Half Lives

Sometimes Cuban socioeconomic differences are directly visible, as in the instances I have mentioned here. Other times, one can see them only indirectly through the media. Yet unlike in countries where the press, visual media, and films routinely allow citizens to see how "the other half" lives through stories, exposés, and special reports—about, for example, how the extremely wealthy and the very poor live—this type of reporting is nearly nonexistent in Cuba. It became evident to me that unless a Cuban had a direct social link to someone in a different socioeconomic stratum, he or she was less likely than I was to know firsthand what other lives looked like.

This became particularly clear after the 2003 release of the film *Suite Havana*,[3] in which the cinematographer took viewers inside the rundown Old Havana district home of a family with a retarded boy. "Wow! Tremendo!" (Tremendous! Something else!), cried David, as we were discussing the movie at length. "The filthy paint and the hole in the wall . . . it actually makes this place look like a palace!" he said, extending his arm to his own apartment. "I know *you* see this kind of stuff all the time when you go to talk to folks, but I don't, and I found it really shocking."

Similarly, on another night when we were watching Cuban TV at David and Tatiana's (on one of Cuba's three state-operated channels at the time), an interview with a famous *telenovela* (soap opera) actress who was launching a new show came on the air. She sat in a sumptuous room, fat candles burning around her on a low table, and she wriggled her carefully pedicured toes as she spoke. David commented sarcastically as we watched, "There are no social classes in Cuba, *pero* [but]... *pero* how come *my* house doesn't look like that?" he chuckled.

David went on to introduce a special "class" of actors, dancers, artists, athletes, and musicians (*farándula*, or show business people, for short), who hold a unique national status through their access to new commodities such as cars and motorcycles,[4] and who have the legal authorization—even government encouragement—to travel and live abroad for periods of time after signing lucrative international contracts. Hernandez-Reguant elaborates on the phenomenon, describing local economic reforms and cultural institutions–turned–copyright industries in the global market:

> Artists prospered, allowing the socialist state to renew, however precariously, its own legitimacy and public prestige, thereby revitalizing its articulation of national culture and identity with the revolutionary project. As a result, a group of musicians, artists, performers, and entertainers emerged as a highly visible elite with transnational connections—their jet-setting lives contrasting with the bleakness of everyday food deprivation, electricity blackouts, and water shortages. This *farándula* immediately became a symbol of a nascent capitalism that was not identified with a socialist ethic of work but with a system of valorization in which wealth accumulation appeared in the public consciousness to be disproportionate to the input of labor. (Hernandez-Reguant 2004: 2; see also Perna 2005: 205)

David also started talking about the class of "El Burguesía Roja"—the Red Bourgeoisie—in Cuba. "They are young people, relatives of Party members—now even grandsons of Party members—who 'live large,' who have access to all kinds of things—cars, computers, clothes. They are not *jineteros*, they are just 'Party people,' but far, far from Revolutionaries. You would never have access to these guys as informants," David told me. "Never. And they are not interested in leaving. They are living like kings here."[5]

In contrast to performers and the Red Bourgeoisie, unsatisfied citizen-consumers must perpetually be involved in *luchando, resolviendo, consiguiendo,* and *inventando,* activities that set them apart as a "class" somewhere in the broad middle of unsteady income earning. The unsatisfied citizen-consumer families I describe in Cuba might fit typical characterizations of "working class" in some dimensions and "middle class" or perhaps "petit bourgeois" in others. There is also considerable variation among them.

However, unsatisfied citizen-consumers, by definition, have some access to dollars and gifts from abroad (even if irregularly). In fact, knowledge of goods and access to dollars are features that fuel their dissatisfaction. Finally, far below them, at the least-privileged end of the continuum, are Cubans who have no access to dollars, receive no remittances, and work almost exclusively in state positions earning pesos rather than dollars, which sets them apart socially as well as economically. I call them the "peso poor."

Analyzing the Late-Socialist "Class" System

I argue it would have little meaning to assign a single, Marxian class category to any of the groups I discuss, particularly since, in reality, there is often an intriguing melding of proletariat and bourgeoisie, rather than a clear pitting of one against the other. I also argue it would not be productive to assign them the traditional but vague categories of upper, middle, and lower class (based on Warner, Meeker, and Eels's 1949 classic scheme); to assign them a class culture based on these categories; or even to categorize them by income, for not one of these elements unites them neatly as a single group for analysis.

Moreover, neo-Marxist paradigms, popular for years in the analysis of Latin American social inequalities, depend heavily on class as a definitive category for analysis of social relations at the local and national levels, and commonly at the scale of the world system. Too often, however, traditional class categories dull analysis since they blur the *emic* definitions of economic means and can obscure the fluctuating ethnographic details that keep a household or business running. This is certainly the case in late-socialist Cuba, engineered to be a classless state. Standard depictions of class do not capture economically significant details, such as the mode of acquisition of tastes for goods, the social pathways and underground routes to certain types of goods or services, the local irrelevance of educational status when education is nationalized or superfluous in the current economy, the social role of financial obligations to local family, dependence on dollar remittances and durable gifts from abroad, and changing employment circumstances. None of these details are contingent on class alone, but rather flow across and outside of what might be considered class categories, giving rise to new categories, social networks, and meanings of their own.

If standard class categories do not fit the Cuban case, this does not mean that the concept of class in and of itself lacks utility. One can quite easily iden-

Table 6.1. Cuba's Late-Socialist Social Classes

Class	Definition
Red Bourgeoisie	*Burguesía roja;* a very small group of privileged relatives of Party members who party and live like kings
Performers/Athletes	*Farándula;* actors, sportspeople, musicians, and other performers who hold special status, allowing them to travel, own expensive consumer items, and live abroad
Dollar Dogs	Legally operating, self-employed workers raking in big incomes: e.g., *casa particular* owners, *paladar* owners; also individuals with direct financial links to a spouse living abroad
Unsatisfied Citizen-Consumers	Ordinary Cubans perpetually involved in *luchando, resolviendo, inventando,* and *consiguiendo* to gain access to goods and services, setting them in a "class apart"; they fall somewhere in the broad middle of the socioeconomic spectrum, experiencing unsteady income earning and irregular remittances
Peso Poor	State-sector employees earning salaries in pesos and with little or no access to dollars; disproportionately Afro-Cuban

tify the class system that has emerged in Cuba since the dawn of the Special Period. As shown in table 6.1, I propose a system that appears to be based around five new culturally and nationally specific late-socialist "classes": Red Bourgeoisie, Performers/Athletes, Dollar Dogs, Unsatisfied Citizen-Consumers, and Peso Poor.

I would not claim that the categories in this table encompass all segments of Cuban society, that the boundaries between them are absolutely fixed (as I will illustrate ethnographically later, through the case of one household), or that they address the constellation of social and economic relationships in rural areas, which are not covered in this book; however, these five groups highlight locally meaningful differences across an emerging and solidifying hierarchy.

Although some have argued that there are no "marginal classes," as there were prior to the revolution, it has also been argued that this might be so "since no one remains beyond the reach of government services, or—what amounts to the same thing—free of government discipline" (Falcoff 2003: 33). Specifically, while government discipline is intensive for those reliant on the state, access to dollars (through certain sources) may precipitate freedom from the state, through decreased economic dependence on—and therefore interaction with—it. So "civil liberties"—defined for now as immunity from the arbitrary exercise of government authority/interference—are what people

Table 6.2. Advantages of Dollars/CUCs over Pesos for Gaining Personal Freedoms

Dimension	Pesos	Dollars/CUCs
Source of employment	Source of income: state Employer: state Immediate coworkers and clients: state workers	Source of income: foreigners, other dollar-earning Cubans Employer: self Immediate coworkers: none or self-selected
Social and discursive networks	Few opportunities to talk to foreigners Little ability to exhange ideas Little ability to complain to foreigners Little ability to speak out against the state (because other Cubans may inform on them).	Access to talk to foreigners Ability to exchange ideas Ability to complain to foreigners Ability to speak out against the state with relative safety (foreigners are ephemeral and do not report to the state).
Relationship to state	Fear of state Gratitude to and dependence on the state for livelihood High exposure to daily state surveillance	Disrespect for state Resentment toward and independence from the state Less exposure to daily state surveillance
Lifestyle	Limited access to cheap products and low-quality services Little ability to vacation/escape Packed buses, long ration and bodega lines, frequent exposure to other peso earners who do not trust one another, minimal talk about political problems	Freedom to choose products and quality of services Freedom for leisure/escape Access to private vehicles and dollar stores; less repression by collective silence
Laws that govern earning	Socialismo Marxism-Leninism Collective inmobilización	Late socialism Some personal liberty Nascent capitalism
Method of political action	Feel discontented and wait . . .	Feel discontented and wait . . .
Leader recognized as legitimate	El comandante en jefe (Fidel or Raúl Castro)	Yet to be elected

gain by functioning outside of the state-controlled peso economy. For the time being, Cuban "civil society" is a realm of social organization and activity not directly under state control.[6] Civil society may be weak, it may be small, and people cannot come together openly in the pursuit of common goals that the state perceives as counter to the revolution, but nevertheless a basic structure exists that allows people to earn privately, to acquire desired goods, and to circumvent the state.

Table 6.2 summarizes the perceived benefits of earning dollars in the late-socialist system, and the dollars' relationship to individual and political freedom on seven dimensions that citizen-consumers find personally and politically important: employment, social and discursive networks, relationship to the state, lifestyle, laws that govern earning, method of political action, and legitimacy of the current regime.

Unsatisfied citizen-consumers explained to me that if your income is tied tightly to the state—if you fear for your well-being and your job—you are intimately aware of the powers and capabilities of the state. The state has great power and surveillance over you because you are directly in its midst. Does this mean that those with ample access to dollars are more able to speak out against the state? I wondered. Their answer was "perhaps," if those dollars were independently earned or obtained. It seems clear however that dollars have become an accessible form of resistance to socialist constraints, and that ordinary Cubans attempt to take advantage of nascent capitalism and *por la libre* (the free market) in order to experience some level of personal liberty as well. Whether or not these individuals choose to speak out against the state, the *psicosis del dólar* ("dollar psychosis"), as Stan the dairy farmer called it, has strong implications. In particular, the division of the population by their access to dollars versus pesos has spawned social changes, and although they may not be as clearly dichotomized in fact as in table 6.2, they nevertheless have strong implications for notions of citizenship, freedom, and Cuba's socialist—or post-socialist—future.

Race, Fe, and Access to Dollars

The relationship between race and access to dollars, which I have noted only in passing, deserves further comment in light of the assertions I have made. I will now emphasize the historical underpinnings of poverty within the new Cuban "class system," drawing particular attention to its understudied racial implications.[7] I do not address race in Cuba at length in this book (but see Martinez-Alier 1974; Kutzinski 1993; R. Moore 1997; Pérez Sarduy and Stubbs 2000; de la Fuente 2001; Safa 2005; M. Sawyer 2005). Rather, I discuss contemporary Afro-Cuban poverty that results primarily from lack of access to dollar remittances from the United States. Anyone who is hard on his luck must be lacking in "fe," as the local saying goes. *Fe* means "faith" in Spanish, but is used as a code acronym for *familia en el exterior*: family abroad who send money. This differential access to dollars had prerevolutionary roots because the flight of white professionals from Cuba in the early 1960s established a base that allowed them to send money back home to their (white) relatives. Since the legalization of the dollar, it has become particularly startling how "white" remittances are, and how much more tightly those Cubans who lack access to remittances are tied to the state for work and resources.

Walking in Havana's neighborhoods and surrounds, one does not find slums or distinctly all-black neighborhoods. One does, however, find increasingly dramatic differences in housing quality between neighbors, and black residents appear to be poorer overall, to the extent that one can judge by material possessions. In a socialist system that claims to have eliminated systemic or institutional racism, that promotes itself as not only egalitarian but also "color blind," it is surprising to see how often this pattern holds true. Thus, it is important to recognize the disturbing link between race and means in the new, two-tiered economy in the late-socialist era.

In the academic literature, one of the commonly cited explanations for contemporary black poverty in Cuba is that black Cubans are not favored for jobs in the tourism industry, as employers prefer a white, "Hollywood" or "Barbie" look. This racial preference is glossed as a demand for *buena presencia* (good appearance) or *presencia agradable* (pleasant appearance), and justified with the reasoning that European tourists and joint venture managers are more comfortable with white than black faces (see Wunderlich 2005). The racialized exception to this is the *jinetera*, where exotic *mulatas* are said to sell better to American and European men than the white Barbie look (N. Fernández 1996, 2001). But blackness has also become associated with prostitution, crime, bad values, and publicly visible poverty. Among my Cuban informants, the most common explanation for Afro-Cuban poverty, cramped living, and multigenerational households was "es su idiosincrasia" (it's their idiosyncrasy), a local stereotype that glosses over lack of Afro-Cuban access to the dollars that would afford them different conditions.

As one summary states, "If Afro-Cubans have benefited most from the Revolution, they have also suffered most during its crisis. Every Cuban needs dollars to survive, and the bulk of the easy money coming in remittances goes to white Cubans because it was their relatives who left early on" (Wunderlich 2005: 68). Specifically, whereas 83.5 percent of Cuban immigrants living in the United States are white, only 16.5 percent are black (Mesa-Lago 2002). Put in monetary terms, "Assuming that dollar remittances . . . stay roughly within the same racial group as the sender, about $680 million of the $800 million that enter the island every year would end up in white hands" (de la Fuente 1998: 6).[8]

The Saízos were an Afro-Cuban, primarily peso-poor family whom I came to know well.[9] They lived in a small, plain, dilapidated, one-story, cement-front apartment with no indoor running water that, oddly enough, was within short walking distance of dollar stores and a small mall in a dollar-rich area of the city. The Saízos were the most overtly communist household with whom I became friendly.[10] Eleven family members squeezed into the two-bedroom space, but the matriarch still declaimed with rather charismatic—and at moments spine-tingling—conviction to me and the ten others gathered around for my visit, "We are poor, but we are dignified." The family audience nodded and chimed in with "Sí, sí," "Verdad," "Gracias a la Revolución" (yes, yes; true; thanks to the Revolution), as if we were in a prayer circle. Energy and unity seemed to be running high. It was my last real fling with socialist revolutionary nostalgia.

"We have no access to dollars because we aren't connected to *la mafia de Miami*," added the eldest daughter at one point, reclining on the narrow twin bed with a sagging mattress she shared with her preschool-aged son. "Not one of us here has a Miami connection."

Historical Legacies and Poverty in Cuba

I want to consider briefly the past and the future of class in Cuba, with a focus on race. Ironically, those who were poor before the revolution too often lack access to dollars today, and loyalty and fidelity to the state may actually penalize citizens economically in the late-socialist era. Those working in state jobs are the most poorly paid and the most highly overseen, in an era where independent economic gain may be the one thing that allows for personal freedom.

It is crucial to note that racial equality exhibited remarkable improvement under the Castro regime, particularly in the early 1980s. For example, in that time period, the proportion of Afro-Cubans and mulattos who graduated from high school was actually higher than that of whites, life expectancy was equal between whites and Afro-Cubans/mulattos, and Afro-Cubans were also well represented among the professions (de la Fuente 1998, 2001). Many such advances in structural racial equality—closely tied to state programs targeting the poor and the laboring classes—have declined with the introduction of the two-tiered economy and the state's difficulties in distributing goods and services to the population during the prolonged economic crisis (de la Fuente 2000; Espina Prieto and Rodríguez Ruiz 2006; Blue 2007).

In Cuba race and class should not be conflated, and the interrelation of race and access to dollars is in need of further research, but remains a phenomenon that is nearly impossible to study systematically under the current regime. Here, however, I summarize the historically contingent cycle of Afro-Cuban poverty: those who benefited most from early revolutionary reforms (primarily Afro-Cubans from the poor and rural eastern provinces) remained in Cuba in the early 1960s, took government positions, and enjoyed a modest pool of resources. As de la Fuente explains, "The revolutionary government never specifically targeted blacks in its social policies, but its program of structural transformations, aimed at improving the lot of the poor and working class, created opportunities for social mobility that were readily seized by the black population" (de la Fuente 1998: 2).

The peso poor are not necessarily Afro-Cuban by any stretch of the imagination, but Afro-Cubans are disproportionately represented among the peso poor. A factor in Afro-Cuban peso-poverty is that, while exchanges of resources may take place between Afro-Cubans in Havana and those living in the eastern provinces, resources rarely have come from abroad, since so few Afro-Cuban family members live *allá*. Such local, dense, and closed family networks, coupled with strict control of the media by the Castro regime, led to Afro-Cubans receiving less direct and frequent information concerning goods and services and political systems outside of their world. With the dawn of the Special Period in the early 1990s, some Afro-Cubans left their homes in the east and moved to Havana in search of more work—tolerating more cramped living conditions in the city and not necessarily faring any better economically (white residents call these darker-skinned labor migrants from the eastern provinces *palestinos*, literally, "Palestinians"). The eastern migrants had trouble entering the tourist industry (because of the previously mentioned hiring discrimination), and could not take advantage of opening *paladares* or *casas particulares* because of their cramped or dilapidated living conditions, a holdover from the prerevolutionary geography of race and poverty.

Not having had regular access to dollars in the intermediate years between the triumph of the revolution in the early 1960s and the legalization of the dollar initiated in 1993, many Afro-Cubans remained at their state jobs, neither able to break into a lucrative black market nor obtain sufficient start-up funds to break into a business, limiting the range of their social network even further, and distancing them socially from the active enclave of new Cuban entrepreneurs. Their continued fidelity to state institutions came partly out of practical necessity (for younger generations) and partly out of historical memory (for older generations).

Some say that Afro-Cuban fidelity is the regime's "secret weapon," that their loyalty is a result of the benefits the revolution has provided them and of the fear that regime collapse would reinstigate hardship and racism, fueled by the return of the white exile community (de la Fuente 1998). That said, it is well known (but not empirically documented) that the participants in the August 1994 Malecón Riot, at the height of the Special Period, were predominantly black. In this event, the first and last of its kind since the revolution, citizens—most estimates range around one thousand or more—took to the streets and damaged public property while shouting slogans about freedom and regime change, indicating a high level of dissatisfaction and obvious lack of loyalty. It is very difficult to obtain reliable details about the riot, since it was short, quickly stopped by plainclothes police, and not documented by the visual media.

While no official statistics are kept, it is a truism in Cuba that Afro-Cubans are the group hardest-done-by in the late-socialist era, making such a riot believable. Part of the hardship is evident in the notable racialization of the lowest-paying state jobs (such as primary-school teachers, bodega shopkeepers, and guards), and of the CDR leadership, whereas more powerful leadership in the upper echelons of the Party are typically white (de la Fuente 1998, 2000, 2001).

Despite revolutionary achievements in health and education, social networks remain dense and closed, and prerevolutionary poverty persists in the late-socialist moment. Afro-Cubans' state-dependent status and low-quality housing stock also do not bode well for their future in the post-socialist era, whenever that may come, since many Cubans plan to liquidate quickly any

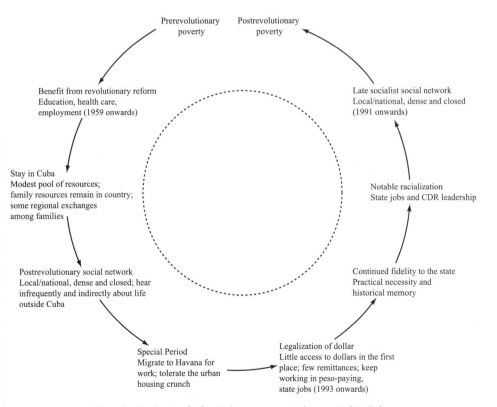

Figure 6.1. Full circle: the logic of Afro-Cuban poverty in late-socialist Cuba

wealth they have through sale of their homes. This is a disheartening prospect for those Afro-Cubans dwelling in deteriorating buildings, some in areas of low real estate value—just one structural legacy that will be difficult to transform in the post-socialist future. These trends are illustrated in figure 6.1.

By Means of a Conclusion

The speech and pronouncements of the matriarch of the Saízo family overtly and explicitly reflected Party messages. For example, she would declare, "¡Comandante en jefe, ordene!" (Commander in chief, we're at your command!) and, in describing Cuba's future, she cheered along and chanted in time with the crowds shown on TV at state-organized marches. She also applied the term *luchando* in the traditional sense, "no matter what, the Revolution lives on, together we will *sigue luchando!*" (continue the struggle). I became curious about whether all eleven family members actually toed the same line, especially some of the younger, well-dressed members of the family, in their twenties and thirties.

One long Sunday afternoon, after several prior visits had revealed no differences among the family members, I sat on the cement stoop with Karlos, a state-sponsored wrestler who had retired in his late twenties with a couple of gold teeth (*por lujo*, for luxury, he explained, when I asked about them). He was tinkering with his shiny red-and-silver, $3,000 Russian motorcycle, his "most faithful woman." We entered into conversation while no other family members were listening. I had gotten the almost immediate impression that Karlos was a somewhat irreverent person, from catching him quietly rolling his eyes at various points during family conversations. Besides giving untaxed salsa lessons, he now worked as one of two armed guards in front of a general's palatial estate in the wealthy Miramar district, on the 7 p.m. to 7 a.m. shift. "What do you have to do?" I asked.

"The dude's never home," Karlos answered, and demonstrated himself sleeping and drooling, slouching with a rifle in his hand. "His place is ridiculous. You should see it. And I don't think he really lives in that one, anyway. Maybe another one."

Karlos went on to describe his international love life. In particular, while on a wrestling tour in Chile he had met Telma, a white, fifty-three-year-old Chilean widow, journalist, and millionaire. She was in love with him, he was not with her, but their relationship provided certain advantages. Telma had then come to Cuba as a journalist supporting Fidel, and after leaving and writing up Cubans' individual stories, decided she no longer supported the romanticized leader. She was the source of the Saízo family's oscillating electric fan, TV, stereo, and framed prints on the wall, he added. Chile, as Karlos experienced it on his wrestling tour, was amazing to him. He talked about the quantity of meat, all-you-can-eat buffets, people ready to serve you. "[Beard-stroke] . . . es un desastre. Carajo!" (He used this word several times to describe the situation in Cuba; it translates roughly as "bloody hell!" or "God damn!")

"But I thought you were communist," I commented.

"No. No young people are," he replied wryly.

"But your family . . . your mother is strongly communist."

He nodded emphatically, "and my father is *even worse* than her, and *she's* a CDR president! Los viejos: son ciegos y locos" (Old people: they are blind and crazy).

Thus, despite the categories I present in table 6.1, even within one household that initially appears state-faithful and peso poor, there is a relatively wealthy wrestler, boasting of an international love interest, who provides cash and material items to the family. The same family, it seems, contains an entire younger generation who never discuss politics with or in front of their parents, but all of whom, I discovered with time, want more, cannot stand the regime, and want to leave. The Saízo family was, in short, emblematic of a certain tension and blending of various lifestyles, including the *doble moral* (double standard), even within the confines of one household, during this long era of late-socialist transition.

III

Free

In just a few days, Petra's émigré son and his young family would be in sunny Cancún, Mexico, for a short working vacation. "So close, I could almost touch them," Petra mused, "The flight takes just forty minutes from here . . . just forty minutes, but I can't leave. I can't see them. My only hope is that I'll see them before I die. I would swim, but the truth is, I'm afraid of the water," she admits, her eyes welling up. She pauses before she continues, "The sea," explained Petra, her voice now soft and heavy with suffering, "serves as the walls of a jail around this island."

This melancholy moment, in which Petra was contemplating a lifetime of separation from her son and his family due to politics and geography, represents culturally shared questions of feeling trapped and finding happiness in late-socialist Cuba. It is also a place to start in considering the Cuban meaning of being "free."

Freedom in Cuba is elusive, since it is not something Cubans talk about in explicit terms. Rather, Cubans' speech is full of metaphors and allegories for having their choices constrained, for being trapped, for attempting to reach out, and for pointing to a desired, external freedom. Within these metaphors and allegories there is also a clear hierarchy with respect to the ease with which particular topics are voiced. It is easiest to complain about the lack of consumer freedoms, options, and autonomy: the most widely circulating and publicly accessible talk is about earning and goods. It is harder for citizens to talk about feeling trapped, though, as I illustrate, Cubans find ways of doing it. Finally, it is hardest to talk about freedom, or *libertad*, itself.

In part III, I discuss what being free means to unsatisfied citizen-consumers, and what specific factors draw Cubans to look outside of Cuba in an attempt to discover it. Specifically, chapter 7 discusses the feeling of being trapped within the confines of the island and considers migration, the exit option to perceived freedom, but more specifically "the un-migration." Chapter 8 discusses freedom, representation, and forms of resistance, Cuban-style. I focus on the roles of forms of everyday, offstage, backstage, and at-home resistance.

7

Un-migration

Late-socialist bureaucracy, and the current ideology behind it, have made it difficult—some claim nearly impossible in recent years—for an ordinary citizen to obtain an exit permit (*permiso de salir*) to travel—far less emigrate— outside of the island. Moreover, if a permit is denied, there is no opportunity for appeal.[1] There are no publicly available official statistics on the number of exit permits actually issued per year, but neighbors sometimes discussed their own experiences or spoke of not personally knowing anyone who had been able to procure a *permiso* in years. If someone were lucky enough to get a permit to travel to the United States, the cost would be a hefty $900 per head.[2] "No los dan" (They're not giving them), people concluded, such definitive talk heightening the feeling of a tightening regime. That was in contrast

Figure 7.1. Havana at twilight, looking toward the Florida Straits, a tangible escape route that haunts restless urban residents.

with the past situation, people claimed, when Cuba's internationalist missions and scholarly exchange programs with socialist bloc countries had meant that many ordinary Cubans had spent years out of the country, experiencing life elsewhere and considering themselves citizens of the world. Now, travel was under strict state restrictions (what I call "trapped traveling"), and the only people who seemed to be able to leave Cuba at will were those with special status—in particular artists, musicians, and actors.

These restrictions have consequences. First, they make the sea even more symbolically and practically alluring, since for common citizens it is the only immediate route of escape (figure 7.1). Moreover, because many people know someone who has escaped by sea, the option seems tangible, if not viable. Second, when physical escape is not possible, which it often is not, Cubans cope in other ways, such as reaching out to foreigners and foreign things, separating themselves from "other" Cubans, and using dramatic metaphors to describe the gravity of their situation.

Shackles, Separations, and the Sea

Felina, seventeen and dreaming of escape and elsewhere, told me of her determined cousin, Silvio, who had invented an odd raft, partially buoyed by discarded Styrofoam. He had left Cuba entirely on his own, promising to contact family upon his arrival in the United States. After a week and a half, when family had heard no word, they presumed he had perished at sea, as many people do trying to cross the ninety miles of water separating Cuba and the United States.[3] But then a phone call came through on her neighbor's line from someone wishing to speak her, she related. It was Silvio: "Guess where I'm calling from?" he asked Felina, his cousin and childhood playmate. "A really nice hospital in Miami." Felina began laughing as she finished telling the story, though moisture had formed in the corners of her eyes. Her tone conveyed a sense of triumph over adversity as she spoke. "He suffered from severe dehydration and sunburn, the *yoma* [handmade boat] was shit and fell apart, but he *swam* the rest of the way. Somebody found him onshore and delivered him, semiconscious, to the hospital. He did not even remember reaching dry land."

"Reaching dry land" is not just an expression; it has become a tangible political status. In 1995, pursuant to an agreement between the Clinton administration and the Cuban government, it was determined that the United States would stop admitting Cubans found at sea (those with "wet feet"), but would return them to Cuba or to a third country. Those who make it to shore with "dry feet," however, are permitted to remain in the United States and qualify for expedited legal permanent resident status and U.S. citizenship, as they have done since the 1966 Cuban Adjustment Act. This policy has become known as the "wet-foot/dry-foot" policy, and is closely associated with Cuban migration (though in reality, the same policy is applied to Haitian and Dominican migrants by sea). This policy also gives seaborne escape from Cuba a gamelike quality, in which speed is of the essence.

Footage of the rough sea slapping against and spraying over the Malecón, Havana's famous seawall promenade, has become stock footage in locally produced films concerning the troubles of contemporary life in Cuba. The recurrent image is usually unnarrated, allowing for ambiguity but nonetheless offering an implicit political message for the public that views it, since they associate this sea—the Florida Straits—with a potential mode of exit and see what lies on the other side as the embodiment of hope, potential and, often, family reunification.[4] There is only ambient noise as troubled waters pound against the cement and stone, unable to break free of their natural place on one side of the wall—and Cubans, filled with longing, unable to escape their political place, are equally trapped on the other.

Getting an exit permit and exiting is one problem, but getting a government-issued reentry permit is another. While some Cuban travelers are perfectly happy not to be "welcomed back" to Cuba and use the bureaucratic problem of reentry permits as an excuse to defect, the threat of family separation, especially from children, is a risk too great for some families to take. Public attention has recently been drawn to this issue since celebrated Cuban author Amir Valle (traveling with his wife and son), discussed it at a book signing in Berlin for his work of nonfiction, *Jineteras*. Valle, in a statement to the international press concerning the bureaucratic delays preventing his reentry, declared, "I am not asking the Cuban government to let me enter the country. . . . I am demanding my right to enter and leave when I decide to, and am in a condition to do so—just like any other citizen of the world" (Snow 2006).

Separations

Petra's next-door neighbor whispers to me that Petra cannot sleep at night, and that they can hear her slamming her bed repeatedly against the bedroom wall in frustration. Petra, continuing the chain of neighborhood gossip, tells me that while I was out at night, old Iris stepped out onto her balcony, shouting out for her daughter, and neighbors had to come to calm her down. She is nearly eighty and beginning to lose hope. "Iris, how are you?" I ask when we cross paths later. We had recently shared a pleasant morning of conversation as she taught me to make *arroz con leche* (rice pudding) in her spotless kitchen. "Aquí" [here], she answered bitterly.

One dark and rainy afternoon, Beatriz receives a call on her downstairs neighbor's phone, and she speaks furtively, wearing the familiar leopard-skin print tank top she washes and wears again every day. "Cuídate mucho. . . . Cuídate" (Really take care of yourself. . . . Take care of yourself), she repeats a few times. Beatriz makes kissing noises into the receiver. "Cuélgalo" (hang up), she tenderly reminds the person on the other end. She begins wiping tears from her eyes even before she hangs up the receiver. "My mother," she explains to me, now letting the tears pour. "It feels like it's been a century since I've seen her. It makes me sentimental." Beatriz was denied an exit visa to visit her mother; the reason given was that she fit the profile of a potential migrant. "What am I going to do?" she pleads. Solutions are limited.

Paulo, a well-loved local neighbor and handyman with a wife and two teen-aged daughters who had settled in Miami, was a public exhibit of these limited solutions. Paulo had been forced to stay behind, but expected to join them whenever it became possible; locally, this was called *divorico a lo Cubano* (divorce, Cuban-style). One evening, Tatiana received a phone call on the line two doors down and returned with a somber message, "Guess who killed himself," she announced quietly to her husband. Paulo had been unable to sustain himself during the wait, had apparently become overcome with hopelessness, and had hung himself in his family home.[5] The entire family—Paulo, his wife, and his daughters—were now gone forever in the eyes of the neighborhood. "I'm covered in chills," said Tatiana, gesturing at her arm, her chin crumpling as she shook her head. "I guess he wasn't able to wait," she concluded. One of Paulo's daughters in Miami was hospitalized from shock upon hearing the news about her father. No one had predicted that the wait would be so agonizing, although no one seemed to judge his act either. Sometimes the wait to join loved ones is unbearable, and the uncertainty and lack of control over reunification seem too remote to comprehend. "He is finally at peace," said Hetta, Tatiana's younger sister, who had been close childhood friends with Paulo's girls, "finally free."

In all of these moments of acute separation and inability to travel to see loved ones, the frequent spilling of tears, and the use of telephone contact—the primary mechanism that allows family members to stay in touch—one thing becomes clear.[6] The repressive travel restriction is often the primary cause that makes ordinary Cubans—but especially the middle-aged and elderly retirees such as those I describe here—feel absolutely lost and alienated from the Castro regime, no matter what their opinions were at the time the revolution triumphed or in the years following.

They detest the fact that the state keeps them from visiting family members before they die, no matter what else it might offer. The restrictions on movement, in short, have built up raw enmity against the mechanism that keeps Cubans unable to travel—and even if this enmity does not lead to direct, collective action against the travel restriction, it certainly generates collective emotional turmoil for those who imagine going, and also for those who have memories of having traveled or lived elsewhere in the past. The result is a culture of frustration and a constant desire to reach out: "those who remain on the island live in mental exile, frustrated because they can't participate in the changing world and their own reality" (Corbett 2002: 11).

Trapped Traveling

Of course, the travel ban is not complete. A small segment of the population does get to leave the country to travel and work abroad, but it is usually only those the government trusts to return, such as merchant marines or, as I have mentioned, performing artists and *farándula* who tour under special contracts, mentioned in chapter 6. (Their return is not guaranteed, but the hard currency they bring in from tours and international contracts is apparently worth the risk.)[7] The scope of internationalist missions (described later) has dwindled because of lack of funding and the changing international relationships of reciprocity, though they still exist.[8] The number of Cubans participating in professional conferences and scholarly exchanges has declined significantly because of increased fear of the participants' defection, although a small number of ordinary citizens do receive permission to leave the country annually.

Some representatives of state agencies also travel internationally in various capacities, although sometimes traveling under state auspices can, ironically, make unsatisfied citizen-consumers feel even more trapped. For example, despite her inability to travel spontaneously to Cancún at the moment her son was there, Petra was lucky in that she had actually been to Cancún three times in the past, sent as an employee of the state travel agency so that she could speak intelligently about the places her travel agency advertised. Specifically, she had been assigned to check out the various luxury accommodations, restaurants, and tourist sites so that she could describe them in some detail to those wealthy foreign tourists in Havana interested in taking a popular side trip to Cancún. Thus, she was dropped off in Cancún for the day on assignment, in her navy blue, state-issued polyester pantsuit uniform, and given a per diem of $5.00 to complete her task that day. "Five dollars for spending money," she scoffed, "I could do little more than enjoy a glass of Coca-Cola." It was citizen-consumer torture of a certain, low-level kind, reminding her of her place in the world and her lack of spending power as she walked down long Cancún tourist strips in her shabby uniform (unable even to pay for a cab), read menus she could not order from, peeked inside hotel suites she could not sleep in, and watched the leisure activities of free-world vacationers and their families unfold around her. She described the sensation of feeling punished and trapped: "As long as you are still a Cuban citizen, you never really get to be anywhere on your own terms, even when you are not in Cuba." And, I would add, when you are a Cuban consumer, the consuming worlds of others seem painfully out of reach, unless you are earning in that economy.

Exit Permits for Citizens of the World

It was hard for young people who had never been outside of Cuba to imagine that there was no possibility of traveling anytime soon. But the sense of regime tightening was especially acute for those middle-aged people who had been allowed to leave the country in the past, or who had participated in the boom of scholarly exchanges or internationalist missions in their coming-of-age years during the 1970s and 1980s.[9] Because of Cuba's internationalist history, I met ordinary people who during the 1970s and 1980s had lived for years as students in the former USSR and its satellites,[10] or as students, architects, or secretaries in Angola, Iraq, and Ethiopia, for example. None had been able to leave Cuba again.

Through Cuba's former internationalism, a significant number of Cuban citizens had inadvertently been given the gift of a diverse, international collective nostalgia, complete with vivid images and personal experiences made possible by travel. They knew from experience, for example, and would discuss, how hot paprika tastes as a spice, whether there is a difference between making love to Eastern Europeans versus Cubans, the physical layout of Angolan villages, the sight of Iraqi babies being handed entire cucumbers on which to teethe, the sensation of living with different music and under a different sky and, of course, having access to different products and services. In summary, the Cuban state had created intellectually curious citizens of the world, which made controlling the movement of these citizens, and withholding information about the world from them, an even more difficult and frustrating experience for them in the late-socialist period.

David was a particularly good example of this. He would keep up with world news, devour paperback novels in any language he could read, and watch a movie per night. To this day he sees every new release before I do, a fact I think he takes some pride in. These were all ways of educating himself and of reaching out to the world—escaping Cuba through personal retreat. Similarly, David's speech was peppered with references to other countries and populations as points of comparison, helping him to define the peculiarity of the Cuban experience. But more than his ways of coping now, David described, at some length, problems he had encountered in Cuba after returning from five years of study in Eastern Europe in the mid-1980s, when he had personally witnessed how things can open up economically and politically.

"About a year after I came back from Central Europe, my friends asked me what I missed the most: clothes, women, food? My answer: 'No, freedom.'" He pointed to his head. David then went on to explain not what he missed from his time abroad, but rather what was most difficult upon his return, for example, the days following Castro's annual Primero de Mayo (May 1, International Workers Day) speech.

"The director of my company sends around a message declaring a meeting at 5:00 p.m. All staff are, of course, in attendance. The director stands up and asks who agreed with Fidel's speech. Everyone raises their hands, of course," narrated David, with an aggrieved expression. "Then the director asked if anyone had any questions about the speech, or anything they wanted to talk about in relation to the speech. A hand goes up. A man said, 'I just want to emphasize how much I agree with El Comandante's speech.' A second hand goes up. A repeat performance. I can't help but laugh, I'm sorry." He shakes his head, pained. "It's a comedy. It's enough. Forty-three years of the same speeches by the same people, 'blah-blah' [using one hand to gesture flapping jaws]. I've grown up with the U.S.–Cuba problem. I'm bored by it. Both governments are to blame, all the U.S. *administrations* and the Cuban administration [emphasizing the plural in reference to the United States]. But we [Cubans] are the victims. There's a double embargo, one by the U.S. government, the other by ours."

"If I lived in Guatemala, I might think that freedom was having a good school to send my kids to, or a good clinic to go to when they were sick. If I lived in Africa, it might be electricity or a TV [points to his TV]. But I'm not. I'm in Cuba. We have those things. I want more. . . . We are not Arabs, we are not Chinese, we are not Russian, we are not South American Indians.[11] We are Cuban. Cubans like nice things. Nice hair, clothes, nails, to go places, to see things, to have things, to live how we want. We are like Americans. We have similar tastes. We just want to be free to have things. We work hard, we love our families, we are proud. OK, medicine and education are important, and they are the positive things about the Revolution, but since then, things have flattened. You have doctors going to international meetings. They see the world changing around them, and then they come back here and it's all the same."

"I call people my age part of the 'Generación Perdida'" (Lost Generation), he summed up. "We didn't see what came before the Revolution, so we have to bear the costs of the changes without a good reference point." Then he concluding by saying, "If I lived outside Cuba I could imagine myself not caring about politics. But here it's unavoidable." He suggested that people like me who grew up in free societies did not and could not fully appreciate the value of that freedom.

Three years later, still unable to travel, David wrote the following e-mail message, linking himself to other unfortunate people in unfortunate places:

Some lucky people spend their free time in travels around the world or fishing or hunting or visiting important museums, etc, etc. But for the larger part of Humanity (us included) those "activities" are only "virtual," seen only in movies, books, or through some friends' stories (also our case). But don't worry, I was only *filosofando* [philosophizing], nothing to worry about. I'm not pessimistic, not at all. I've a wonderful family and wonderful friends (you both included), we're all in good shape and "luchando," as always. It's just that sometimes a man dreams, and his dreams help him to make his life easier, more bearable.

Reaching Out and Away from "Other Cubans"

If one cannot leave, weaving dreams about life away from home makes life in Cuba more bearable, or at least it helps pass the time. Reaching out, or linking oneself to life outside of Cuba, is a crucial coping mechanism, practically and emotionally, as is separating oneself from, or transcending, what one wishes to believe is the "Other": those trapped Cubans with which one finds oneself surrounded.

E-mail Elena was a fantastic example of this, in the extent to which she presented herself as a worldly, open-minded Cuban, unique in her individuality and desire for self-expression.[12] This persona manifested itself in two ways. First, she rarely missed an opportunity to put "Other" Cubans down. She would accuse them of being *llanos* (literally "flat" or "plain," but by implication "simpleminded"), *Isleños de la mente* ("Islanders of the mind"—a common way that Cubans describe "Other" Cubans), or *loros* (parrots), who just go on repeating what they hear. She also complained bitterly about Cubans' propensity to "step on other people's heads" in order to better themselves. "Cubans are the biggest capitalists," she explained, "but they don't even know how to be capitalists." It was Cubans' disrespectful exploitation of others, not an appealing ability to earn capital creatively through innovation, to which she referred. The inability to appreciate innovation was another of her standard complaints. It was best represented by one story she found particularly depressing and symbolic. Her son, a talented artist, had hand-drawn in a classic cartographic style a lovely, detailed map, which she proudly hung on her wall. Other Cubans (those lucky enough to enter her apartment) had asked, peering at the unfamiliar map, "es una fotocopia?" (Is it a photocopy?), she mimicked in a nasal voice. "A photocopy?!" Elena raged. "This is the kind of place where no one recognizes talent or something new or special, because they can't. Where would it get you? Why bother?"

The second way Elena would attempt to transcend Cuba and Cubans was to construct herself, in contrast to other Cubans, as a person who understood and was connected to foreigners, and was affiliated with things outside of Cuba. Thus, her pride in her ability to speak foreign languages, in her sophisticated personal tastes, and in her declared love of innovation and the modern mentality. For example, she often mentioned her pleasant associations with foreign things and experiences. She later told me she was willing to do things that other Cubans were not, such as refraining from gossip, respecting the privacy of others, and not caving into "misinformed taboos" and "silly superstitions" (saving locks of blonde hair or setting up elaborate Santería shrines at home to ensure good luck, for example). She saw herself as rising above such provincial or backwards conventions, and as being able to accept and respect differences, even regarding intimate details in life (such as circumcising baby boys, breastfeeding for extended periods, and washing other people's underwear).

During one conversation, for example, a little palm-sized plastic photo album with some pictures taken over recent years served as our centerpiece. As we flipped through it, she showed me a picture of a young French couple who had honeymooned in Cuba and who had graced her by renting a room in her house while in Havana. Elena was charmed that they loved the cool, silky feel of the tile floor, and had happily allowed them to break the Cuban taboo against going barefoot indoors, in order to let them to enjoy it.

Elena was another member of that club of middle-aged Cubans who had spent significant time abroad the 1980s.[13] She had lived and studied in the Dominican Republic, and had fond memories of those years, and of flying in and out of Cuba. Her children had also spent some of their formative years in the Dominican Republic and had "non-Cuban" tastes because of it. For example, years after returning, they still preferred bread, pizza, cheese, and eggs—"American-style food"—having never really taken to rice and beans as staples.

I also learned that several unusual items in her house—such as a jumbo pack of Crayola crayons and another of one hundred Magic Markers, and even the modern color television set—were hand-delivered gifts from an American man called Wellington, who had once visited Cuba and whose Christian values had led him subsequently to send Elena's family a $100 monthly cash transfer through Western Union (or "El Vestern," as she affectionately referred to it). "A godfather, sent to me through God and providing a lifeline for my family," was how she described him. Wellington, balding, potbellied, and bearded, smiled up from the album, sitting comfortably in front of his laptop in his home office in California. Elena had also included shots of his modern home, furnished in soft beiges and oddly unpopulated in the pictures. But these images apparently held some allure or importance for Elena, as they were included alongside her more prominent family portraits.

As my relationship with Elena developed, I came to realize that her detachment from her countrymen served as a temporary psychological escape while physical escape was as yet impossible. Putting other Cubans down and associating herself with things outside of Cuba were both forms of escape. Elena coped by presenting herself as a singular, free-thinking individual with personal tastes and broad visions, standing apart from "the pack" of state-monitored citizens. By distancing herself from other Cubans and what she perceived as the limitations of Cuban "mentality," she could distance herself from the experience of being trapped in Cuba. Essentially, through her self-representation as un-Cuban in her beliefs and behaviors, and her dislike of Cuban mores, she was constructing herself as ready to live elsewhere or as belonging elsewhere. Ironically, this mode of self-presentation, while extreme in its intensity, was very much part of a common stream of conversation among Cuban unsatisfied citizen-consumers in general. Many of my informants were attracted to foreign things, and a certain type scorned fellow citizens and had a great desire to move.

Asphyxiation and Breathing as Metaphors

Being unable to obtain an exit permit; having memories of travel but being unable to travel again; traveling under state restriction; being prevented from seeing family, perhaps for the remainder of their lifetimes; and wanting to escape the presence or mentality of "other" Cubans: each of these traps or entrapments—whether related to a specific event or relationship, or in a more overarching and persistent context—was commonly expressed in the form of metaphors or allegories.

The most common verbal metaphors for being trapped were references to cages, jails, walls, restraints, being stranded on an island, or living in a bubble. It was also common to link the contemporary Cuban experience to historical atrocities such as concentration camps, slavery, indentured servitude, state terror, *el puño de hierro* (the iron fist, combined with the gesture of smacking one's thigh with a fist); or to link it to other dictatorships (usually fascist, specifically Stalinist, but also Nazi and, most recently, Saddam Hussein's Iraqi regime).[14] However, one of the most frequently used and overarching metaphors for the sensation of being closed in, of not being able to breathe easily or freely, and of having to guard everything from watchful and powerful eyes, was *asfixia* (asphyxiation).

At moments when unsatisfied citizen-consumers talked about being stifled or suffocated politically or economically, they often brought their hands to their own throats. In discussing how Fidel was holding back the country or keeping it backwards (*atrasado, muy atraso*), the corresponding hand gesture was to grip one's own wrist in a choke hold with the other hand.

Ironically, asthma seems to be a medical, psychosocial, or embodied metaphor for constriction as well.[15] For reasons not fully clinically explained, rates of bronchial asthma and chronic obstructive pulmonary disease in Cuba are among the highest in the world.[16] There are many lay explanations relating to the "bad air," the "bad atmosphere," too much of one thing, or not enough of another. As one author puts it, highlighting the link between material want and obstructed breathing, "Cuba has the highest rate of asthma in the world, from the dust and the mold and the humidity which they can't get rid of or escape from, for lack of parts" (Tattlin 2002: 181–82).

Tristan was a recent migrant to Costa Rica, who had arrived in the capital city of San José only two months before I met him there in 2003.[17] He had suffered from an acute, lifelong case of asthma in Cuba, which required treatment with an inhaler, often more than once daily, to subdue his wheezing and the feeling of constriction in his chest. Although he had reservations about certain elements of Costa Rican culture with which he was not impressed, he announced to me in amazement that from the moment he had arrived in Costa Rica, his condition had suddenly disappeared: "My asthma is gone, my asthma is completely gone! I can't remember the last time I used my inhaler. When I talk on the phone to my mom, she always asks, 'y tu asma?' and I have to keep on reminding her: 'Mamí, you can stop asking me! It's over. It's gone.'" A possible cause of the disappearance of his symptoms and spontaneous healing was that the change in climate had an effect on his airways (though San José is notoriously polluted). Tristan himself, however, had a "magical" explanation he found equally plausible: because he was able to earn on his own again, he was able breathe on his own again.

"Even with tight regulations," explains one author, describing the creeping pace of economic reform in Cuba, "a little taste of economic freedom goes a long way. 'It was like giving an asphyxiating patient a breath of oxygen,' says Marta, who rents [out] a room in her house. 'First he recovers. Then he wants more'" (Barbassa 2005: 17–18). Also, as noted in a well-known travelogue written a decade ago, "an aging Fidel Castro is struggling to maintain his grip on a population yearning for aire libre, or at least Air Jordans" (Hunt 1998).

Cubans cope with chronic stress and feelings of asphyxiation in various ways. When I first met Tatiana, she offered me a Popular cigarette from her pack, stored in her tidy kitchen cabinet. "I do two things to keep myself from tearing my hair out in Cuba," she explained, tugging at her hair and then lowering her hands to grasp her throat, "smoke cigarettes and drink plenty of coffee." Paco, the hippie musician and practitioner of yoga, who avoids such toxins, explained to me the importance of breathing as a coping mechanism, metaphorically and practically: "Breathing and emotional health are linked," he explained, sitting up straight in his chair to demonstrate proper posture. "When we breathe freely, the diaphragm moves without restriction, and we experience health and well-being. But when it is tight and restricted, the result is a limitation of feelings and flow of energy. But it's not so easy to breathe here sometimes, so you must actually practice," he said, closing his eyes, demonstrating a deep inhalation, and encouraging me to imitate it.

In order to understand what Cubans mean by freedom—a state of being that is difficult for most Cubans to articulate—one must first understand its opposite, feeling trapped. The sensation of being trapped serves as a point of departure for defining freedom itself. Thus, Cuban unsatisfied citizen-consumers imagine freedom as the state of becoming citizens of the world again, traveling on their own terms, being able to reunite with family, breathing freely (metaphorically and physiologically), and transcending the "Other": trapped Cubans. Finally, freedom also encompasses the ability to earn one's own keep without economic dependence upon, or fear of political retribution from, the state. For many, the wait for these freedoms has been too long, leaving them with only one option: to exit as a migrant. It is to that option I now turn, and in particular, to the relationship between freedom and imagined emigration.

Migration

It is impossible to discuss contemporary Cuba at any length without mention of migration. Before 1959 there was very little migration from Cuba, since it was one of the most prosperous Latin American countries. In contrast, migration, in both extraordinary waves and ever-present trickles, has been an intrinsic part of Cuba's history, politics, and economics since the eve of the revolution,[18] and the macro-strokes and historical contours left by the major exoduses, or waves, of migration have been dramatic.[19] More than one million Cubans have left for the United States alone, and there are notable Cuban communities in many other countries as well.

This chapter is not about migrants or migration per se. Likewise, the book up to this point does not represent an ethnography of migration, although migration is a specter that implicitly haunts unsatisfied citizen-consumers. Rather, the unsatisfied citizen-consumer fits the ethnographic profile of someone in the phases of potential migration through pre-migration; that is, the period when no concrete steps toward migration have yet been taken, whether or not the individual has made a tangible decision to emigrate. In other words, in this chapter, more than *emigration* itself, I describe the "migration not taken" and the genesis and quality of that unfulfilled state of being. I argue that there are countless potential migrants who are waiting to leave or never make it to their imagined destinations. Who are they? How are they produced? What happens to them? Finally, what sort of collectivity do they constitute?

In the literature on migration, the *making* of migrants remains the lesser-told and harder-to-capture part of the migration story. Life before one has gone anywhere excludes the dramatic, punctuated moments that occur once the migration process has been put into motion: the departure, the journey, the arrival in the receiving country. It also excludes what has become the best-studied part of the process: the measurable outcomes after the migrant leaves home and the "transnational homelands" that become established with return, cyclical, or recurrent migration.[20]

Here, then, I remain focused on the *making* of migrants through examining the social production of unsatisfied citizen-consumers and their shared social imaginary. Up to this point, I have documented the collective motivations and triggers for dissatisfaction, the strong emotions behind dreams of a better lifestyle, and the events leading up to the climactic decision to actually leave home. But in Cuba, more often than not, migration may be foiled, deferred, and then ultimately fizzle into a subjective but shared state of mind. In other words, the migration not taken should be understood not only as the migration not *yet* taken, but also as the conditions of either living in a state of thwarted migration for an undetermined length of time, or of being disaffected with what your own nation has to offer and continually dreaming of something better, other, and elsewhere.

I suggest that not migrating—"un-migration"—is culturally productive in its own right. This book represents the ethnography of a social process (S. Moore 1987), located mainly before the "final stage" of actually leaving home. I capture how private desires concerning lifestyle and migration translate into collective public moods (a cultural process of externalization), and how collective public moods likewise penetrate private wishes (a cultural process of internalization), which produces unsatisfied citizen-consumers.

Through a series of case examples of informants we have come to know well, I describe ethnographically the turning points and announcements of intent to migrate, what they lead to, and what they mean for contemporary Cuban culture. Finally, I address potential problems of defining freedom in terms of migration.

Literature on Motivations for Migration

The conditions that motivate migration and the profile of prospective migrants are standard parts of the migration literature. It has been established that "in general, research from around the world finds that immigrants come from somewhere in the middle of the wealth distribution—rich enough to be able to finance a trip but poor enough to have unsatisfied ambitions at home" (Massey and Aysa 2005: 7, quoting from Massey et al. 1998; see also discussion in Portes 1995).

On the face of it, the standard portrait of a migrant maps neatly onto unsatisfied citizen-consumers. Yet what is generally missing from the migration literature is an essential qualitative component: the capacity to describe the *specific* background conditions and social networks that predict migration—not just the classic economic profiles and appeals to long-standing rational choice theories. The problem is that pre-migration and potential migration have been understudied, both ethnographically and empirically (as described in Winchie and Carment 1988). For the most part, the reasons given for migration in the existing literature are usually "post-hoc reflections of migrants about their prior behavior," rather than migrants' "pre-move motivations" (as stated in De Jong and Fawcett 1989).

In other words, migration literature often suffers from what is called "sampling on the dependent variable" in sociological literature. This post-hoc perspective is beginning to change, however, reflecting an emerging genre of "ethnography of migration" that considers ethnographic components in the sending country (for example, Portes and Rumbout 2006; Miles 2004; Sayad 2004) and that points to a "culture of migration" (Piore 1979; Massey et al. 1987; Massey et al. 1993; Kandel and Massey 2002; J. Cohen 2004; R. Smith 2006). What remains underrepresented (with the notable exception of Sayad's works on Algeria), however, is a description of the *emic* meaning of migration to the emigrant.[21]

There is also an evolving demographic literature that looks beyond neoclassical economic models of migration toward the role of networks and the emergence of a self-perpetuating "culture of migration." It assumes that "families, households or other culturally produced units of production and consumption are the appropriate units of analysis for the study of migration, not autonomous individuals." It recognizes that at the community level "migration becomes deeply ingrained into the repertoire of people's behaviours, and values associated with migration become part of the community's values." Furthermore, it considers how experiences of migrants influence "tastes for consumer goods and styles of life that are difficult to attain through local labor," presumably also influencing those who have not yet migrated (Massey et al. 1993: 452; also see the classic exposition in Piore 1979). Finally, it produces a "powerful internal momentum resistant to easy control or regulation . . . outside of the reach of government" (Massey et al. 1993: 453; see also Kandel and Massey 2002).

Trajectory of Unsatisfied Citizen-Consumers toward Migration

The making of migrants and un-migrants is of particular interest to me because, with the fullness of time, it became clear that every person who appears in this book, with the exception of some individual communist hard-liners (see appendix), wanted to leave Cuba. Moreover, this desire did not usually express itself as some vague dream; individuals almost always had made some concrete plans: what to sell, what route to take, how long the journey would take, and exactly how much money would be needed; many even had the money set aside and ready for the moment escape became possible. At the same time, even those with the most concrete plans knew at some level that escape might never become possible.

Here I summarize the logical progression from dissatisfaction to migration (see "Trajectory from Unsatisfied Citizen-Consumer to Migrant" sidebar). I refer to the numbered items in the sidebar as "stages" and conceive of them as subphases of the potential migration and pre-migration phases. Because throughout the book I have focused on stages 1 and 2, depicting the unsatisfied citizen consumer, in the section that follows, I focus on stages 3–5, the prospective migrant, in an attempt to illustrate some of these stages through ethnographic description.

The Trajectory from Unsatisfied Citizen-Consumer to Migrant

Unsatisfied citizen-consumer

1. Private dissatisfaction with lifestyle; entry into underground economy
2. Public dissatisfaction with lifestyle; dreams of elsewhere

Prospective migrant

3. Turning point: decision to leave home
4. Concrete plans put into motion
5. Migration not undertaken: holding pattern

Migrant

6. Target: departure, journey, arrival in receiving country

Note: This sequence serves as a heuristic device rather than a strict, linear progression. For example, (1) there are feedback loops between stages 1 and 2; (2) elements of stage 2 carry on indefinitely; and (3) there are feedback loops between stage 4 and 5 that fuel frustration and increase tension between state and citizen.

Progressive Revelation

A process of progressive revelation leads up to the announcement of intent to migrate. Although informants usually stated a degree of dissatisfaction with their standard of living from the first time I met them, many also stated convincingly, in their own spontaneous narrations, that they wanted to stay in Cuba, though that position gradually changed. At first, they claimed that they could not imagine leaving family, and also expressed reservations concerning the discomfort, risk, separations, and drastic changes in daily life that leaving home would doubtless bring. Whatever they were processing privately, they publicly rejected the possibility of migration, regardless of what neighbors, family, and friends may have done, deeming it an unworthy solution given their personal values and circumstances. In general, they were committed to scraping by and expanding their involvement in the underground economy to generate more income.

Although the informants' statements to me were partially attributable to secret keeping and lack of disclosure, there was also an element of progressive revelation as they continued down a course of increasing dissatisfaction and pressure for a resolution to their situation. I watched the progression of citizen-consumers to an endpoint where they could not stand the thought of sticking it out through tough times any longer and became determined to leave the country. Even though I spoke with some of these informants daily, their decision to migrate—or the timing of their informing me of their decision—seemed sudden, and genuinely surprised me.[22]

The trajectory of unsatisfied citizen-consumers from the point at which they privately recognize their dissatisfaction with their lifestyle is familiar. First, they ask themselves basic questions about the quality of their lives: Can we buy what we want? Provide nice things for our children? Own a home? Occasionally enjoy leisure time? Plan for our future? Usually, the answer to these questions is no, but through earning on the side or entering the underground economy in much more extensive ways, they may temporarily resolve some of their problems (stage 1 in sidebar 7.1).

If, after these citizens enter the underground economy, the answer to these questions remains no; or if they decide that they still want more than they have, that they are tired of living frugally and using coping strategies or of living by the *doble moral,* a new set of questions emerges. Because these questions are decidedly more geopolitical, at this point the search for a better life, which initially appeared mundane, takes on a dramatic, transformative quality, personally and politically. What country in the world has the better-paying jobs that we want? If good jobs are not available locally, why not? Where in the world will we have the freedom to earn? What are we willing to do and where are we willing to go to live more comfortably? (stage 2 in sidebar 7.1) Asking this second set of questions is what separates unsatisfied citizen-consumers from prospective migrants and opens the door to a potential large-scale migration project.[23]

In summary, when the questions shift from *what* it is possible to have to *where* it might be possible to have it, the desire for more and dreams of better give *elsewhere*, and all that elsewhere represents, a new status. Elsewhere falls within haunting and imaginable (although not always realistic) reach, fueling a willingness to take the risks of leaving family and homeland behind for an imagined something that is worth the sacrifice (stages 3–5 in sidebar 7.1). And if the individuals actually pack up and leave, their story is added to that timeless stock of stories about people who have "gone off to seek their fortune," the quest and shared imaginary of today's economic or labor migrants across the globe (stage 6 in sidebar 7.1).

Turning Points and Announcements

Neither the anthropology of migration nor a description of the culture of unsatisfied citizen-consumers can be explained through experience-distant discussions of core-periphery relations and capitalist hegemony (as critiqued by Kearney 1986, 1995; Marcus 1998) or neoliberalization as a disembodied force. Using examples of four informants I have introduced earlier in the book (David and Tatiana, Elena, and Karlos), I provide three brief vignettes of the transition from unsatisfied citizen-consumer to prospective migrant, presuming that we have gained sufficient background knowledge now to be somewhat familiar with their private dissatisfactions with lifestyle, entry into the underground economy, public dissatisfaction with lifestyle, and dreams of elsewhere (stages 1–2 in sidebar 7.1). I now highlight the moments at which these unsatisfied citizen-consumers announce themselves as prospective migrants, attempt to set the process into motion (stage 3), and ultimately, begin to wait (stage 4).

David and Tatiana

Initially, David explicitly said he planned to stay in Cuba, not wanting to separate from friends and family, and being too curious to see "how the story ends." Despite the constrictions and limitations of life in Cuba, he just could not imagine himself in Miami with "a bunch of guys" at "some bar," as he described it, "talking about American sit-coms and sports." Over time, however, he disclosed more and more dissatisfactions, and it became clear that talks David and Tatiana had been having alone in their bedroom had evolved into a version that they were now having with me.

One typical afternoon, Tatiana stopped by with a load of freshly laundered cloth diapers. I showed her the bottle of deodorant I had just purchased; she approved, and said she even had the same kind but in blue. As was par for the course, we chatted about the dollar boutique where I had purchased it. She informed me about other specific products made by international manufacturers that I could purchase there not too expensively, although she warned me most things cost much too much—*really* too much. "Listen," she said lowering her voice, "when you are in Costa Rica. . . ." Given the topic of the conversation thus far, I was logically expecting her to ask me to bring her back a certain product, but then she threw me a curve. "Can you figure out a way to get us out?" I tried to hide my surprise.

"Because, if you can," she continued, "I'm out of here." She took one palm and slammed it on the other, simulating a jet plane taking off, arching quickly into the sky.

She then got up and closed my front door to carry on the rest of the conversation. She believed there was a possibility of obtaining a work contract that would allow them to apply for a special kind of visa. A letter of invitation, a way to leave Cuba for a visit, was usually only extended to adults and did not include children; it was imperative that Wendy come too. We discussed things briefly and agreed to hold a meeting that night that would include David, whom she assured me was on board with the plan, despite our many conversations to the contrary. "Please," she said, stating the obvious, "Do not mention this to anyone." Having selected us as an escape valve, she had implicitly entrusted us to keep her secret. I told her we would stop by her apartment that night to discuss plans in further detail.

That night when I walked in, David and his daughter, Wendy, were sprawled on the couch watching a kung fu movie with Spanish subtitles in front of the electric fan. David's eyes met mine with a certain sadness. We closed all the doors. David had wanted to conduct the meeting in English, so that Wendy could not overhear, but he could not—"it's not coming to me," he explained, and Wendy was sent off to play games on Petra's computer. This is how the conversation started: "I don't want to cry," he said, "but we need money. I can't even take Wendy to a swimming pool on a hot summer day."

He produced a brief, simple, handwritten résumé, and we moved to the dining room table for the conference, bringing our series of conversations about consumer dissatisfactions and political problems to their logical conclusion. It became clear that David was not just dreaming and seeking out possibilities. He was serious and ready to make actual plans. They would use Costa Rica only as a trampoline, and then find a way to head north to Miami.[24] So all they wanted at this point was a labor contract that would allow them to get the visa to leave. Our job would be to find someone there who could draw up a work contract, even it was a "dummy" work contract, but it would be most believable if it matched David's and Tatiana's skills and experience.

David remained emotional and uncomfortable throughout the conversation. He portrayed Tatiana as the somewhat more impulsive one. He told us that he had asked Tatiana with concern whether asking us for such a favor might be abusing our friendship. "No one, no one knows about the plan. Not parents, not sisters, not brothers, not friends, no one." During the course of the conversation, a couple of neighbors and one family member walked in to borrow things or ask questions, at which points we abruptly switched to an unrelated topic and tried to appear casual.

I asked Tatiana how she would feel if she missed the upcoming birth of her sister's first baby. "I can see pictures," she replied, shaking her head dismissively and rolling her eyes. David stressed that any communication by e-mail after we left the country would not be completely secure, and that we needed to write in code, even though they had complete trust in the neighbor whose computer they would be using for the correspondence, and so we came up with words that would signify various ideas related to the move. No one wrote them down. David remained somber and surprisingly sure as he spoke about the family decision, but also vulnerable and human about the thought of leaving.

We eventually moved to the living room. David sat on the floor, his wrists resting on his knees. His chin wrinkled and his face contorted a couple of times as he described how hard a decision this was, the hardest decision he had ever made in his life. "But we have to do it. We have to do it. There is no future for us here."[25] He stated that he loved his parents, and leaving his brothers was extremely difficult, but he thought he could do more for them there than here. He hoped all members of the family would eventually meet up again.

Despite the high energy and strong emotions, the shuffling around, and the increased use of sotto voce after the decision had been made, and finally, the planning and research I did for their family in Costa Rica, we were able to procure neither labor contracts nor letters of invitation, due to shifting Costa Rican laws allowing only next-of-kin to arrange migration. As of this writing, David, Tatiana, and Wendy are still living in Los Árboles, where they feel nothing has changed and that they are in a liminal holding pattern to this day (sidebar 7.1, stage 5).

E-mail Elena

Elena, despite her desperation, did have something precious that not every Cuban has: $100 ($25 for each family member) that arrived faithfully into her Western Union account every month from the United States. Wellington, the man who sent the money, had renewed Elena's faith in the church, both spiritually and as a practical means of survival in Cuba. Wellington "is a good Christian" she explained, "at the level of Lucius Walker, sent to her by God, and a godfather to her three children."[26] While Elena always spoke of Wellington with passionate respect, with the passage of time, her relationship with him deepened. Here, I include a sample of Elena's e-mails to Wellington, to show their progression. As her scribe, I had the opportunity to observe the transformations in the tone and content of the e-mails she cast his way.[27]

> Dear Wellington,
> How are you doing? We are praying for you and your family. Let us know about you.
> Love Sincerely,
> Elena and the Kids
>
> Dear W,
> I am very worried about the current events here and the ones who captured those yachts to travel to U.S. (murdered).[28] Really, I don't know what will happen here. I went to Western Union last Saturday and the money was still not here. Tomorrow, Monday, I will go again. Now I'm watching a Press Lecture (conference) on TV offered by Cuba's Foreign Affairs Ministry, and he is denouncing those who receive money from NGOs (as family aids to support Cuban "agents" for them here). Thank God that is not our case, and I pray to God that we may always receive aid because it is our survival. Pray for us to see if God may favor us with what is convenient and more favorable for this family. My only sin has been today to denounce what is not fair or just for us. . . . I write to you by Internet because it is the only secure way to make contact abroad.
> Sincerely and with too much love,
> Elena and the Kids.
> P.S.: We still wait for the Bombo [lottery],[29] a journey that would be Thanksgiving Day for us, if it comes, with the blessing of God. Today is Sunday, and I will attend a musical concert for Easter at my Church.
>
> Hi, W,
> How are you, W? Please do not ask me to decide or to think if my ex-husband's return is good for me or not, because too much time has passed since we got divorced, and he does not love me. He is doing this to us. I mean, if he were to appear after six years, he would see that we were going ahead without him. Now I ask you to think if you are in the position to move Ahead with this family. The kids love you and they are pleased with you, and all the efforts you have made without being their

father. They say you are their godfather, for God sent you to look after them when we were alone. In relation to me, let me tell you that I have been waiting for you without dating, taking care of my kids and me and praying for us all, including you. I also dream of being in California one rainy day to smell that wet soil. . . . Please, Darling, I do not know what will happen with the aid from there, but it is summer season and I have finished my private tutoring job, so I was wondering if you could send us some aid prior to May 20.[30] That day the president will speak to say what he decided to do with the family aid coming to us. . . . Here in Cuba we are very eager and worried what will happen that day. What will happen after your president speaks. Since you know there are many families living from the family aid that comes from your country. I do not know how we are going to receive our aid, but in case it is not possible to send it to me because it is a determined amount every three months, you could send it to Daniela [Elena's youngest daughter] in case. Western Union continues functioning up to now.

Love, Elena

In the process of casting her net wide, a net that would allow her to endure, to improve her situation financially, and finally, to escape, Elena had begun to refashion Wellington as a marriage partner. Her e-mails to him started out as brief and polite, but with time became more politicized and also emphasized their shared Christian connection. Eventually, they became more intimate, pushing for a more formal family connection that would allow her to migrate.

The fantasies Elena conjured up about her relationship with Wellington reflected her tendency, in all of her correspondence, to magnify the potential of every existing social connection she had. It was also part of a more general and risky strategy of asking the most she could from every person she knew abroad, no risk being as great in her mind as the prospect of staying indefinitely in Cuba—thus, the increasing intensity, wildness, and social inappropriateness of her e-mails to Wellington and, as she became increasingly frustrated and desperate, to a host of other recipients. Ultimately, none of her e-mails to Wellington or anyone else gave her what she so desperately wanted. They were just messages in bottles, floating out in a virtual sea, unanswered, despite her hope and faith. Nevertheless, during my tenure as her scribe, she wrote e-mails in her children's voices to take on different tones; she offered herself as a potential bride for a Spanish suitor, sending digital photos of herself posing in Flamenco outfits with castanets and fans; she tried to pawn off her eldest son as a priest to an international brotherhood; she tried to convince her ex-husband she needed more child support; and she ratted on a priest's bad behavior to the archbishop of Havana, hoping to win some level of support from this powerful figure of dissent.

But her supplications and attempts to escape are classic parts of the contemporary Cuban story. So, too, is her failure to realize her plans. Elena remains in Cuba, stuck in a holding pattern.

Karlos

In one of our first meetings, I asked Karlos, a former member of the Cuban national wrestling squad and member of an avowedly communist family (casually and in private), if after visiting Chile he would ever want to live there. He answered defiantly that he would not, although he also mentioned that very many Cubans want to leave, and that Telma, his older, wealthy girlfriend, wanted him to join her. "But it's too cold," he said, "it even snows in the southern region, and after all, I'm used to being here." His answer seemed authentic at the time, especially since he actually did return to Cuba after enjoying a three-month visit to Chile.

Karlos's attitude began to unfold a little differently as our relationship developed. At first, he started talking a little bit more about Chile and things he had experienced there. In fact, the turning point for him concerning his views about Cuba was living in Chile for three months and "seeing, realizing, comparing details about the two places." He thought about how hard everything was in Cuba, even getting food. He described a meat restaurant that was *tenedor libre* (literally "free fork," the Spanish term for all-you-can eat), quantities of meat the likes of which he had never seen, how he felt he couldn't stop eating, and how he was sure one must be able to recognize other Cubans at these buffets. He also described how he had never received such good service as he had there, with people waiting to serve him. And his girlfriend owned things: a farm, a bank, a restaurant. And she was a freelance journalist who could write whatever she liked. He had never seen or experienced any of these things before in his life.

"I was a fool for rejecting her," he admitted, showing me a blown-up, eight-by-eleven-inch photograph of the couple when Telma visited Cuba. Karlos, muscular and smiling, was dressed all in white, with fresh cornrows; mirrored, iridescent sunglasses; and several gold chains and rings. He stood next to a white woman in her early fifties, with wrinkles and a somewhat fallen face, also wearing abundant gold jewelry, as well as a long flowered dress. "I don't love her, but I know she's coming back for me. I know it. And when she comes this time, I'm leaving Cuba with her forever. This time, *voy a quedarme.*"[31]

Karlos is like many Cubans who find themselves in a situation where they may have to trap themselves in a marriage of convenience in order to leave. They are willing to exchange one trap for another: an unbearable state-centered trap for a bearable marital one with a partner they like reasonably well in an otherwise free state. Yet Karlos's fate, like those of David, Tatiana, and Elena, was eternal waiting. When I embraced Karlos goodbye upon leaving Cuba, I whispered, "Maybe I'll see you next time in Chile," and he placed his fist on his heart. Telma, however, was calling less and less. Karlos, in other words, had found but lost his ticket out of Cuba and was left waiting. Apropos of the Cuban migration story, "to hope" and "to wait" are expressed in Spanish in one and the same word: *esperar*.

Cumulative Push Factors

These moments of revelation and announcement are important to the unsatis-fied citizen-consumer story, but looking back on the moments that led up to the revelation is equally significant in understanding the phenomenon as a whole. One important aim of this book has been to reveal how the local avail-ability of affordable, quality goods and services, and their role in everyday life, act as push factors in migration decision making in late-socialist Cuba. This process can be identified only through observing the fine-grained details of households in the home, or sending, country, since it is only through familiar-ity with these details that observers can hope to decode the series of hidden, backstage dramas that lead to the moment of the migration decision itself as the ultimate solution for avoiding or remaining out of poverty, and for escap-ing the tight clutch of state control.

In addition to laying out the trajectory of unsatisfied citizen consumers (but without indulging in extensive ethnographic detail to illustrate my point), I wish to summarize other elements of discourse, gesture, emotion, and desire that I found to be signs leading up to a migration announcement and to con-tribute to cumulative push factors. These are summarized in the "Typology of Signs and Symptoms of Dissatisfaction Leading to Migration" sidebar.

Conclusion: Equating Migration with Freedom

Is escape freedom? Is migration from Cuba freedom? Freedom from what? The prospect of migration holds the allure of freedom to earn one's own keep and provide for one's own family. The most pressing problem for unsatisfied citizen-consumers in Cuba is that the state forces them, as one study of citi-zens under formal social security put it, "to live according to a set of rules that strongly limits their opportunities to seek their own solutions to their mate-rial problems" (Snel and Staring 2001: 10). The second pressing problem is the ongoing friction between limited public provisions and social rights and their dependence on a state that forces them to violate laws in order to survive. Im-

Typology of Signs and Symptoms of Dissatisfaction Leading to Migration

1. *Transferring feelings of asphyxiation onto physical spaces:* not liking walls, grates, bars; placing one's hands around one's throat as if being choked when speaking about being a citizen in Cuba.
2. *Becoming increasingly curious concerning details of life outside the island:* learning about products and services and their exact costs, smells, sounds, as well as patterns of daily life, all of which lead to a heightened perception of deprivation.
3. *Exhibiting growing impatience with* having to wait in lines, dealing with ministries, receiving inadequate services.
4. *Making negative comments concerning a specific problem regarding a nationalized service:* Irritation turns into anger when articulating the problem as part of a pattern.
5. *Framing government promises or citizens' rights as lies.*
6. *Feeling depressed or anxious, or both, mixed with subdued hope if signs point to change.*
7. *Describing life as "futureless" in Cuba and in one's current situation.*
8. *Expressing increasing irritation and complaints about one's country and the mentality of fellow citizens:* avoiding public rituals, events, and meetings; avoiding contact with state officials and ministries when possible; perceiving oneself as existing "outside of the system."
9. *Transforming desires into actual planning:* looking into obtaining a visa or investigating routes or modes of escape, saving a specific amount of money for migration-related expenses, increasing activity on the informal market while trying to increase income.
10. *Heightening one's desire for secrecy and privacy:* talking about plans using a different tone of voice or lower volume, perceiving people and the community around them as things that will soon be in their past.

plicit in Cuban citizenship is criminality. Ribas (1998) attempts to answer the "freedom from what" question, suggesting that migrants seek at least freedom from the "ethical duality" upon which socialism (and I would add, particularly late socialism) is based.

A conceptual framework that considers the dialectical relationship between order and freedom is relevant to this discussion, in that it suggests freedom is not just a passive experience or a "state" one can leave or enter. Rather, it is something that can be created through meaning (see Sanday 2004 on public interest anthropology). Applying the concept of culture as "webs of significance" that humans spin while simultaneously being suspended within them (Geertz 1973: 5), freedom corresponds with the "spinning," and order with the "being suspended."

Within the Cuban late-socialist context, migration has come to have a certain meaning, to represent a certain kind of order or logic, and to serve as a certain kind of solution. It has become part of the social field, as Sanday (2004) puts it, which is "upheld and legitimated by historical cultural meanings justifying values and norms." Specifically, leaving Cuba has come to represent a moment of choice in which one chooses to resolve one's conflict with the state through exit. Consequently, leaving Cuba has come to represent freedom in the abstract whereas, in actuality, it represents a certain existing social order in which Cubans are "suspended": citizens dream about leaving rather than transforming the political system, which leaves them in fact generally trapped within the existing system.

As such, leaving has come to replace the construction of solidarity, which yields new webs of meaning supporting new, previously unimagined possibilities for social relations among Cubans, and between Cubans and the state apparatus. In other words, although migration may appear to be freedom, it is actually part of the existing order or cultural logic among citizen-consumers that allows the existing system to prevail.

Freedom as opposed to order becomes possible "when existing social relations or situations are contested as people challenge the determinism of *social fields* or *the tyranny of custom* in responding and seeking correction to the *disorders* that confront them" (Sanday 2004, n.p.). Nevertheless, Cuban unsatisfied citizen-consumers face special challenges because they lack a clearly identifiable public sphere, which as Calhoun puts it, would serve as "a setting for the development of social solidarity as a matter of choice," where "new ways of imagining identity, interests, and solidarity make possible new material forms of social relations" (Sanday 2004, n.p., quoting Calhoun 2002). Yet the freedom of citizens does not apply only to societies with a strictly identifiable public sphere. What importance do forms or acts of resistance have within the constraints of "state-spun" webs of significance? Can they influence the existing political order or identify an emerging public sphere? I consider these matters in greater depth as I continue my discussion of freedom in chapter 8 and in the conclusion.

Freedom Offstage

If migration is the shadow public's exit from a crumbling state, as I described in chapter 7, quiet, offstage forms of criticism are a form of voice in that same system.[1] Members of the shadow public are not notable citizens. In other words, they do not try to stand out or make their voices heard. Again, they are not therefore—nor can they be—activists. For example, they do not participate in the mild dissident activity that has surfaced following Fidel's ceding power to his brother, such as gathering for a silent demonstration in a public park (International Human Rights Day, December 2006) or wearing white rubber bracelets that have "cambio" (change) inscribed on them (November 2007). They are certainly not engaging in riots or circulating public petitions.

The absence of public political activity does not mean that members of the shadow public can be described as politically apathetic, individualistic, purely materialistic, or in need of having their consciousness raised. In fact, they frequently are quite educated about local, national, and often international politics. They express political views, have visions of change, and occasionally express ideas for intentional collective action, even if they do not follow through with it. But they no longer see the state as "a means to address their own interests, nor the broader concerns for their society, [so] they have little incentive to be engaged in civic life," as Powers (2001: 238) said of Argentina. Furthermore, they cannot justify spending time and energy on the unpaid work of activism, especially if that might lure a bugaboo state—a state that causes persistent fear, worry, and problems—any closer to the family hearth.

Discussing "offstage" resistance and "hidden transcripts" (à la Scott 1990) has largely fallen out of favor in contemporary analysis of Cuban citizen protest. Hagedorn (2001), Hernandez-Reguant (2004), Frederick (2005), Fernandes (2006), and others have demonstrated the problems that arise from imposing readings derived from dualistic models such as offstage versus onstage on categories of engagement, such as dissent, censorship, or participation. A growing body of scholarship has documented increasing tolerance in Cuba, particularly after the 1990s, that have opened up new spaces of critique and public expressions of disagreement, especially in the world of Cuban art, music, and film. In fact, since the 1980s Cuban films have regularly contained critiques of totalitarianism. Furthermore, recent scholarship has also demonstrated the difficulty of differentiating the state from society. It argues that daily practices follow a multiplicity of agendas that are not always self-consciously defined vis-à-vis government ideology; and that engagement and disengagement, identification and dis-identification are at times intertwined. This stream of analysis is an important one. It does not, however, shed light on the shadow public, whose members remain in intentional obscurity, criticizing the state in private while withdrawing from public expressions of disagreement.

Thus far, I have described how the shadow public engages in criticizing or subverting state domination, but usually only in ways that will better their families' economic condition in the short term, keep their families free from harm, and improve, or at least invest, in their quality of life. Yet despite their lack of overt activism or contribution to a broad, popular call for political change, they are nevertheless social and political agents whose dissatisfaction can challenge the limitations imposed on them by the state (see also analysis by Kittrell 2004). Although I situate shadow public concerns and actions in the late-socialist era, scholarship regarding Cuba in the 1960s and 1970s reported on similar patterns; for example, nonmembership or nonparticipation in officially sponsored so-called mass organizations. In particular, the Lewis, Lewis, and Rigdon (1977–78) anthropological project in Cuba documented lack of engagement with officially sponsored themes or forms of participation at the individual level, indicating that problems of disengagement and development of a shadow public have existed for some time. I suspect that the intensifying social and economic problems of the Special Period and its aftermath have likely caused the shadow public to expand.

In this chapter, I focus on what I argue have been three common offstage forms of state criticism in Cuba: in-house protests to broadcasts of Fidel's televised speeches on TV; using metaphors and aphorisms among friends to criticize the socialist (welfare) state; and withdrawal from state-orchestrated political rituals. These rituals include elections, political "debates," and "citizen organizing," but I focus particularly on the practice of avoiding marches. Using Randall Collins's (2004) analysis of ritual interactions, I describe how the shadow public has created more meaningful offstage ritual counter-gatherings for themselves on march days. I identify these acts of criticism and withdrawal as more politically explicit than the types I have previously explored (that is, complaining about goods, working for dollars in the shadow economy, and migrating) and as more connected to unsatisfied citizenship than to unsatisfied consumption.

I acknowledge the improbability of large-scale protest or the development of powerful interest groups in Cuba, and explain how the forms of protest I identify do not represent a unified, national opposition movement of any sustained potency. These acts of political criticism—as limited, dispersed, and fragmentary as they may appear (Taylor 2004)—combined with consumer dissatisfaction, nevertheless point to a broad base of the population that no longer supports the current socialist regime and that collectively and cumulatively may be wearing down Cuba's existing political fabric (see also Chazan et al. 1992).[2]

While unsatisfied Cubans have found niches for criticism (of state-imposed broadcasts, state-provided services, and state-orchestrated political rituals), I point out that these are not the same as having one's voice accurately represented. Consequently, I discuss who is entrusted to provide the official interpretations and representations of Cuban events and experiences, and under what circumstances, and I frame the discussion around a conversation with Mariela Castro Espín, the daughter of Raúl Castro. I conclude with a consideration of freedom, representation, and expression in late-socialist Cuba.

Fidel on TV: Waning Respect for an Aging Leader and the "Cootacracy"

Throughout the active years of his forty-seven-year rule (1959–2006), Fidel Castro was the dominant fixture in the Cuban media, known for his frequent public appearances and trademark marathon speeches, both of which were imposed upon the broadcast network (and secretly resented by many Cubans). Since August 2006, this situation has changed drastically. Fidel Castro has appeared only occasionally in photographs (in one, holding *Granma*, the official Communist Party newspaper, with the current date prominently displayed, to assure people of both the photo's legitimacy and of his continued existence) and in a few brief, nationally aired videos in Cuba. In all cases he wears a tracksuit rather than his traditional green military gear, indicating a more casual role in leadership.

No hint of this change in Fidel's public presence was in the air when I attended a family gathering in 2003, on the outskirts of Havana. Fidel appeared on TV in a rebroadcast of a recent speech, and laughter rippled throughout the crowded room. "Turn it down! Turn the sound off!" someone demanded. "He's crashing the party!" With a quick turn of a knob, Fidel went silent, his image now providing an animated backdrop for the banter that ensued.

"That's your father, there on TV!" said Fredrich, throwing a mock insult at me and laughing. "No, I mean your *grandfather*. No, no, what am I saying?! That's your *great-grandfather*." The salsa is turned up on the stereo, and Fidel is left to move his hands to the music, his mouth emphatically forming words; he occasionally raises a fist to punctuate his silent oratory, but his message is intentionally drowned out by the merrymakers, some of whom continue to snicker and comment on how his gesticulations oddly keep time to the music, creating the effect of a music video.

"If you live in a free state," Benny, a taxi driver, explains to me with passion during the same party, "with freedom of the press, of speech, you can stand in a public place and say 'Bush is a bastard! Down with Fidel!' and that's your right. Nothing will happen. But *here*" (making a motion as if to slit his throat with the side of his hand).

It was rare to hear people speak so explicitly about freedom. The only parallel I could think of was something David had said some time back, when I had asked, "It seems like people talk about desires for economic freedom. Do they also talk about desires for political freedom?"

"Sure they do," he replied casually, taking a sip of his drink, "but they're in jail."

Apparently it was easier merely to make fun of Fidel on TV,[3] or to scrutinize his appearance the way Petra did. Petra, entering the long days of early retirement, liked to sit in her rocking chair in the evenings, with the TV on and the volume low. This Saturday night she preferred my company. She was really looking forward to the pleasant escape of the Saturday-night movie and had planned her evening around it, but instead we found ourselves watching another Fidel speech. Petra paid no attention to the substance of the speech. She was actually quite angry and depressed about being obliged to watch it. Fidel occasionally referred to a text with a blue transparent cover in front of him on the table. He was sitting down, looking pale, his age spots standing out, his eyes dark and watery.

"He looks old today," Petra murmured, "old and a bit frail. Don't you think?" she asked me hopefully, studying Fidel's face. Some days I was not sure whether Petra could take another disappointment, but luckily in this instance I agreed with her anyway. "His voice is much weaker than I expected," I assured her quietly. She nodded and rocked in contented agreement.

Another time, at a small gathering at an architect's house, guests were sitting on the floor, drinking *cafecitos* (demitasses of espresso) and homemade *batido de fruta bomba* (papaya milkshake), eating *torticas* (Cuban sugar cookies), and talking about local Cuban kitsch and bad taste in Miami. I noticed that there was more than one TV in the small apartment. I asked why. "Why do you think?" Armando joked, "so that when Fidel appears on TV to give a speech, we can watch him in stereo. . . . I also turn on the radio, para el Surround Sound!" The group of architects laughed. "¡Oye! [Hey, listen!] We'd better watch what we're saying," joked another one, "she might be a spy, and there's a tiny microphone hidden in the baby's diaper, recording everything we say. Why do you think she's always carrying that baby around?" he asked, referring to my infant son, whom I often had in my arms. This comment was followed by more unrestrained laughter and thigh slapping.

I asked around about people's blatant disrespect for Fidel, in particular during his TV appearances. "It's true!" one hissed to me in what sounded like excitement. "Times are really changing. Even the kids, even the *kids* make fun of him now! It did not used to be that way." In fact, Fidel's speeches increasingly seemed to do no more than get in people's way; for example, by preempting movies or other shows on TV. Indeed, this was so much the case that people hoped that an *apagón* (blackout) would miraculously fall during a Fidel broadcast, so that they could feel free not to tune in and, equally importantly, feel free that they were not being watched not tuning in. Reacting to Fidel on TV was a common form of criticism among the shadow public but, of course, only offstage, within the safety of living rooms and bedrooms and among family and close friends.

While this pressure has lifted since the sudden disappearance of broadcast Fidel speeches in 2006, the feeling is still that Cuba's late-socialist state is completely run by old socialists, many in their seventies and some approaching their eighties. As one author describes it, the Cuban leadership is full of "old coots," a "cootacracy": "bearded, fragile, isolated, in ill-fitting clothes, unchallenged, long-finger-nailed, muttering to itself, obsessing about the reality forty years ago" (Tattlin 2002: 210). The cootacracy is in direct opposition to the youth, who cannot imagine a future in the Cuba where they live.

Shadow Opposition

When I asked if any of these small-scale, domestic forms of criticism and the strong sentiment against an aging and out-of-touch leadership could turn into actual, large-scale protest, informants definitively claimed they could not. The opinion of many ordinary Cubans reflects an array of scholarly analysis as well. Mesa-Lago and Fabian (1993: 362) acknowledge that there is "a large silent segment—a majority?—of the population that does not actively oppose the regime . . . but is dissatisfied and wants some type of change." Rosendahl (1997: 123), too, has directed her research toward exploring the "backstage" in Cuba, noting the "deep discontent with the lack of democratic rights" and the need to "read between the lines" to detect criticism of the regime. Eckstein (1995: 30) has argued that "nominally nonpolitical forms of resistance . . . did more to erode government legitimacy than the work of formal dissident groups." As Scott (1990: 199) might say, these acts and attitudes fall within "the immense political terrain that lies between quiescence and revolt" (see also Kittrell 2004 for more analysis).

What prevents outright revolt? For years, middle-aged and older people (but generally not today's youth) believed that the charismatic power and physical presence of Fidel continued to make people weak in the knees. Now that Fidel himself for the most part has been removed from the public stage, the combination of people's fear for their families and their fear of a military response continues to prevent popular protest. Local lore, for example, has it that there is an entire battalion of underground tanks beneath Havana ready to roll up to the surface in the event of a popular uprising or invasion. Ironically, this is in contrast to the Batista period, when there were enough civil liberties and government ineptitude that Fidel and his band could amass arms and use the press to rally people to their cause, as David explained. Either way, the general sentiment among those most embittered with the regime was not one of public protest but of resignation: "Who is going to do it? We, like everyone else, just want to stay afloat and take care of our kids."

If popular protest is improbable, the changes in the structure of Cuban society during its transition into late socialism have allowed for the emergence of at least one interest group with the potential to adopt relatively strong positions vis-à-vis the state. This group is the self-employed, in particular those self-employed who are relatively less dependent upon the state and its resources. In practice, however, this is much less an interest group than an atomized set of individuals who would not benefit from collective action. As B. Smith (1999: 56–58) notes, "complaining to local citizen's groups, formed under *Poder Popular* [People's Power] initiatives of the 1980s, accomplishes very little. . . . Organizing also attracts the attention of state officials, which was clearly a disincentive to organization. . . . Overwhelmingly, they simply wanted to be able to work for themselves in peace."

This attitude to popular organizing, I would argue, is the overall sentiment of the shadow public in Cuba, and perhaps of Cubans at large. Smith continues, "The biggest advantage to self-employment, even more so than increased earning power, was freedom. They could make their own hours; if they did not want to work, they did not have to . . . this was a new experience for Cubans, and they cherished it" (1999: 53). Yet cherishing this new freedom did not carry over into mass action, in part because the self-employed did not want to endanger that freedom.

Critiquing the Welfare State

While some Cubans are developing a taste for increased earning power through self-employment, the power and restrictions imposed by the socialist welfare state still loom large in daily life. In my profile of Cuba in chapter 1, I discussed the importance of the welfare state in this project as the shared context, the macro-institutional structure or "enclosure and regime through which subjects pass" (Willis 2000: xiii). I defined a welfare state as one that provides or directly subsidizes basic social security and other social welfare "consumption needs," and I emphasized how this creates an uneasy intimacy between citizen-consumers and the state on which they depend as a paternalistic provider.

In fact, there is considerable tension around this intimacy. On the one hand, my informants expressed genuine concern that the future transition from the current "Fidelista" system would undermine the universal healthcare and education services to which they were so accustomed. On the other hand, despite this concern, the lived experience of receiving state welfare under Cuban late socialism was overwhelmingly negative, as expressed indirectly through widely circulating metaphors, allegories, aphorisms, or *cuentos* (which Tanuma 2007 defines as ironic jokes or stories). In the sidebar, I list aphorisms and *cuentos* that specifically define the role of the state provider as an incarcerator, along with brief explanatory notes. These sayings are quietly circulating among members of the shadow public.

Late-Socialist Aphorisms and *Cuentos* with Commentary

Tu Padre (Your Father)

Your father says, "I will send you to any university you want; if you get sick, I will send you to the best doctor; you choose a sport, I will pay for all of your lessons. But you can only read what I tell you to read, and nothing else; you will eat only what I offer; you will date and marry whom I say." What would you say to that? Of course, most people would say, "No thanks, I'm leaving home, keep your money." But if you are dirt poor, you might have to live *con tu padre*.

Castro is the father, and the Cuban people, his children, too many of whom are trapped because they are "dirt poor."

Gallinas sin Plumas (Featherless Chickens)

If you have a featherless chicken, and it gets cold, it will snuggle close; if it is hungry, it will come close to be fed. Keep your chickens featherless, and you will keep your power.

It was said, by word of mouth, that Stalin had propounded this statement. Poor families who were faithful to the regime, holding low-paying state positions and never criticizing the government, its leaders, or its policies, were described as featherless chickens, not ideologues. David also expressed concern about featherless chickens out in the traditionally more pro-revolutionary eastern provinces, imitating a nasal, rural accent, accompanied by a downtrodden posture: "Por lo menos [at least] my kids have food, por lo menos my kids can read, por lo menos we have a doctor." Unsatisfied citizen-consumers do not generally have a *por lo menos* attitude toward their situation.

Pájaros en la Jaula de Oro (Birds in a Gilded Cage)

You are given a nice little house, where you get your allotted food, like an exotic bird in a gilded cage. You are spoon-fed and given a little bath in a golden tub and kept in a gilded cage for life. Beautiful things, in a beautiful cage, but still imprisoned. The iron cage of bureaucracy, the golden cage of the largesse of the welfare state, it's still a cage.

A strong central government with socialist/communist policies is also sometimes referred to as a "birdcage" government.

La Telenovela sin Parar (The Never-Ending Soap Opera)

When will it end? Chapter after chapter unfolds, it is a long, ongoing telenovela with endless installments, and no one knows when or how it will end. If something happens, people say, "It's just another chapter, just another phase." If nothing happens, they say the same thing.

This is an apt metaphor for a political situation that is stagnant but still has its ups and downs, one that people watch to keep themselves amused, but where nothing really changes. This metaphor also highlights citizen detachment and powerlessness as "viewers."

Él, el Abuelo/Viejo Caprichoso
(Fidel, the Capricious Grandfather/Old Man)

Fidel is like a capricious old man, suddenly starting crackdowns, changing policies, getting in a bad mood, changing his mind. Sometimes he enforces a rule rigidly, other times he overlooks it. Having a sudden desire he demands, "I want this!" He's living in the past and reminiscing about the "good old days." On top of that, he seems occasionally to exhibit symptoms of senility, dementia, or Parkinson's disease.

Estamos Mamando el Pecho del Estado
(We Are Suckling at the Breast of the State)

The population is accustomed to "feeding at the breast" of the state, of "Mother Cuba," and doesn't know how to manage on their own. They will have to be weaned, since this kind of connection can't go on forever. If the breast is taken away without warning, however, people will not know what to do or how to sustain themselves.

Fredrick, the self-made, cigar-pilfering entrepreneur, adds that there are going to be problems, no matter what happens. Even if people are ready to be weaned, they drink from the breast out of necessity, not desire. (Of course, while Fredrick is self-made in the sense that he earns his own dollars, even he is quite accustomed to taking advantage of state resources via the cigar factory.)

El Mejor Comunista Está en la Opuesta
(The Best Communist is in the Opposition)

The best communists are those not currently in power, but rather those desiring power but still in the opposition party, campaigning and dreaming about all the amazing things they will be able to do: provide for the people, and provide for all the people equally. Communist dreams are appealing, communist reality is a trap.

Cuentos in Political Perspective

Overall, these sayings highlight the paternalistic style and authoritarian intensity of Cuba's state provision of welfare, and the citizens' perception of an excessive level of control over their lives, both of which lead to feeling trapped. Most of the sayings also emphasize the damaging effects of loss of self-sufficiency and autonomy.

The origins and paths of circulation of these aphorisms are elusive. Most people do not know where they come from or when they started circulating. They are also careful not to attribute them to an individual person or source.

It is clear that these aphorisms are, for the most part, spread orally and repeated only among trusted friends and family members.

In the fields of anthropology and folklore, it has been widely recognized that meaning, history, and polity can be brought into being through lyric discourse as well as song (George 1993), poetry (Abu-Lughod 1986), and myth (Urban 1991). It is also recognized that metaphors, maxims, allegories, and aphorisms are particularly important forms of daily discourse, in that they serve as metacultural commentary (Urban 2001). Elsewhere, metaphors in particular have often been described as being rooted in the cultural categories within which speakers construct their conversations (Ben-Amos 2000: 153; see also Ricoeur 1977; Sapir and Crocker 1977; Ortony 1979; Kittay 1987; Lakoff and Johnson 1980). The metaphors contained in these aphorisms may represent either cognitive categories or a more "compact" form of speech that carries implicit meanings—particularly useful in regimes where longer or more explicit forms of talk can mark you as a traitor.

Jokes historically have also proven particularly useful in regime criticism, although not in terms of direct political change: since they are "at once an assertion of defiance and admission of defeat . . . no public change is effected" (Cochran 1989: 272; see also Mañach 1991 and Tanuma 2007 for Cuban jokes in historical perspective).[4] The truth of this statement depends, of course, on how one is defining public change. Yurchak notes that socialist jokes, or *anekdots*,[5] helped sustain the contradictions of everyday life during late socialism in the Soviet Union, laying a groundwork for change (Yurchak 1997; see also Ries 1997). As Brandes (1977: 331) explains, "when people live under politically repressive circumstances, they are likely to vent their anger and frustration through . . . jokes . . . or related genres, and thereby create for themselves a temporary escape from omnipresent and severe restrictions on freedom of expression." Also writing about jokes under repressive regimes, and touching on the formation of publics, Oring states

> The joke rejects conventional logic and with its own counter-logics affirms the independence and integrity of tellers and hearers. [Jokes] objectify that opinion and crystallize it in aesthetic forms. And while no genuine public is created for this opinion, in some sense, the jokes stand as the oral artifacts of an "alternate moral universe" (Scott 1976: 240)—monuments of a buried civilization. (Oring 2004: 227)

All of the verbally circulating sayings I have listed may indeed be shared and passed down by a cultural group or community of speakers (a more commonly used term), but only rarely has such communication been used to identify the formation of a public. Is it possible to conceive of a public as those individuals who are attracted to the use of the same metaphors and allegories to describe their situation? What if their speech is circulating only verbally and in certain, limited contexts? Would these aphorisms help identify "reliable traces of people's inner dialogs, hidden fantasies, suppressed anxieties or unstated preferences"; or their "interests, complaints, demands and aspirations . . . attitudes in the loose sense of the word" (Tilly 1983: 462), allowing for the identification of a shadow public discourse?

Shadow Political Rituals

Discourse aside, state mechanisms that control citizens' ability to assemble freely remain solidly in place in Cuba. The Cuban state apparatus (through its subjects) must make it appear to the outside world, and perhaps even to themselves, that there is some type of public sphere. As Taylor writes, the public sphere is such a central feature of modern society that "even where [the public sphere] is in fact suppressed or manipulated it has to be faked. Modern despotic societies have generally felt compelled to go through the motions. . . . All this takes place as though a genuine process were in train, forming a common mind through exchange, even though the result is carefully controlled from the beginning" (Taylor 2004: 84).

"Faking," or "going through the motions," is utterly routine, although sometimes painful, to the shadow public. As I mentioned in chapter 1, Cubans widely consider that voting does not make a bit of difference, because no one elected at the levels of government where there are direct elections—for example, the syndicate level—has any power to innovate; thus, people just try to get elections done as quickly as possible. There is a mutual understanding among the electorate that hands should fly up to vote for the first candidate presented to them, so that they can turn on their heels and go home.

Cubans also endure skimming editorials allegedly expressing individual opinion—or more recently, since his illness, editorials written by Fidel Castro himself—that appear in *Granma*,[6] *Trabajadores* (Workers), or *Juventud Rebelde* (Rebel Youth), the three national news organs, all quite similar in content. They tune in and out of "Mesa Redonda" (Round Table), a news show featuring politicians and party members allegedly debating political issues. "You can detect that something is seriously wrong," Cubans warned me, "because the whole time, the people are just sitting around agreeing with each other. It's the most boring show in the world, but it might be worth it for you to watch it once, just for the experience." Some feel obligated to join what appear to be large grassroots organizations for women, workers, or youth, the *organizaciones de masas*. These organizations represent a form of "communist civil society: extremely coherent, fully inclusive, . . . thin in real content and driven from the top down rather than the bottom up" (Falcoff 2003: 181).

Marchas

Marchas (state-orchestrated marches or mass demonstrations), held seasonally, annually, or "spontaneously" in support of a certain cause and, as Taylor (2004: 84) might say, "purporting to give vent to the felt indignation of large numbers of people," pose the greatest opportunity for intentional political withdrawal by the shadow public. In fact, defiantly but quietly not attending marches seemed to be something of a litmus test for identifying members of the shadow public, and they took a certain pride in successfully avoiding such events. I had assumed that attendance at marches was mandatory, but many people I spoke to said, "I'm not going," and I was surprised at the number of younger people, usually under thirty, who declared, "I've never been to a march in my entire life."

I was warned against attending marches myself by people who wrinkled their noses and said with distaste "tanta gente!" (so many people); or wagged a forefinger at me and announced, "Not suitable for children." As for themselves, they begged off with "It starts way too early in the morning. I'm not getting up for that." They had alternate plans: "mañana es feriado! [tomorrow's a public holiday!]. No work! Are you coming over for la fiesta? . . . Excellent. Join us for a drink. It will be nice and tranquilo [calm/peaceful], and we can really talk. All the chivatos [snitches, squealers] will be at the march. . . . Am I going to the march? Of course not. I'm *for* the thing they're marching *against!*"[7]

The preferred way to spend a public holiday among the shadow public was to enjoy intimate in-house parties and gatherings, drinking, dancing, listening to music, and spending time with friends and family. The mechanics behind avoiding a march involved buying supplies and making plans with like-minded friends in advance, closing one's shutters, locking the doors, keeping all the lights off, and sleeping in, making it appear to CDR members (who knock on doors at the crack of dawn to round up the troops) that one's family got an early start in order to secure a good spot at the plaza. After the coast was clear and everyone had gone, the shadow public festivities could begin.

Randall Collins (2004: 49–53) recognizes that the gathering of family and friends is a natural interactional ritual, and consequently, a more likely setting for the generation of high emotional energy, shared mood, and feelings of group solidarity than the formal or forced ritual of the march itself.

That said, some people felt the weight of obligation to march at certain points in their lives—for example, to obtain or maintain a desired professional post or a private business license, or to avoid an uncomfortable or even threatening confrontation with a CDR president. For those forced to go to the marches even though they had no attachment to the cause behind them, there were other ways of coping with participation. Many Cubans would get drunk early in the morning, turning the event into a rum-drenched haze with plenty of chanting in unison in the company of friends, and the opportunity to obtain free revolutionary T-shirts to add to one's wardrobe or for later sale to tourists.

All these avoidance strategies pointed to the unavoidable contrast between the emptiness of public protest in Cuba compared with what a real political rally should or could be. Many people highlighted the formality and the forcedness of the political ritual by mimicking the coercion to shout a certain meaningless slogan over and over again, or by exhibiting how they would shuffle their feet and carry signs apathetically or raise a limply balled fist, shouting with vigor only when they suspected that someone was watching. These experiences reflect what Collins (2004: 49–51) calls a "ritual failure": a formal ritual that is an "empty going through the forms, even a dead ceremonialism" resulting from what he describes as "little or no feeling of group solidarity; no sense of one's identity being affirmed or changed; no respect for the group's symbols; no heightened emotional energy—either a flat feeling unaffected by the ritual, or worse yet a sense of drag, the feeling of boredom and constraint, even depression, interaction fatigue, a desire to escape."

Regardless of people's personal feelings about them, what role does the persistence of these seemingly unanimous acts of mass demonstration play in the progression of late socialism or the socialist transition? Using late-socialist Russia as his example, Yurchak describes the way Soviet citizens participated in "ideological rituals and events," and his observations may shed light on the phenomena developing in Cuba. He writes that the overwhelming majority of citizens *did* participate in May Day and Revolution Day parades in Soviet cities, and came to do so with very few negative emotional associations. In fact, they often had quite a bit of fun: "in practice . . . most people in the parades paid little attention to the slogans and many were not aware who exactly was depicted on the Politburo portraits they carried." Furthermore, "in most contexts these unanimous acts, gestures, and utterances of support did not refer to the literal meaning of ideological statements, resolutions, and figures, but rather performed a different role" through what he refers to as a *performative shift* (Yurchak 2005: 15–16). The centrality of the repetitiveness and exactness in the performed act or form of authoritative discourse (vote, speech, report, slogan, meeting, parade, election, and so on) actually began to counter the constraints of their literal meaning, thus paradoxically opening up an avenue for the actors to assign new interpretations and unanticipated meanings to the rituals themselves. This is the same process that might take place in any ritual prayer or ceremony. Perhaps Cuba is not far enough in the late-socialist trajectory for these "new meanings" to open up, or perhaps many among Cuba's shadow public are not as committed to socialism itself as Yurchak's informants seem to have been. But his interpretation of mass participation is nonetheless compelling and may at some point be relevant to the Cuban case.

It remains difficult to know what such a large group of people as the Cuban shadow public are experiencing individually or collectively—whether their attitudes reflect Collins's idea of a "ritual failure," duplicitous "faking it" or dissimulation along a public/private divide, Yurchak's version of a performative shift, or something else entirely. To David, however, the more important issue was how these mass demonstrations were being interpreted in the outside world. "I'm afraid that people will see the quantity of people filling the streets and think, 'Wow. Look at the support!' How are they going to know what we're really thinking when they just see so many bodies, so many people waving flags?" His concern was a legitimate one, but I countered that Cuban marches were not televised with such frequency throughout the world as they were within Cuba. When they were broadcast internationally, viewers also were aware of the long history of citizens being required to demonstrate by totalitarian governments, and critically thinking people outside Cuba would be skeptical of scenarios of unanimous support. David was not fully convinced.

Freedom and Representation

How is the battle against unanimous support fought at home? Who in Cuba are the "authoritative actors" with the liberty and the influence to circulate "authoritative discourse"[8] and to provide the world with interpretations and representations of life in Cuba? Ordinary Cubans see self-representation as an uphill battle and one in which it is hardly worth engaging. With the exception of informal, individual contacts with visiting foreigners, Cubans have few if any opportunities to express their opinions freely to the outside world (particularly if they lack secure access to the Internet to join the Cuban blogosphere),[9] making concerns about Cuba's collective outward appearance, such as those voiced by David in relation to the *marchas*, important.

The way that authoritative discourse is filtered in formal interviews was one of the contexts where I first noted the problem of official representation. Particularly striking was one life-history interview with a young Afro-Cuban mother, Zemmi, from what I would call a particularly peso-poor family. Her mother worked for MINFAR (Cuba's Ministry of Defense) and her father was a merchant marine, so their family's livelihood was tightly connected to the state. Her father stood in the background as I conducted the interview, and I could detect discomfort in his voice as he tried to shape what Zemmi was saying on tape, resulting in fear and formality on Zemmi's part that was quite unlike the tone of our other interactions.[10] She spoke haltingly (even talking about one's favorite foods as a child or where one was born can become a politically sensitive topic given recent changes in the economy and health care), while her father frequently and loudly interjected "gracias a la Revolución" (thanks to the Revolution), to punctuate key points in his daughter's narrative. Zemmi would then dutifully repeat the phrase, making clear how recorded speech constrained her ability to tell her life story as she might have wished.

Recorded interviews are met with *desconfianza* (mistrust), as is speaking with the international press, an activity not considered a safe form of popular dissent. Cubans, when they do speak to journalists, are extremely cautious. If they do not toe the Party line on a particular issue, they give vague or ambiguous answers to questions about it, and if they do choose to say something that might appear critical toward the government, they are quite nervous and never want their real names in print. The Cuban "voice" to the outside world, therefore, is left in the hands of carefully selected official representatives. These authoritative actors inevitably and invariably showcase the success of the system despite hard times, and the involvement and commitment of Cubans from below.

A Conversation with Raúl's Daughter

I had an opportunity to speak with Mariela Castro Espín, Raúl Castro's daughter.[11] During our conversation at CENESEX (Cuba's National Center for Sex Education), Mariela wore hip clothing and large, modern pieces of artistic silver jewelry. There were no framed pictures of Raúl or her Uncle Fidel adorning the walls of her government office wall. Rather, a funky, psychedelic Che, the now-copyrighted late-socialist icon, presided over her large, flat-screen Toshiba computer and sleek Sanyo microwave. Tasteful, exotic knickknacks, which she had picked up while traveling to international conferences all over the world, decorated her shelves.

Like Mariela's belongings, her depiction of Cuba and her profound style of nationalism were so radically different from anything I associated with ordinary, non-Party-affiliated citizens that it was difficult for me to conceive how she could be talking about the same time and the same place as my shadow-public informants. For example, she encouraged me to study what she called the "Responsible Parenthood Movement" (a local intervention program promoting couples education and communication), which she described as follows: "Without resources, a motivated nurse set this program into motion, and it took off. In Cuba, people talk [making talking gestures with both hands], people *mobilize* . . . and a program goes off running!" [making her fingers scurry gracefully through the air]. "¡Y me gusto eso!" [and I like that!], declared Mariela, wrinkling her nose and shrugging her shoulders with pride and pleasure, "¡Sin recursos!" [without resources!] she emphasized a second time.

Mariela painted a picture of a strong, grassroots Cuban population, with the freedom to start programs and enough commitment to do so without a single peso to carry them out. This official story of popular mobilizing did not fit with anything else that I had seen or heard, given both the prohibition on freedom of assembly and people's time-consuming struggle to survive, provide for their families, or simply enjoy the little that they do have.

Also painting a different picture than the one I had seen, Mariela described the government benefit of a year off for lactation to promote breastfeeding. "Cuban law dictates a year off work for women post-partum. And now Cuba is working for a father's year off as well, so that fathers can be more involved in the process and really enjoy that first year with their child. "*Paid* leave," she stressed, "Other, much more developed countries have this model" she added, not mentioning, of course, how little that pay is or what people really use that year for—namely, to engage in the underground economy.

When I asked my citizen-consumer informants for their interpretations of the lactation year off and its proposed expansion, their response was unanimous: the plan was masquerading as a socially progressive policy but was just one more temporary solution to a mounting economic crisis brought on by poorly paid underemployment and inefficiency.

At one point during our conversation, Mariela lowered her voice and admitted that there are still tremendous problems with the granting of research visas: "Yes, there have been times when people have come in to do research and have written reports that have said this, that, and the other about Cuba and the Revolution." She rolled her eyes and threw up her hands in confused dismay at this disrespect for the revolution, which she framed as progressive and deserving of respect despite running counter to liberal-compact values associated with freedom of the press and of information. She referred to the revolution as if it were a recent event that people were still becoming accustomed to, and spoke of Cuba as if it had almost perfected itself, just needing to tweak some things to become a little more progressive, advanced, or even ahead of the times.

"Mariela," my informants explained, "Does not know Cuba at all. Never in her life has she ever stood in line at a bodega. Everything has been delivered to her doorstep. Essentially, she does not have any idea what it is like to live in Cuba." Their cynical response to her vision of grassroots Cubans talking, gathering, mobilizing, and solving their problems was "escalofriante" (creepy) and "espantoso" (horrific, appalling).

Nevertheless, Mariela is one of Cuba's key public faces and authoritative voices in certain circles. She frequently travels to international meetings and conferences in order to discuss and promote Cuban sexual health education to the world. She is assigned to meet with visitors, and is entrusted with the power of official interpretation and official representation, all of which results in the broad circulation of a particular story about Cuba's achievements and Cubans' commitment to the system. She, in other words, is an important cog in the wheel of information dissemination and a key deployer of authoritative discourse, even if she masks her opinions as "ordinary" and downplays her personal, familial connections to the political elite.

While it has been difficult to obtain accurate information from the Cuban government on Fidel Castro's health since his emergency surgery and ceding of power in August 2006, Mariela met with news agency representatives. A resulting report stated: "Castro Espín, 44, said she had no inside knowledge, but thought that illness and age would prevent Castro from coming back as the full-blown leader of Cuba. . . . 'My impression as an ordinary Cuban is that we are going to have him in another role, as the wise 80-year-old leader that now is going to take care of himself,' she said" (Valdez 2006, n.p.). At some point "ordinary Cubans" without such tight links to the Party and its protection, and truly without any "inside knowledge" may be more comfortable stating their names and giving their opinions on the future of leadership in their country, but for now, Mariela serves this role.

Conclusion: Forms of Shadow Struggles

Understanding the spectrum of visibility of resistance remains the central challenge to the cultural study of relationships of power. The shadow public's criticisms may be shrouded, but they are still observable in the Cuban case, particularly in living rooms, bedrooms, and alleyways; on rooftops; and next to clotheslines. I have borrowed Scott's (1990) term "offstage" to conceptualize those arenas in which criticism and opposition can comfortably take place. One can argue that offstage acts performed within the confines of one's own social group and conducted through joke-telling, anti-state aphorisms, and avoidance do not circulate in the same way as critiques within the realm of expressive arts, and certainly do not resemble outright revolt. Yet such practices nevertheless mark the existence of an unsatisfied group.

Other shadow public forms of adaptation to tough times in the late-socialist area include adopting a *doble moral*, reappropriating revolutionary words to create a Special Period lexicon with alternative meanings referencing the margins of legality, depending on *socioismo* more than *socialismo*, diligently earning dollars on the shadow economy through *trabajo particular* (private work), evading the reach of state control while loafing on and pilfering from their state jobs, and planning to migrate.[12] These acts and forms of expression have started to become viewed locally as "culture as usual" in the late-socialist era. But in fact, embedded within this culture as usual are codes and attitudes that may contradict outward expression of deference and reveal an alternative perspective of the sociocultural order (see Sewell 1999: 41).

Communicative acts are therefore rebellious in their content but masked in their execution: jokes, aphorisms, or complaining about goods are culturally acceptable forms of discourse that allow the shadow public to conceal their opposition while nevertheless marking their dissatisfaction with relations of power. By examining the form and structure of opportunities to express opinion publicly and freely, we can gain insight into how power flows, how significance within late-socialist culture is shaped by social actors, and how agency and action—even when dispersed, fragmentary, and unprinted—are possible within the confines of late-socialist state structure.

9

Conclusion

Citizens, Consumers, and Shadow Publics
in Time and Space

In conclusion, I expand my argument in order to consider two larger political categories that encompass the shadow public, and that the category of shadow public shapes in turn: *citizens* and *publics*. Specifically, I distinguish real versus ideal types of citizens, a model that can be mapped onto late-socialist Cuba but may also be useful in other contexts. I then go on to consider what kind of public the unsatisfied citizen-consumers constitute, solidifying the concept of a shadow public to which I have referred throughout the book. With this as my backdrop, I consider Cuba's unsatisfied citizen-consumers as a shadow public in the context of Latin America as a region, in a period dubbed "the end of politics" (Colburn 2002). Finally, I end not with a discussion of Cuba's imminent future, but rather, using post-socialist states as a guide, with a discussion of the future of nostalgia for citizen-consumers.

Citizenship

A discussion that involves citizen dissatisfaction, a shadow economy, migration desires, and lack of coherent revolt brings into question definitions of good citizenship and of citizenship itself. What is citizen loyalty if citizens know that if they are not satisfied, they may be able to take their citizenship elsewhere? When does this happen, and what does it lead to? The citizenship I define—based on local meaning—differs from the classical definition whose "ideal type" assumes direct citizen-state interaction and citizens' active participation in the state. I propose that it is central to reconsider models of citizenship in the late-socialist context.

What is the culture of citizenship in a late-socialist welfare state where there is widespread citizen discontent? What are forms of participatory, or active, citizenship in Cuba's national context, where civil society and the public sphere do not conform to standard definitions? What are the realistic options in Cuba for ordinary citizens who want change? Both the official restrictions placed on citizens and citizen-driven alternatives to classical participation are best captured by the citizen metadiscourse of entitlement and deprivation.

For example, hard-working, tax-burdened Cuban citizens see their dissatisfaction with the goods, services, and overall quality of life available to them as legitimate grievances, even if the welfare state provides them with the benefit of "free" social rights (see Marshall 1965). They frame themselves as "deserving" or "entitled" citizens (emphasizing citizenship-as-legal-status), even if they do not see themselves as "outstanding" or even as "good" citizens (deemphasizing citizenship-as-desirable-activity).[1] Such metadiscourse on citizenship cultivates public opinion and generates ripples of belief and behavior, even as active citizenship and interface with the state is avoided. Avoiding the state, as I have discussed, ultimately results in migration from Cuba.

Trends in the scholarly literature on citizenship in the "flowing '90s" popularized the analysis of unprecedented streams of global migration. During this period, citizenship became framed as something that was not locked in relationship with a given nation-state, but rather traversed permeable borders, engaged with cultural motion and diffusion, and cultivated identity politics. In anthropology in particular, citizenship was being theorized as "flexible" (Ong 1999), while the "global ecumene" was making the nation itself a weak container for its citizens (Hannerz 1989; R. Foster 1991) and wandering social imaginaries were leading citizens to new global "-scapes" (Appadurai 1996).

I wish to point, however, to the countertrend, the central paradox of a global age in which national boundaries are once again making citizenship more relevant as a fixed category (see Basch, Schiller, and Szanton Blanc 1994; Trouillot 2001; Al-Ali and Koser 2002; Sassen 2006). At the precise moment when Cuban citizens have become highly aware of available goods, wages, and freedoms in other societies through social networks and media exposure, developing the tastes of another reference group, few of them are legally allowed to enter other countries to live and work.

In other words, I argue that understanding the meaning of citizenship is important not only for those who actually migrate, but also for those who do not get that chance. The flowing '90s have left unaccounted for and undertheorized the growing number of dissatisfied citizens in the world who know of life in another place, who dream of it, and who shape the public culture in the nations where they live, whether or not they actually contribute to today's global population flows. International borders and immigration laws continue to tighten, travel visas become more arduous to obtain, and new technologies are deployed to track and deport visitors who have overstayed their welcome. We have entered a historical moment in which potential migrants are more likely to remain stuck and discontented at home for longer periods of time than ever before, making the themes of this book increasingly socially relevant in other locations all over the globe and making unsatisfied citizen-consumers, as a culture and a public, even more important to define.

Cuban Citizenship

Citizenship in the contemporary Cuban context is often experienced as an official, national belonging that presents a collective sense of both relative privilege and relative deprivation.[2] The current value of national belonging to Cuba is therefore placed in direct relation to the limitations with which one is confronted, and how those limitations measure up to the situations of other national "reference groups" can function either as standards of comparison or sources of normative attitudes (Hyman 1960). The lived experience of citizenship in Cuba highlights an acute awareness of other available options for living and earning in the world, but in the absence of an actual ability to do so, given legal constraints imposed by one's own nation-state or others.

Throughout the book, I have described Cuban citizens' relative privileges and relative deprivations, how they have come to be seen as such, how they are communicated between fellow citizens and to outsiders, and finally, what concrete traces of ethnographic, material, and historical evidence citizenship-as relative-deprivation—the attitude of a citizenry—leaves.

My definition of citizenship deviates from the classic, contractual definition: "A native or nationalized person who owes allegiance to a government and is entitled to protection from it" (Britannica 2006).[3] Yet citizenship-as-relative-deprivation is still inherently contractual, and the balance between allegiance and entitlement is still crucially important in the Cuban case.

This is because, as Tilly might suggest, the character of the contractual relationship between citizen and state is "variable in range, never completely specifiable, always depending on unstated assumptions about context, modified by practice, and constrained by collective memory, yet ineluctably involving rights and obligations sufficiently defined that either party is likely to express indignation and take corrective action when the other fails to meet expectations built into the relationship" (Tilly 1997: 600). In this reciprocal characterization, it is not only the state, but also the citizen who can take such "corrective action."

Types of Citizen-State Relationships

An alternative way of visualizing my definition of citizenship is to frame it in terms of types of citizen-state relationships, which come in a number of forms, as shown in figure 9.1.

In a traditional vertical orientation, citizens look up to a paternalistic state to protect them and provide a certain standard of living (diagram 1 in figure 9.1; these citizens are represented in Cuba by the peso poor, or "featherless chickens"). In an ideal-type liberal compact, there is more active participation on the part of citizens, both amongst themselves and in open exchanges of ideas and interaction between them and the state (diagram 2). Alternatively, and perhaps particularly in the absence of a healthy civil society or public, citizenship can also take the form of organized, grassroots social movements or outright revolt (diagram 3), where citizens implicitly redraw the contract between themselves and the state in order to secure their standard of living or enshrine some other collective good.

In diagrams 4 and 5, the relationship between citizens and the state is dramatically different. To the extent that there is any contract whatsoever, it takes one of two forms. It can be horizontal, as citizens conspire to facilitate certain freedoms and a particular standard or quality of living (diagram 4).

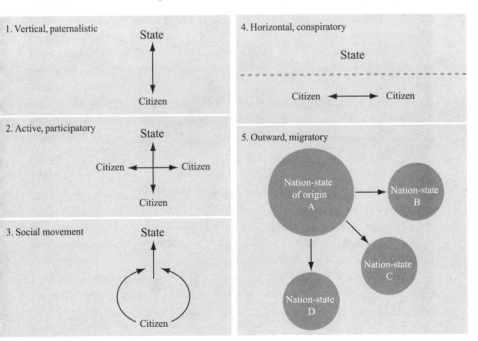

Figure 9.1. Types of citizen-state relationships.

Otherwise, it is outbound, meaning that citizens decide to migrate in order to achieve a certain standard of living. At some level this involves giving up or sacrificing their citizenship (diagram 5).

I now discuss the relationships among these types of citizenship in more detail. Even with no notable collective action, there is something inherently cultural and "lateral" about citizenship, because it binds "whole categories of persons, rather than single individuals to each other" (Tilly 1997: 600). Citizenship is directly predicated upon citizenry, creating a bounded "we," even if there are divisions within that "we" (see discussion in Urban 2001: 93–144). Furthermore, it may be argued that, behind the formal membership definition (for example, vertical), there is also a substantive definition: "the array of civic, political, socio-economic, and cultural rights people possess and exercise" (Holston and Appadurai 1996: 190),[4] hinting both at the breadth of affiliations and activities within a nation-state and at its detachment from vertical allegiance. I have addressed the solidity of this "we-ness"—lateral orientation, substantive activity, how it is represented, and what circulates within it—in my discussion of unsatisfied citizen-consumers, particularly in their desire for the private (chapters 2–3) and their relationship to goods and means (chapters 4–6).

Horizontal allegiance and "substantive" activity are most visible once vertical allegiance has eroded. The shift to horizontal allegiance allows citizens silently to enter vast gray-to-black-market networks, develop the culture of an informal economy, evade taxation, bribe officials and law enforcement officers, or not report one another's crimes and misdemeanors against the state to the authorities. In effect, horizontal allegiances establish a second, "under-the-table" realm of governance, a normative and widespread option for securing a material standard of living that they feel they are being unjustly prevented from having.[5] More roughly stated, "bad" citizenship is a common local option for "living better" at home. It is within this lateral relationship, in its mundane but sometimes dangerously illicit forms, that nearly all of the action of citizens in late-socialist Cuba takes place.[6]

When living better at home itself becomes unsatisfactory (which it often does), and a citizen's reference group is not just next-door neighbors, but also international communities of citizens and consumers, there is something pressingly global about citizenship's outlook. Citizenship, particularly in Cuba (and throughout Latin America), is outward-looking and often outbound.[7] Citizenship-as-relative-deprivation in late-socialist Cuba is a comparative and relational phenomenon in which citizen-consumers cannot describe their experience without an external point of reference. Usually this is the urban or suburban United States, if not Miami specifically—places they have never witnessed firsthand but about which they have detailed information.

As cultural logic dictates, if a citizen-consumer is not satisfied with the quality of life where he or she lives, the solution is to attempt to leave and to try his or her luck elsewhere. This move is often to a location where there is already a dense cluster of compatriots or at least same-region exiles, refugees, asylum-seekers, or undocumented migrants, as well as an opportunity to join the reference group to which he or she has been comparing himself or herself, along with a chance to change citizenship. Migration is the specter that lingers over most Latin American citizen-state relationships, and does so in Cuba more than any other Latin American country next to Mexico.

In summary, if citizens come to believe that the state is not fulfilling its end of the bargain, citizen indignation and corrective action, individual or collective, involves a shift in orientation and allegiance. Here, I have presented models of ideal and real citizen-state relationships;[8] broadening my scope and applicability beyond dollar versus peso freedoms, I argue that the actions of unsatisfied citizen-consumers represent the most common "real" responses to difficulties with the state and I lay down a template for a shadow public.

A Shadow Public

Having defined real citizenship, I now ask, What kind of group is the "unsatisfied citizen-consumer" within the citizenry? An interest group? A culture? A public? What defines these categories, what exactly does this group of people share, and what makes unsatisfied citizen-consumers an analytic and politically significant category in Cuba, and perhaps, in any national context?

The shared *interests* of the group I discuss are clear, since it is these interests that identify unsatisfied citizen-consumers as an easily recognizable subcategory of citizens. Put simply, they want affordable, quality goods and services to be available locally; remuneration for their hard work through a salary commensurate with the cost of living; and minimal contact with those state organs that invade their sense of dignity, privacy, and ability to support themselves. They want to eliminate the friction between limited public provisions, social rights, and dependence on a state that forces them to violate laws in order to live as they wish (see Snel and Staring 2001: 10). They also want to eliminate the stress, exclusion, constraints on opportunities, and constraints on choice—as citizens and as consumers—that result from their material conditions and national situation (see Powers 2001: 11).

Yet it is not their interests alone that define unsatisfied citizen-consumers. They also share a common *trajectory of action* and *inaction*, as well as certain patterns of practice, making their group membership even clearer. In particular, they explicitly avoid activism as a political tool to raise their standard of living, preferring ritualized civic participation (or resistant nonparticipation), engagement in the informal economy, and ultimately, migration as practical strategies that circumvent or extend beyond the reach of state control. Their practice is bound to their shared "social imaginary" in at least two senses of the popular term.[9] They share a forward-looking *social imaginary*, in the sense of Appadurai's use of *imaginary* as "a constructed landscape of collective aspirations" in the context of global flows (Appadurai 1996: 31). They want *privacy* (in family life and in enterprise), *means* (material and financial), and *freedom* (personal, social, and political); and despite—or perhaps because of—a socialist state apparatus that controls them, they believe that private *means* free; that privacy defines freedom. This is useful in understanding the imagination as an organized field of social practice and in recognizing that imagination, as a social fact, also holds the potential to be a central form of agency (Appadurai 1996). Furthermore, it is particularly relevant when one is discussing the state as a structural constraint, as I have here, and the forms of resistance or withdrawal unsatisfied citizen-consumers choose.

I have argued that in late-socialist Cuba there is a limited "'repertory' of collective action at the disposal of a given sector of society. These are the common actions that they know how to undertake all the way from the general election, involving the whole society, to knowing how to strike up a polite but uninvolved conversation with a casual group in the reception hall. The discriminations we have to make to carry these off, knowing whom to speak to and when and how, carry an implicit map of social space, of what kinds of people we can associate with, in what ways, and under what circumstances" (Taylor 2004: 24). The result has been an analysis that emphasizes the need to focus on the articulation of citizen-state relationships and the power of ordinary consumer desire. Specifically, I have attempted to illustrate the ethnographic importance of "unofficial" conversations that have an "extrapolitical" status (Taylor 2004: 89), and to show how diffuse, private, unprinted discourse still produces a shared social imaginary of unsatisfied citizen-consumers. Charles Taylor's construction of the imaginary, embedded in the here and now, is also important to this conversation. In particular, this relates to the ways in which ordinary people imagine both their social surroundings and their social existence, and specifically, "how they fit together with others, how things go on between them and their fellows, and the deeper normative notions and images that underlie these expectations" (Taylor 2004: 22).

In their amalgamation of interests, trajectory, practice, and imaginary, do unsatisfied citizen-consumers constitute a public? There are an increasing number of definitions of a public, but most definitions, at a minimum, identify a group of individuals with common interests or characteristics who are also linked by sharing the same social space, common aims, and discursive arena. A public can be a subdivision of a citizenry but is not usually as large as a national citizenry. Finally, a public harbors the potential to coalesce and to make its collective voice heard in a way that influences state decision making.

According to this definition, unsatisfied citizen-consumers have a clear common interest and common characteristics, which I have outlined at length. Their discursive arena, however, is by far their weakest asset. In fact, unsatisfied citizen-consumers, as a shadow public, usually do not know specifically who the other members of their group are, as their constituency is large and widespread, with boundaries so unclear that it does not exist as a unified body, even though individual members of the constituency share a general sense that they are normal and represent a majority. Cubans often consider their condition an immutable national trait that shapes their character. On the other hand, in Cuba, their discursive arena is inexplicit, kept invisible, and made politically dangerous by the state.

Therefore, Cuban unsatisfied citizen-consumers do not come together as a public, even though they likely constitute a plurality of their nation. There are, of course, other variations on a public. To borrow Fraser's widely discussed term, it appears that Cuban citizen-consumers could constitute a "weak" public, because they have a "deliberative practice [that] consists exclusively in opinion formation and does not also encompass decision-making" (Fraser 1992: 134). Accordingly, the deliberations and dialogue of weak publics do not circulate easily in the wider discourse and have little impact on social and political change.

I have considered to what extent and in what form unsatisfied citizen-consumers' interests circulate in the wider discourse and whether they have an impact on social, cultural, and political change. I have also considered whether weak publics serve as a sufficient analytical model for considering how citizen discontent still manages, one way or another, to create public opinion and citizen practice, even if it lacks unity or vocality. Yet Cuban unsatisfied citizen-consumers cannot even constitute a weak public, at least not yet, because their discursive arena is too limited. Their locus of discourse takes place only in private, or at most in semipublic settings such as kitchens, bedrooms, out by the clothesline, at ad-hoc social gatherings or household parties, or in furtive words spoken to an ephemeral tourist.

Unsatisfied citizen-consumers are not a subaltern counter-public either, because they are mainstream and silent, and their ideas do not circulate in print, unlike Fraser's countercultural and vocal counter-public.[10] Nevertheless, it is helpful to think of subaltern counter-public spheres that exist in nonphysical and nonpermanent spaces, such as the ones I list, as ephemeral common spaces that serve the purpose of allowing Cubans to voice their opinions without threat of state retribution, and that offer a prototype for a Cuban public sphere.

Public Sphere and Civil Society

In writing about citizens and public, I also brush up against *public sphere* and *civil society,* other terms that are worth considering now. Jürgen Habermas (1974, 1984, 1987a, 1987b, 1989) has been instrumental in shaping the conceptions of the ideal (even utopian) space or discursive arena for "communicative action." As Habermas explains, "by 'the public sphere' we mean first all of our social life in which something approaching public opinion can be formed. Access is guaranteed to all citizens. A portion of the public sphere comes into being in every conversation in which private individuals inform a public body" (1974: 44). In this utopian public sphere, the precision of the speaker's arguments, not the status of the speaker, would take precedence. Scholars have argued whether there actually is a generalizable bourgeois public sphere and how it remains a valuable heuristic device in which to frame a public for analysis. While this utopian ideal is inapplicable to the national context I discuss, there are compelling examples of how the public sphere can be reshaped to suit various sites.

Civil society, the bedfellow of the public sphere, is an idea related but not equivalent to the public. As "a realm of social organization and activity not directly under state control" (Calhoun 1992: 195) it emphasizes the social arena where social issues circulate and people come together in pursuit of common goals (Sanday 1998; see Keane 1998 and Gray and Kapcia 2008 for the Cuban context). Civil societies are, of course, associated with Western liberal democracies and the guarantees of freedom of association, self-government, and equality. Undissected, this would not seem a realistic model to impose upon Cuba, particularly because that country does not guarantee such rights. However, as Taylor suggests, civil society is not solely a medium for democratic politics, but rather is a structure that may check the political process. Civil society, like the public sphere, can exist in alternative and supplemental but recognizable forms (Taylor 1995: 208, 287). One of my goals throughout this book has been to uncover these forms, describe if and when they overlap with the public sphere, and determine how they check the political process of the state. The answer is only in ephemeral forms and constituted by ephemeral members.

I conclude by reiterating what I think unsatisfied citizen-consumers are: they share interests, characteristics, a social imaginary, and a trajectory and practice, but their political silence, underground economic activity, and secret identity as prospective migrants casts a shadow over them. They are therefore a *shadow public*:[11] an uncoalesced but potentially powerful group that engages in resistance to state domination, but without a public sphere and only in ways they believe will allow them to remain invisible while maintaining or even improving their families' economic condition, keeping their families free from harm, and improving their quality of life. Ultimately, the shadow public—even if they do not assemble or take collective action, but deliberately remain publicly silent—do take "corrective action" (Tilly 1997: 600) that in the medium to long term eventually "wears down the existing political fabric" of the nation (Chazan et al. 1992). In Cuba, this wearing down is one of the key factors responsible for driving the country into the late-socialist phase.

Unsatisfied Citizen-Consumers in Space and Time

In closing, it is worth revisiting the opening words and key arguments of the book: in particular, that unsatisfied citizen-consumers in Cuba are those Cubans who are unfulfilled because of both public government and private material shortcomings; and that their political silence, underground economic activity, and secret identity as prospective migrants mark the boundaries of a significant shadow public in Cuba's late-socialist era. I have illuminated the social, cultural, and political importance of this Cuban citizen type in three distinct sections that together point to the key interests and concerns of this growing population. Specifically, I have defined *private, means,* and *freedom* in late-socialist Cuba through a focus on day-to-day life, thick description, metaculture, and discourse. This focus opens up new categories for the analysis of Cuba in transition, a topic that is gaining prominence and generating increasing public interest and analysis about change and Cuba's uncharted future, particularly as Fidel Castro has stepped down.

Rather than concluding by summarizing the principal concepts in each of the three parts of the book, I would prefer to pull together two relevant themes that allow us to think in broader terms—geographically and temporally— about the ideas I have introduced. First, I place Cuba in a broader regional context and consider how well the unsatisfied citizen-consumer model can be mapped onto the rest of Latin America. In particular, I explore how citizens' responses to hardship and citizen-state relationships have been framed for analysis within Latin America. I argue that, despite Cuba's exceptionalism as the longest-standing socialist dictatorship and welfare state in the Western Hemisphere, the unsatisfied citizen-consumer model could have utility for Latin America at large. This is particularly true in light of the fact that, over the last two decades and throughout the region as a whole, there has been a calming of popular uprisings, an ever-thriving informal economy, and an increase in out-migration

Second, I look forward in time and consider the future of unsatisfied citizen-consumers as Cuba makes the transition from late socialism to post-socialism. I frame this section as an alternative to the more run-of-the-mill predictions about leadership, constitutions, and strategic affiliations. Remaining in the realm of the lived experience of unsatisfied citizen-consumers, I offer a speculative glimpse at the future of nostalgia using the post-Soviet and post-socialist world and its transition to capitalism as a vital point of comparison. Indeed, lately, there has been a boom in reporting on and analyzing "socialist nostalgia" as it has emerged in post-socialist Eastern and Central European countries in the last several years. While popular conversations about social-ist nostalgia rotate around consumer desires (fashions, goods, and products, not political systems) I also consider at what point socialist nostalgia becomes political and connected to an older form of citizenship or belonging—citizen desires—cycling my topic of the citizen-consumer back to the future.

Latin America, Unsatisfied Citizen-Consumers, and the End of Politics

At first glance, it might appear that Cuba is just too different, too much of an exception, to map the citizen-consumer or shadow public model devel-oped in that context onto the rest of Latin America, a region that has taken a different road to development—particularly in reference to capitalism. These differences are reflected in laws concerning ownership, finances, distribution, incentives and consumer choice, and civic rights (Mesa-Lago 2000). Further-more, if democratization is a sign of regional progress and a point of com-parison, then Cuba is certainly lagging behind. Thirty years ago, authoritarian regimes dominated Latin America's political systems, and regional analysts were pessimistic about the possibilities for political democracy. Yet by the end of the 1990s, every country in the region except Cuba had experienced some form of transition to democracy, though the quality of those democracies has varied.

Despite Cuba's exceptionalism, there are still some key links between Cuba and countries throughout Latin America, particularly in terms of migration, a vast informal economy, and lack of collective citizen action to address tren-chant social problems. Democratization, in other words, is not all that it may seem. Although some of the new democratic regimes have proved robust, many have continued to be beleaguered by economic crises, rampant social inequalities, unbridled corruption, tenuous judicial institutions, inefficiency, monopolies, and feeble regulation and enforcement. Moreover, others have not been successful in upholding the rule of law, guaranteeing basic rights of citizenship, and programmatically countering social and economic distress, overall reflecting Guillermo O'Donnell's (1993) concept of "brown areas"; that is, systems that reveal the problems of having formal trappings of democracy without democracy on the ground.[12]

And what of citizen response, the key focus of this book? To extend the argument, if the "old" Latin American masses ever turned to labor organiz-ing and grassroots solidarity movements to solve their problems, the "new" masses—those I suggest are unsatisfied citizen-consumers—are much more likely to adapt to hardship through informal and black-market micro-entrepreneurship and migration, just as Cubans do. This suggests that unsatisfied citizen-consumers define one of Latin America's public groups, its boundaries delineated by a transnational culture of citizenship whose aim is to avoid the reach of direct state interference—as depicted in diagrams 4 and 5 of figure 9.1.

I am not alone in this assessment of the region or its citizens, although it is not the most popular assessment in the academic literature. Forrest Colburn, in a slim volume of essays entitled *Latin America at the End of Politics* (2002), on which I draw substantially here, notes the multiple attempts to institute socialist or socialist-style reforms throughout the region. He argues that throughout the twentieth century, Latin America was galvanized by numerous and almost sequential efforts to redistribute wealth and income. The collapse of utopian ideologies marks the end of an era and provides a starting point for a broad inquiry into Latin America (Colburn 2002: 4–5). Furthermore, although socialism has allured Latin America for some time, in the way it "collected disparate concerns about poverty and inequality, offered an explanation for their continued presence, and promised a just distribution of wealth and a future of equitable economic growth," it did not prove to provide a solution. "Utopia vanished, and with it went political activism" (Colburn 2002: 31).

Along similar lines, and focusing on the absence of popular uprising, K. Roberts (1997: 137) declares, "The boom in the study of Latin American social movements in the 1970s and 1980s, manifested a high degree of faith in the transformative potential of popular organizations. . . . The course of events in the ensuing years has not been kind to this romanticized vision." Challenging left-wing academics and political activists, he provides a critique of "celebratory but unconvincing" arguments concerning popular organizing, and presents a new set of literature that, in a more sober but realistic tone, attempts to understand the dynamics of social movements in the neoliberal era. This small body of critique considers the limitations of the dominant paradigms of Latin American citizen discontent following the "collapse of utopian ideologies" and focuses in particular on contemporary Latin American citizen inactivity since the 1990s.

Colburn frames his "broad inquiry into Latin America" by building on a similar argument concerning the lack of popular organizing: "There is an end to ideological confrontation and contestation. . . . The impetus for remaking state and society has withered. . . . The ideal of egalitarianism has been smothered by political fatigue and aspirations for acquisition" (Colburn 2002: 7). Such lack of activism and "aspirations for acquisition" are also considered by O'Dougherty in *Consumption Intensified: The Politics of Middle-Class Daily Life in Brazil* (2002) in which she discusses how Brazilians had "limitless ability to adapt to the chronic inflation and economic instability" (O'Dougherty 2002: 190). These strategies allowed families to maintain the "middle-class" lifestyles they desired, but did not galvanize resistance. She quotes informants who describe Brazilians as "too calm, accepting, perhaps docile" or "accommodating, conforming, or resigned." Concerning the economic crisis, a Brazilian explains, "'in the beginning people just got very, very mad at the government. They talked badly about it, but no one had the courage to do anything. People here don't fight for their rights. They always take a paternalistic attitude and wait acceptingly'" (O'Dougherty 2002: 193). O'Dougherty also mentions "the discreet sales of the middle class" (black- and gray-market sales) as a silent coping mechanism, which reflects a phenomenon throughout the region.

Perhaps most famously, the Peruvian economist Hernando de Soto examined discreet and not-so-discreet sales by "informals" (a world of trade that exists without permits, receipts, or tax payments), as well as the greater structures behind the Latin American shadow economy. Among his key contentions is that although much of Latin America lacks an integrated formal property system, leading to informal ownership of land and goods, a market system full of organic entrepreneurs is already in place and is waiting to be unleashed; in the meantime, these individuals remain extralegal and frustrated (De Soto 2000, 2002, 2004). While De Soto is widely read by high-level American policymakers and the general public, and his book *The Other Path: The Invisible Revolution in the Third World* (originally published in Spanish as *El otro sendero,* 1989) was a best seller in Latin America, his ideas are not widely applied in social science analysis of the region, and certainly not by anthropologists.[13]

Finally, in addressing migration, the other regionally pertinent topic, Colburn links exodus from the region with political conformity, claiming that it is "a result of having the disaffected, the ambitious, migrate. For political elites, this migration is a 'relief.' Individual 'exit strategies,' as a common solution to grave problems, serve as a political and economic 'safety valve' for regimes that might otherwise be overwhelmed by demands for radical change." Furthermore, he claims "Gonzalo" (Colburn's Chilean interlocutor) would say "that radical change would only be disruptive, forcing still more to flee. Gonzalo is looking forward to buying a new car" (Colburn 2002: 125).

Plenty of scholars are talking about Latin American migration; in fact, there has been a crop of Latin American "ethnographies of migration" addressing transnational networks and migration in the new millennium, effectively creating a genre that links and blurs homeland and country of origin through multi-sited research (see, for example, Menjívar 2000; Levitt 2001; G.

Pérez 2004; R. Smith 2006; Stephen 2007; Olwig 2007). These transnational migration stories are arguably becoming the most popular way of analyzing change in Latin American society in the age of globalization, though they do not feature citizen-consumer discontent as the force driving the problem or connect migration to the problem of disengaged citizenship in the region.

Despite these regional similarities which might suggest that the citizen-consumer phenomenon envelops Latin America, and although scholars are forced to touch on popular "apathy,"[14] the informal economy, and migration, there has yet to be a cohesive paradigm that addresses the constellation of citizen problems I discuss. Moreover, if there were a chance of such a paradigm emerging now, I fear that what is being called the "leftward swing" of populist or socialist presidents sweeping Latin America, and the burgeoning groundswells against free trade and neoliberalization (see, for example, K. Roberts forthcoming), endanger it.[15] These new movements may engender a new generation of celebratory analyses of citizen discontent and, in so doing, continuing to overlook what I have called "the backdrop or the broadest and most stable base: the quiet majority of 'ordinary' citizens" (see the introduction). I suggest that part of the reason for this lack of focus and absence of thick description of citizen-consumers or related citizen types is that in Latin America consumer tastes, desires, and related concepts such as lifestyle, quality of life, living well, or desires for nice things and a good life are too often glossed with experience-distant and morally tinged words such as *materialism, Americanization, globalization,* and *modernization.* In both the popular and academic presses, such desires are explicitly blamed on power structures reflecting imperialism, the spread of capitalism, commercialization, and increasing cultural homogenization through hegemony.

The metadiscourse reflected in each of these terms is that things in Latin American culture are becoming more (or "too much") like North America, which could not be good for anyone. In other words, Latin American things are losing their authentic Latin American-ness, partly because Latin America is looking to North America and to things from North America for its answers (see Berger 1997: 17; but also see D. Miller 2001b for a related critique).

Just what *is* that thing flowing between Latin America and North America? Do citizens of Latin America really come to desire it? Why? What happens once they do? How does it shape Latin American citizen logic? These are important and largely unanswered questions that I have begun to address throughout the book.

Interestingly, neither citizen discontent within the region nor the process of democratization have led Latin Americanists down the same paths of analysis as their post-Soviet and post-socialist counterparts. Talking about goods and consumption and the discourse and practice of dissatisfaction in the post-

Soviet world is considered hip, cool, and relevant. Indeed, consumer desires often framed a creative form of resistance and, therefore, have not been met with the same level of moralizing and judgment as they are in Latin America.

Here, too, Cuba may arguably prove to be an exception. Something about Cuban poverty and consumer frustration definitely captures the popular imagination. North American and European readers have a fascination and empathy with these stories of material struggle and ingenuity, judging by the barrage of books, documentaries, websites, blogs, research groups, and print media discussing them. Cuban poverty, in short, is apparently more fascinating than "drab" Bolivian or Honduran or other poverties in the region that in many cases are more dramatic but do not receive the same attention.

This may be because in Cuba there are no alienating highland ponchos and few thatched huts to have to work around. More likely, however, it is because Cuban tastes and desires are much closer to those in the developed world. Poverty is more palatable and evokes more empathy if we can relate to what it might be like to experience it; for example, to want for a disposable baby wipe, an Internet connection, or pantyhose—all of which are easier to imagine than what it would be like to want for food to survive. Cubans, furthermore, at least in the popular imagination, are esteemed as literate, talented, musical, highly educated, physically attractive, multiracial, and sensual. They also carry with them some nostalgic, leftover fairy dust of the utopian socialist ideal, even if that reality is drifting farther and farther away.

Back to Cuba, Back to the Future

What should stand as Cuba's point of reference or comparison as we look forward? What future should Cuba be expecting or preparing for? Here I do not engage in predictions or forecasts, although many predictions could be made. For a few years now, U.S. political analysts have been publishing books with titles such as *Cuba: The Morning After—Confronting Castro's Legacy* (Falcoff 2003); *Cuba after Castro: Legacies, Challenges, and Impediments* (Gonzalez and McCarthy 2004); and *After Fidel: The Inside Story of Castro's Regime and Cuba's Next Leader* (Latell 2005), which overtly paint leadership demise and regime change as imminent.

There was a piece of "news" that really scared people in Cuba before Fidel's illness was made public. On a popular Spanish-language call-in show featuring a psychic (captured, of course, by illegal satellite), a woman dialing in from Miami asked when Fidel would die. The year 2014 was the menacing answer that gave the chills to those who tuned in to hear. Such an explicit and hopeless answer spoken aloud was too much. Cubans themselves never dare to predict such things themselves, but rather throw up their hands and say,

"Solo sabe Dios" (God only knows) or use sign language (a thumbs up that then doubles over) to refer to the unspeakable possibility of the final passing of their leader.

A new wave of predictions concerning Cuba's future flourished in the international news media following Fidel's temporary cession of power to his brother Raúl in 2006, but this has quieted somewhat since the transfer became permanent. What comes next, and what role citizens will play in Cuba's national transition, remains unclear. Certainly, Cuba has not experienced the type of citizen protest evidenced during the wave of communist state democratizations in the late 1980s and early 1990s, even though the Cuban people have experienced conditions of daily life much worse than those in Eastern Europe in the 1980s (Eckstein 1995: 23).

Nevertheless, as I have mentioned throughout the book, I think that the post-Soviet world and its transition serves as a vital point of comparison for Cuba, particularly in terms of citizen-consumer relationships in the late-socialist era. In terms of the future, history tells us little, since there is no single model for post-socialist transition. For example, we do not know whether Cuba will follow China in liberalizing elements of its markets and economy while repressing political (and religious) freedoms; whether it will embrace a more ambitious, perestroika-style model in which citizens' voices are allowed to be heard; whether it will undergo a big-bang "shock therapy" as Poland did or a more gradual transformation à la Hungary (see Åslund 1992 for a comparative discussion); or whether, eventually, it will move closer to a Costa Rican–style mixed model of social democracy, open markets, and relatively effective social safety nets (Mesa-Lago 2000). We have no way to know, but one thing is certain: there will be change in Cuba, since that is written into its current late-socialist character, and this era will inevitably slip away with the passage of time. Consequently, it is on that level that I now leap ahead, to conclude this section with a discussion of "the future of nostalgia" (Boym 2002).

Coda: Socialist Nostalgia

When we were talking during his party, Benny, the anti-Castro taxi driver, at one point said, "Now is not the time to say anything too loudly—in five minutes a CDR meeting is about to start." Benny was surprised when I told him I had not yet attended a CDR meeting and was thrilled to provide me with the experience. He clapped and rubbed his hands together with delight as we were surreptitiously preparing to go. Along with Fredrich, he warned me what to do, and what to say and not say. "Don't take photos," Benny cautioned. "If you do that, you run the risk of them opening your camera and removing the film and confiscating it." Fredrich encouraged me to carry a hidden tape recorder, but to place it in his pocket rather than my own, so that I would not get into trouble. "You'll want this on tape. Now, here is what you are going to say: raise your hand and ask the following . . . [Benny starts laughing before he can get the words out]: 'Are there any social problems in Cuba?!'"

"I was born a capitalist," Benny told me, wiping his eyes. "I've never supported the Revolution." A loud, unfriendly rap suddenly sounded on his door "¡Ya empieza la reunión!" (The meeting has already started!) Benny gave me a thumbs up as he shouted back, "¡Ya me voy!" (I'm coming right now!)

I jotted the following in my field notes after this event: "But I saw Benny loving to hate the CDR meeting, and I wondered, if his wish to leave Cuba was granted, if he would deeply miss some elements of Cuban culture, like forced community meetings, or if he would become lonely, disillusioned, or even nostalgic."

I observed another "it's so bad, it's good" comment—this time related to a consumer rather than citizenship issue—while Felina stood in the area of her tiny apartment that served as a kitchen, sipping La Niña brand *leche condensada* (sweetened condensed milk) straight from a hole punctured in the tin with a knife. She offered me a sip from her tin, and then prepared a typical drink purported to give breastfeeding women energy and calories: *leche condensada* poured into a glass and mixed with Bucanero *malta* (nonalcoholic black beer). "It's too sweet, but it's funny, actually. I don't think, even if there were anything else, anywhere else, I can't imagine I'd drink another *marca* [brand]." What would she do, I now wonder, if those brands suddenly faded away along with the regime she complained so much about? Would she have nostalgia for the drink she enjoyed while breastfeeding her first child in Cuba?

Consumer Nostalgia

There has been a boom in reporting on and analyzing "socialist nostalgia," chiefly as it has emerged in post-socialist Eastern and Central European countries. This nostalgia is a particularly relevant topic with which to conclude this discussion on citizen-consumers. Socialist or communist nostalgia was made most widely known and understood by the wildly popular film *Goodbye Lenin!* (directed by Wolfgang Becker, 2003). The film portrays an East German mother and avowed Communist Party member who, on her way to a Socialist Unity Party rally in 1989, witnesses her son being arrested at an antigovernment march and promptly has a heart attack, going into a coma. When she emerges from the coma eight months later, in 1990, she is so fragile that her children and neighbors, in an effort to prevent a fatal relapse, lovingly allow her to believe that the Berlin Wall is still standing and the GDR is still in power. Her son, Alex, therefore re-creates the conditions of the world she remembers, in large part through dressing in old clothes, returning their apartment to its dreary, pre-transition state, and with extreme difficulty, scavenging socialist-era food jars and refilling them with Western products, all so that his mother never becomes aware of the transition and can continue living in her secure world.

Lately, socialist nostalgia, as it is captured in the popular press and popular imagination, mostly centers on the revival of commercial products and relics from the communist era. This is part of a broad phenomenon that leads people to "embrace the products they [once] shunned" (Schweizer 2006). For example, companies in Hungary, Poland, the Czech Republic, and the former East Germany have been able to sell soft drinks, cosmetics, sports shoes, and laundry detergent that were only available in the socialist era. Sometimes these products appear in their original packaging. The phenomenon extends to communist-style pubs; and youth—those who came of age just before or after the transition—throw communist-era parties (see Purvis 2006 on the former East Germany).[16] In sum, there is "a growing fascination with the paraphernalia of everyday life under communism" that is part of an "evolving relationship with consumer culture and nostalgia for old times" (Karanova 2003: 33).

As is true of any retro fad or craze anywhere in the world, consumers often return to old products and fashions because they see them as unique, or they remind them of their childhoods or youth. Companies for their part are willing revitalize the image of an old product, tapping into nostalgia as a marketing tactic. This, coupled with the fact that once they have access to "previously unobtainable western goods, people soon became disenchanted with their overrated quality, cost and monopolization of the local market" (Karanova 2003). Declares one Hungarian, expanding the argument, "Our past should not be colored solely by politics. We must realize that there were nonpolitical achievements in the previous era that have a universal value. Perhaps young people who applaud Truabi [grape soft drink] and Tisza [sport] shoes will help the older generation to overcome their past."

Citizen Nostalgia

Popular conversations about socialist nostalgia rotate around fashion, goods, and products, not political systems. But when, if ever, does socialist nostalgia become political and connected to an older form of citizenship or belonging?[17] What is the mechanism behind ever-evolving social memory? Who is or becomes nostalgic, and what are they nostalgic for? Do people, for example, miss the "rigid certainties of life in a totalitarian state?" (Purvis 2006). To some, the narrative strategy of nostalgia—speaking warmly of an era gone by—is more a function of allowing people to make sense of their present existence than making sense of their past. This sentiment is captured by Andrei Codrescu, the Romanian-American journalist and literature professor on his first trip to Cuba:

> The [hotel] room and the elevator put me in an indescribably happy mood caused doubtless by the similarity, down to the tiniest smell, between the Capri and the Bucharest hotel by the same name where I'd stayed in 1965 before leaving Romania. Say what you might about socio-economic–religious conditions, the fact remains that all places can be known and connected by smell. . . . The commie smell was here, transporting me right back in time. I was suddenly nineteen years old, defiant, irreverent, filled with an insatiable appetite for the unknown.
>
> There was no way I could explain this to my [American] companions who were waiting for me in the lobby, looking fairly excited, but also cautious.
>
> "It's my world," I exclaimed, "The police are watching! Love is in the air!" (Codrescu 1999: 51–52)

There are other textual and visual references to citizen nostalgia for socialism. In her paper on Yugoslavia's Noć Reklamoždera (The Night of the Ad-Gorgers), Greenberg (2006) describes a six-hour public media event for viewing advertisements from all over the world, scheduled for November 29, ironically the former Day of the Republic in socialist Yugoslavia. "Guests were greeted with cheap, red scarves to tie around their necks in the fashion of Tito's socialist youth pioneers. Each person coming in received a ticket on which was printed an updated version of the pioneer oath taken by all good little boys and girls until the early 1990s." The oath "ironically dictated them, as good comrades, to carefully follow, enjoy and appraise the advertisements through audience response, which they did, and in larger numbers than a socialist-era rally could have conjured up" (Greenberg 2006: 181–82).

Citizen and consumer nostalgia, just like citizen and consumer reality, is not so easy to separate. This is particularly true since "individual memories of life in state socialism were the lack of desired goods, the culture of shortages, and the 'dictatorship over needs'" (Luthar 2006). Like the lived experience of state socialism, memories of state socialism also blend the roles of citizen, consumer, and the penetration of state power into those roles (see also Shevchenko 2002 on the meaning of durable goods in post-soviet Russia).

I read these reports and wonder about Cuba's transition from late socialism to post-socialism, and about when and how *la nostalgia socialista* might kick in. Will Cubans go back to sipping Bucanero and Cristal beers, or splashing themselves and their babies with Suchel Camacho colognes after bathing, particularly *agua de violetas* (violet water, the people's eau de toilette, which some claim is *the* smell of Cuban hygiene). To cook their rice and beans, will they stock up on indestructible Pronto pressure cookers, which in my experience are far higher in quality than those available in the West? Will they attend CDR revival meetings, or gather to watch reruns of old Fidel marathon speeches for nostalgic entertainment?

Right now, these scenarios seem ludicrous and unlikely, but as Felina explained about the future: "Vamos a ver que pasa. Es que cada día da tanto vueltas. Que uno no sabe de cual parte hay. Me entiendes? La vida da tantas vueltas." [We'll see what happens. It's just that every day it's something new. You never know what's coming. You know what I mean? Life always has unexpected turns.].[18] Material associations and the emotions and associations they provoke can run deep (figure 9.2). Whenever the transition in Cuba does come, I suspect we will see the rediscovery of certain elements of contemporary consumer culture and the paraphernalia of everyday life under Castro, but before that happens, some time has yet to pass.

Figure 9.2. A Havana primary school pays homage to the commander-in-chief, 1959–2008: "Thank You, Fidel."

Epilogue

I revisited Cuba in February–March 2008, wanting to see what had changed in the two years between my completing my research and this book going to press. Serendipitously, I landed in Havana on the quiet, humid evening following the historic announcement that, after Cubans had experienced nearly fifty years of daily life under Fidel, Raúl Castro had been appointed the new commander in chief. I was greeted in the darkened corridors of a familiar district by air fragrant with night-blooming jasmine and gasps of surprise from old neighbors.

Waking early the next day, I immersed myself in the hum of the morning crowd, finding that the news of the new president was met with tremendous calm. People got up, bathed, splashed on some *agua de violetas*, made their way to work or school in pressed uniforms, and went about their normal business of contraband, *cafecitos*, daily struggle, family life, and romance. "El mismo perro, diferente collar" (same dog, different collar) was the explanation for the palpable lack of shift in energy, despite the notable change in leadership.

I made the rounds to find eggs, bread, and coffee; confirmed that papaya and guava were in season; and desperately tried to locate a pen or pencil, having decided against bringing any electronic equipment on this visit in order to remain as anonymous a researcher as possible. After engaging in the ritual search of several shops, I purchased an overpriced ballpoint. This was not, however, the device my Cuban friends hoped I would be using for documentation.

"You mean to tell me you didn't bring un flash?!" (USB flash drive or memory stick) chided David, still my key informant, in disbelief, holding his head in his hands. Flash culture was rapidly diffusing through Havana in 2008, creating new possibilities for Cubans to share clandestine images and information discreetly and quickly. In fact, David owned three with different storage capacities, one a James Bond–style drive hidden within a slim golden pen. Besides their usefulness for discreetly downloading the most recent film releases from the U.S. market via illegal Internet hookups and burning them onto CDs—an increasingly popular practice—flash drives were enabling the circulation of more specifically political material as well. For example, a flash drive had allowed Cuban blogger Yoani Sánchez to document, in vivid and provocative detail, daily hardships and download them onto her "Generación Y" web page since April 2007. Her readership reached 1.2 million worldwide, and she was awarded the prestigious Ortega y Gasset prize for digital journalism in Spain (though the site is sometimes blocked for periods of time in Cuba, and she was not allowed to leave the country to receive the award in person).

In a similar cyber-underground spirit, I soon found myself peering into an old personal computer as I sat next to David, illicitly viewing a recorded question-and-answer session between Cuban National Assembly President Ricardo Alarcón and an earnest student named Eliécer Ávila, whom David identified as "puro guajiro" (a "total hick" in Cuban slang). The student's accent identified him as from the poor eastern region of Las Tunas.

Cuban citizens and consumers had never seen anything like it before. In a town-hall-style meeting that took place at the computer science university in February 2008, the student had stood up and asked: "Why do hard-working state employees earn in pesos but have to buy basic goods in CUCs, the convertible currency meant for tourists and foreigners?" David nods. "Why are we not allowed to travel outside of the country, even if we had a million dollars to do so?" David nods enthusiastically. "Why can't we access the Internet freely?" David catches my eye. "Why can we not have more direct contact with state officials in order to address questions like these and be truly represented?" David nods again. Alarcón was flustered, "unprepared" as he put it, to answer such "ignorant" questions of today's youth, whom he implied had little understanding of the history or nature of sacrifice. Waving his hands, he evaded the questions as best he could for thirty minutes.[1]

Alarcón's shadow audience, in front of computer screens across the city, snickered and rolled their eyes at his inept replies, and the video clip spread like wildfire, flash-to-flash, between residents in Havana, referred to casually as "la respuesta" (the response). Cubans asserted that the student's questions had crystallized some of the important issues of the day, but more than that, they also heard other individuals voicing problems that really mattered to them in a public venue, even if the program was never aired, could only be watched in the comfort of private settings, and did not represent collective action.

This open confrontation with a state official was a celebrated moment. It suggested that the digital age may be facilitating Cuban citizens' ability to circumvent state restrictions on the flow of information in historically unprecedented ways. The flow of digital information, along with other shifts in the availability of certain kinds of goods and services and modifications in policies since the core of this book was written (2004–2006), indicate that a process of aperture and liberalization is taking place in Cuba. These changes are not, however, tangible enough to quell citizen-consumer dissatisfaction. On the contrary, it seems that every change is accompanied by a complaint or disappointment.

First, Yutongs, the new fleet of hundreds of shiny green or white Chinese buses, have changed the urban landscape and improved transportation throughout the country. Residents in Havana, however, still complain that there is not good control over the routes and the timing, and that while the vehicles are new, they are still packed to overflowing and do not provide change for passengers. Instead, the excess fares are clearly pocketed by employees who collect fares at the front of the bus.

Second, the oil-for-doctors program may have ended the long-endured *apagones* (blackouts), as fuel now pours steadily in from Venezuela, but it has also drained away local medical staff, approximately 22 percent of whom are working abroad.[2] The result is that the once-bustling neighborhood *consultorio* remained dark, its windows shuttered, without hours posted on the door, no one delivering cups of coffee to the doctor on duty.

Third, gay rights are improving. CENESEX (Cuba's National Center for Sex Education), under Mariela Castro Espín's leadership, has made revolutionary strides in promoting education and legislation regarding sexual diversity and sexual orientation. The pendulum is now swinging from years of persecution and incarceration of homosexuals to talk among members of the politburo about legalizing gay marriage, to a symbolic same-sex wedding ceremony (two brides) on a state ministry lawn, to free sex-reassignment surgery approved by the Ministry of Public Health, and to attempts to plan the first gay rights parade. But here, too, these changes are not the product of open dialogue, and to the relatively conservative crowd of my unsatisfied citizen-consumer informants, these reforms are capricious, morally dubious, top-down, and not representative of their most pressing concerns or interests.

Fourth, although more nondurable consumer goods are available in the hard currency stores, too many of these items are deemed insignificant. For example, informants, shaking their heads and shrugging, reported that rather than increased availability of affordable staples such as rice, beans, milk, cooking oil, or meat, I would find a proliferation of Colombian, Chilean, and Brazilian sweets and crackers in colorful, crinkly packages; expensive pasta; lots of imported contact lens solution; and deodorant.

Finally, when I revisited my informants in Havana in 2008 (see the postscript for specific biographical updates), I found that, compared to 2003, more of their homes contained microwaves, electric rice cookers, private phone lines, DVD players, computers, new bathroom tiles, toilet seats, and artificial flower bouquets. This was not a sign of progress or development, they explained. On the contrary, the material accumulation was both superficial and illegal. In the 2003–2008 period, not only had nothing improved in terms of daily political liberties among ordinary people, but economically, the situation had grown markedly worse as the disparities between salaries and goods available for purchase had grown, making the black market an even more essential part of daily life than when I had originally documented it.

Adaptation, Off the Record

Citizen and consumer adaptations to changes in migration, shopping, earning, education, and family life continue to remain obscured. For example, residents sense that neighborhoods are simply emptying out as more and more people emigrate, leaving those remaining with a wistful sense of being left behind. Petra systematically counted off people she knew who had gone for good, making it into the fingers of her second hand.

There were certainly window-shoppers waiting in line to gawk at the new products for sale. Yet Paula, the owner of the new *casa particular* that friends had booked for me, claimed she simply never entered stores anymore and had little need to, since contraband and supplies of every kind are now being carried around in lumpy backpacks all over the city, available at much more affordable prices and often delivered right to her door. Others echoed her assessment, and I was offered an array of basic supplies for stocking my kitchen, all *por la izquierda*.

Others, including David, told me that among the best-paid workers these days are private property assessors who visit homes and estimate the value of the dwelling and the belongings within, should one choose to liquidate everything. Also doing exceptionally well these days are housing and business inspectors, who wander the streets, picking up twenty CUCs here and there as built-in payoffs for not reporting infractions. There is even a trickle-down effect: a little old Afro-Cuban lady sits watch in front of the booming second-story *peluquería* where I got my hair cut and highlighted, greeting customers and getting a cut of the payoff for warning the hairstylists if she sees an inspector on the way.

There has been a recent mass migration of teachers from the public schools, because peso salaries are no longer sufficient to sustain them. Instead they have "gone private," offering night courses, particularly in Spanish, English, and math, to small groups and charging in CUCs, creating yet another wave of *servicios particulares*, and one that is sowing the seeds of a Cuban private education system. The impact does not stop there: those teachers who quit are being replaced by young, inexperienced teachers sometimes only a few years older than the high-school students they instruct. Some teachers are migrants from the east who are known to dislike city kids, their entitlements, and their attitudes. Tatiana brought out her daughter, Wendy's, composition notebook with its smooth, bleached pages and blue lines. She was convinced that this higher-quality notebook—which she had purchased because the pages do not disintegrate when pencil marks are erased as the standard ones do—had led to a spate of resentful grading on the part of her daughter's new eastern school-teacher. For example, points had been subtracted from one of Wendy's essay for mis-punctuating the date and deviating from the standard length, and stern, formalistic comments had also been scrawled throughout in red pen. Tatiana also recounted what she described as a well-known (but unpublished) incident in Havana that involved much more than petty grade deflation: an angry teacher had allegedly hurled a chair at a student's head, fatally wounding him.

New class and regional tensions are not only evident in urban schools. Pilar, a teenaged student at *el pre* (*preuniversitarios*, or *escuelas en el campo*, the compulsory pre-university boarding schools in the countryside) stood jauntily in her state-issued miniskirt sporting the latest Cuban schoolgirls' fad—knee-socks and a navel ring—and spoke animatedly about the decreasing safety of *el pre*. Dark eyes flashing, manicured fingernails flying, she complained that the schools have become a pit of crime and rampant theft. One can't even leave one's *bloomers* (panties) out to dry on the line: they'll be snatched in a second by someone in greater need. In addition, eastern kids now carry knives to get what they want. One morning, while waiting in line to use the iron to press her uniform, a black girl from *Oriente* (she emphasized highlighting acutely perceived racial and regional differences) grew impatient and stabbed another girl in line. I was assured that all of these incidents go unreported in the press, though each detail rocks the revolutionary pillar of free, high-quality state education among comrades.

Visiting Cuba in 2008 with a baby in tow helped me connect with other families, as it always had in my past research. Yet, another sign of the economic woes was my informants' reaction to the birth of my third child. It seemed at times that carrying him around with me was an excessive display of wealth: people politely congratulated me as they might have if I had rolled up in a third luxury vehicle. His presence prompted narratives from those who knew me and those who did not alike, lamenting that whereas Cubans used to have one or maybe two children—even during the height of the economic crises—there is a new trend of couples choosing not to have any kids at all. There is not enough money and even less hope.

"There are good and bad things about Cuba" and "I love my country" I was often reminded by informants concerned about giving a balanced picture of their country and not wanting my reporting to be overly negative. But there is nothing positive about the current economic situation or the way it is being managed. Rumors are swirling in the air, some causing fear and discomfort: Yet another currency might be introduced. Cuba is going to go free market, starting in December 2008 with the liberalization of the bakeries, but free elections will never happen while Fidel is still alive. The key word of the era, I was told, is *desesperanza* (hopelessness). Perhaps the wait for real change has simply grown too long.

Winds of Change

Just after my final visit in the spring of 2008, Raúl introduced a cascade of reforms. Although intended to draw attention to his more rational, practical leadership, they also threw the relationship between citizenship and consumption into sharp relief in Cuba and abroad, drawing explicit links between political and economic reform. First, it was quietly announced in *Granma* that the general public could legally purchase a variety of electronics and appliances for personal use for the first time since the revolution: cell phones, computers, TVs of all sizes, video players, microwave ovens, motorbikes, and electric pressure cookers. As the opening line of one *New York Times* article asked, "Can a rice maker possibly be revolutionary?" (Lacey 2008). This loosening of restrictions on consumption was followed by the announcement that the ban on citizens entering tourist hotels and resorts had also been lifted.

These are potentially important reforms. They mark the official end to illegal accumulation of certain durable goods and to "tourist apartheid." The problem, of course, is that such changes in policy do nothing to solve any of the structural problems that make it so difficult to actually pay for the newly legal commodities or for a hotel vacation. This leaves them well out of reach for most Cubans. It will likely also increase the outward signs of inequality amongst them. Raúl's desire to remove state wage restraints—a fundamental communist mainstay—and to introduce incentives based on employee productivity might increase Cubans' earning potential. It is no surprise to Cubans, however, that this radical new proposal is on hold and they must lower their expectations yet again, the global economic recession will force belt-tightening and therefore delays in state salary improvements.

Perhaps the most significant change in terms of deep-seated transformation is the declared intent to decentralize agricultural production; that is, to allow abundant state land currently lying fallow to be cultivated by private farmers and cooperatives. (Since an estimated half of agricultural land in

Cuba is either fallow or underproductive, Cuba is unnecessarily dependent on agricultural imports.) In an unparalleled deregulation, farmers will be allowed to plant crops of their choice, sell produce at market prices, and do so in the marketplaces that they choose rather than those mandated by the state (to whom they previously had to sell 75–80 percent of their crops for distribution). They can also freely purchase equipment, tools, and supplies for the first time after decades of state control. Each of these reforms pushes the new system further from state socialism (see Alvarez 2004 for a comprehensive history of Cuba's agricultural sector). This reform is more likely than any other mentioned so far to have real effects on the urban shadow public since, by stimulating agricultural production, it should both drive down food prices for Cubans all over the country and perhaps also raise the value of the Cuban peso (especially in light of current world food and oil prices). That said, agronomists predict that it will likely take several harvests for the effects to be felt, and therefore it requires a patience of which the shadow public has run short.

What I have described here are the most publicized reforms and those that have been covered by the international press (see *Havana Journal* 2008 for a chronological compilation of the reforms and easing of restrictions). Cumulatively, these reforms mark the beginning of Raúl's new era and point to some measure of regime shift. Yet my informants convinced me that the problems I discussed in the book have, if anything, intensified and magnified. Just like the drive to attain dollars between 1994 and 2004, the drive to attain CUCs from 2004 to the present continues to shape the contours of Cuban society, creating new breeds of poverty, wealth, and concepts of access and deprivation born of the two-tiered monetary system.

Conclusion

Change in contemporary Cuba, I once again found, is embodied in details: Which rice cooker? How much? Who is selling? Where? Who actually bought? How did they get the money? Details push beyond an "experience-distant" analysis of sweeping change (Geertz 1983), and beyond a categorization of the Cuban system as communist, authoritarian, democratic, capitalist, state socialist, or late socialist. This means that consumer details and familiarity with daily life will remain the litmus test by which to measure the extent to which any transition in Cuba is solid rather than symbolic, or to measure the depth of the reforms. I remain committed to the argument that the experience of citizenship is continually penetrated by consumer interests, complaints, demands, and aspirations, and that these consumer concerns, in turn, are connected if not inseparable from political discourse. One cannot be analyzed without reference to the other.

In the past, political opponents of Cuba frequently predicted its transition from socialism, but since Fidel's illness was made public in August 2006 and Raúl took power in February 2008, change in Cuba is brewing more obviously, and change at this historic level is of interest to a broader audience, adding greater consequence to the ethnographic details in this book. I have argued that Cuba's social and cultural transition out of orthodox socialism has long been in process, and I suggest that despite their lack of public voice and intentional withdrawal from civic life, the shadow public has significantly weakened Cuba's existing political fabric. It is my hope that this book will not only be received as a contemporary ethnographic text describing daily life in late-socialist Cuba, but also serve as a historical record of the lives of ordinary Cubans as they experienced them in the shadows of social and political change.

Postscript: Updates on Key Informants

Beatriz, the owner of the black-market daycare center, has gone to join her kin in West Virginia, following a successful family reunification process, and is now sharing in the middle-class luxuries of wall-to-wall carpeting, Maytag washer-dryers, and backyards she viewed so many times on her VCR.

Benny, the taxi driver who claims he was born a capitalist and never supported the revolution, no longer has to attend CDR meetings. He won the *bombo* and lives in Miami with his family. He considers himself a refugee and has not yet returned to Cuba for a visit.

David and Tatiana remain in the neighborhood, and we remain in regular contact, keeping our friendship alive through the exchange of information and ideas. They are still desperate to leave but refuse to separate as a couple in order to do so. As David nears fifty, he is thinking more pragmatically in terms of retirement plans, of their daughter Wendy entering her teenage years, and of language and location. They are giving up on their dreams of America and are now actively hatching plans for a Central American destination.

E-mail Elena still hits the Internet café a couple of times a month, though nothing has come of her efforts and she admits she has lost a little faith. (She's lost none of her paranoia, however.) She has also lost touch with Wellington, who had been regularly providing funds for the family in the past, but she has found a new Italian godmother for her daughter. She continues to pray before meals and attends church regularly.

Fredrich and Felina's barbacoa, once chock-full of possessions, now stands utterly bare. Fredrich sold every last item and went to a major European city where he is painting houses and sending money back when he can. Felina continues to live in the empty dwelling alone with her son, Fredrich Jr., and sports a couple of new gold-capped teeth. She hopes to rejoin her husband some day.

Ingrid and Humberto stopped renting their *casa particular,* unable to keep up with the growing state demands and regulations. Humberto passed away unexpectedly not long ago, and Ingrid, now living with her son, tries to keep busy by getting out each day, though because she works as a ministry secretary and earns only pesos, she feels the impact of a salary and lifestyle downgrade.

Iris, the elderly expert in rice pudding who had shouted over the rooftops that she just wanted to see her daughter before she died, did receive a visit from that daughter, but because Iris is now afflicted with Alzheimer's disease, she did not recognize her. She mistook her for a distant cousin from the countryside.

Jinori and Stan, after the brief purchasing and home-improvement spree enabled by their sale of dairy cows in 2003, have put a curb on their spending. Their home remains exactly as it was when I last saw it, and Stan continues to farm and watch his growing collection of bootleg videos.

Karlos, the former state-sponsored wrestler, moved out of his cramped natal home, as did the eight other younger residents, leaving the elderly, pro-revolution mother and father living there alone. Karlos now lives with a new girlfriend in Central Havana, though he claims his motorcycle remains his most faithful woman. He still guards Party officials' mansions. His sister, *Zemile,* also moved out after her boyfriend left for Europe and provided her with rights to his residence. She predicts from the CDR meetings she attends that Cuba will go the economic direction of China, a country the new comandante respects.

Paco and Pratha have split up, but Paco has met a new woman in his peso-paying security job. He enjoys listening to Phil Collins's greatest hits on his new CD player and cordially served me a cold cabbage-and-tomato salad and some Cuban wine, having run out of basic supplies.

Petra felt the relief of living in Argentina for two years when she joined her daughter on a diplomatic mission. She was very happy to receive my gift of queen-sized pantyhose, though she showed me she had also picked up some in South America. She still prefers L'Eggs brand though, as they are sheerer.

Stuart, owner of the four-bedroom *casa particular,* continues to live large and has repainted the rental rooms in glorious tropical colors, upgraded all of his appliances, hired new staff, and reprinted his business card. At a rate of thirty-five CUCs a night, his rooms were fully booked when I stopped by to visit.

Appendix

Informant Profiles

Alias	No. of Children	Age	Housing	Occupation/Vocation	Political orientation/ Migration Plans
Arturo	0	55–60	1-bedroom apartment	Former state architect, now in private practice on the black market	Anti-Castro
*Beatriz	3	40–45	2-bedroom apartment	Operator of black-market daycare center, beautician, masseuse	Anti-Castro, applied for *bombo* (later emigrated to join family in West Virginia)
Benny and Helena	2	35–40	2-bedroom apartment	State-sponsored taxi driver and housewife	Anti-Castro, actively planning to migrate (Later they did win the *bombo,* and the family resettled in Miami.)
Daniel	4	40–45	1-bedroom apartment	Parking lot guard with *permiso* to work in Spain in a cookie factory	Actively planning to migrate
*David and Tatiana	1	35–45	2-bedroom apartment	Former director of marketing for a central planning site now works in public relations, marketing, and international finance for a joint-venture company. Tatiana does manicures, cleaning, and laundry on the black market, while David has a video rental service.	Anti-Castro, actively planning migration, applied for *bombo* and attempted to obtain foreign work permits
Daniela	4	85–90	1-bedroom home (rural area outside Havana)	Retired	Children arranging her migration (she lived in Miami, but wanted to return)

(continued)

Alias	No. of Children	Age	Housing	Occupation/Vocation	Political orientation/ Migration Plans
Dolores	1	66–70	1-bedroom apartment	Former state-sponsored interior decorator, now retired and supported by daughter	No active plans
Diki	2	60–65	2-bedroom apartment	Retired film producer	Applied for *bombo*
Doli and Néstor	1	35–40	Remodeled 2-bedroom, first-floor apartment with private patio	Former secretary, now *casa particular* owner and sportscaster	Communist Party affiliation
*Elena	3	40–45	2-bedroom apartment	Freelance translator, editor, and English tutor	Actively trying to migrate; has refugee no.; applied for *bombo*
Ernesto	2	35–40	2-bedroom apartment	Translator for NGO	Unknown
Federico	0	15–20	2-bedroom apartment	Studying for a bachelor's degree in theology; intends to become a priest	Actively trying to migrate
Frances	1 (expecting second)	30–35	2-bedroom apartment	Operator of black-market daycare center	Unknown
Fredrich and Felina	1	15–25	1-bedroom *barbacoa* in a *solar*	State-sponsored cigar industry worker engaged in black-market cigar sales, and housewife	Anti-Castro, actively trying to migrate (Fredrich later emigrated to Europe, where Felina hopes to join him.)
Giego	1	50–55	Dilapidated *solar*	Freelance English teacher, state gallery guide	Anti-Castro
Gregorio and Wilma	1	40–45	2-bedroom apartment	Operator of neighborhood gym and professor of pedagogy	Communist Party affiliation
Ingrid and Humberto	1	55–65	2-bedroom apartment	Former upper-level Ministry secretary *casa particular* owner; former restaurateur in Europe as undocumented migrant before returning to Cuba	Anti-Castro, high Party connections (heads of ministries, senior generals, Party leaders)
Iris	2	70–75	1-bedroom apartment	Former cigar roller for private company before revolution and state company afterward; now *casa particular* owner	Anti-Castro
Jenica and Hernando	1	35–40	2-bedroom apartment	Former owner of *casa particular* (fined and shut down), now black market child-care provider; Ministry of Culture–sponsored performing artist	Unknown

Alias	No. of Children	Age	Housing	Occupation/Vocation	Political orientation/ Migration Plans
Inori and *Stan*	1	30–40	2-bedroom stand-alone cement-block house built by micro-brigade (semirural area outside Havana)	Dairy farmer and housewife	Proud of status as campesino, some unsatisfied consumer desires
Carlos	6	25–30	Dilapidated 2-bedroom apartment	Former state-sponsored wrestler; armed guard at mansion of upper-level Party member; black market salsa instructor	Ostensible Communist Party affiliation but anti-Castro to outsiders; actively planning migration
Laline	3	40–45	2-bedroom apartment	Legal pizza stand	Unknown
Lara and Diego	3	40–45	2-bedroom apartment	Former assembly-line worker in factory; now gives black-market home manicures and runs black-market *paladar* and international construction brigade, now retired	Unknown, children want to migrate
Lila	1	25–30	2-bedroom apartment	Married to a European who lives abroad but supports her financially	Satisfied "dollar dog"
Mariela Castro-Espín (not alias)	3	35–40	Restored mansion	Director, CENESEX National Center for Sex Education; sexual rights activist	High-level Communist Party affiliation. Raúl Castro's daughter.
Marta	1	40–45	2-bedroom apartment	Former state-sponsored daycare worker, now operate black-market daycare center	Unknown
Mauricio and Fifi	1	45–50 and 55–60	2-bedroom dilapidated, solar (prerevolutionary hotel)	Merchant marine and secretary at National Armed Forces	Communist Party affiliation
Mona and Pipo	2	60–65	2-bedroom apartment housing 11 family members	CDR leadership/state bodega management and gardening/security	CDR president and Communist Party affiliation
Naomi	2	35–40	2-bedroom apartment	Nurse for family doctor program; illegally rents out room in apartment	Applied for bombo; actively planning to migrate
Nolga	0	60–65	Unknown	Retired, seeking odd jobs	Unknown
Nora	1	55–60	Unknown	Secretary for a judge; cook/cleaner at relative's *casa particular*	Anti-Castro
Olivia and Ricardo	4	55–60	1-bedroom apartment	CDR leadership	Communist Party affiliation
Oni	1	15–20	Lavish, refurbished 4-bedroom mansion	Assists family in black-market *paladar*	Anti-Castro, actively trying to migrate

(continued)

Alias	No. of Children	Age	Housing	Occupation/Vocation	Political orientation/ Migration Plans
Paula, Yido, and Pilar	1	35–40	2-bedroom apartment	Casa particular owner, dollar store employee	Anti-Castro, applied for bombo
Paco and Pratha	2	35–40	1-bedroom apartment	Ministry of Culture musician and emergency room nurse	Loyal to Party but with consumer desires
*Petra	2	55–60	1-bedroom apartment	Former subemployed travel agent, now retired	Many family members have Communist Party affiliations; vocally anti-Castro outside family; applied for bombo
Petrita and Kyle	1	30–35	2-bedroom apartment	Ministry of Communication computer specialist and European embassy repairman	Communist Party affiliation but anti-Castro
Poncho and Gloria	2	60–65	1-bedroom apartment	Retired, working odd repair jobs and selling coffee on black market	Unknown; children in Europe
Quincy	2	60–65	Unknown	Former agricultural worker, now cook/ cleaner in relative's casa particular	Anti-Castro
Quito	Unknown	55–60	1-bedroom apartment in dilapidated, colonial-era building	Landlord, kingpin in black-market housing rental network	Unknown
Reinita and Paulo	1	35–40	2-bedroom apartment	Former state-sponsored daycare worker now operating black-market daycare center and state-sponsored taxi driver	Unknown
Solomon and Jaya	0	20–25	Rented room in casa particular during visits	Religious outreach leaders from Israel and Argentina, unable to obtain visa to continue work in Cuba	Actively trying to migrate to Cuba
Stuart and Ursula	2	40–45	Refurbished 4-bedroom apartment	Casa particular owner and medical internist	Communist Party affiliation
Tamara	0	65–70	Unknown	Retired, depends on Jewish community for supplemental meals	Unknown
Ulanda	2	30–35	Unknown	Professor of medicine	Actively trying to migrate
Yelina and Estelle (sisters)	1	35–30	4-bedroom casa particular	Museum educator and high-school teacher, illegally serving meals	Yelina migrated to Spain and returned
Yudit and Yehuda	1	40–45	2-bedroom apartment	Owns legal pizza stand	Actively planning to migrate

Alias	No. of Children	Age	Housing	Occupation/Vocation	Political orientation/ Migration Plans
ame		30–35	Unknown	Social worker at state maternity home	Unknown
amile	1	25–30	2-bedroom apartment housing 11 family members	Bodega guard	Communist Party affiliation
emmi and *stevan*	1	15–20	Unknown	Zemmi raising child while Estevan lives in the east as a sugarcane worker	Communist Party affiliation

otes: * and *italicized:* key informants with whom I had daily contact.

alicized: secondary informants with whom I had regular contact.

Notes

Introduction

1. I categorize Cuba as authoritarian based on the following characteristics: its rule by a one-party system for fifty years (forty-eight of which were under a single commander-in-chief); citizens who are subject to arbitrary enforcement of state authority and reprisal in many aspects of their lives; and lack of core civil liberties such as freedom of speech, press, assembly, and travel, features I document ethnographically throughout the book. That said, defining Cuba as authoritarian is contested. Some scholars and commentators have contrasting opinions, arguing that Cuba exemplifies a deep form of democracy based on real representation and collective decision making for the common good (see, in particular, Roman 2003, as well as Cole 1998; August 1999; Alarcón de Quesada 2000).

2. I adopt Verdery's (2002: 14496) definition of socialist societies in this book: "Socialist (also known as communist) societies constitute a class of twentieth-century societies sharing two distinctive features: the political dominance of a revolutionary—usually a Communist—Party, and widespread nationalization of means of production, with consequent preponderance of state and collective property." See Lampland (1995); Verdery (1996); Yurchak (1997, 2005); Maier (1997); Barker (1999); Ho Tai (2001); Zhang (2001); Erjavek (2003); Hernandez-Reguant (2004, 2009) for ethnographic illustrations of late socialism in various parts of the world.

3. I place this racial designation in quotation marks because while many informants in this research identified themselves as white, they would be considered Latino/Hispanic or mixed race in other contexts. An increasing number of Cubans are of mixed race or ethnicity, with a quarter classified as "*mestizo* or *mulato*" in Cuba's most recent (2002) national census report (Arrington 2005). Although black or mixed race informants provided crucial perspectives, particularly on the role race plays in economic inequality, migration networks, and financially dependent relationships to the state, their presence was not dominant in the neighborhoods where I conducted research (see also chapter 6 for more on race and economic means).

4. I have changed all neighborhood names to protect the anonymity of their residents, but sometimes mention municipalities of Havana by their actual names to provide accurate context.

5. Dollar stores, originally established for tourists, sell "luxury" or imported items in dollars, and now in Cuban convertible pesos (CUCs), a phenomenon I will describe in greater detail later.

6. It is remarkably difficult to tell how big this group is because, although the Cuban government may keep reliable statistics on formally reported household income, including remittances sent through formal channels, it does not make such data publicly available. In addition, there are other important undocumented sources of household income (e.g., cash-in-hand remittances, equipment that is sold on the black market, etc.) that the Cuban government, like any government, can estimate but has no mechanism to document accurately. Most informants and many Cuban studies scholars would agree that the phenomenon I discuss is apparent and widespread throughout Cuba, but particularly so in Havana.

7. In this book, I do not address in depth the unemployed or those living in chronic or abject poverty. I recognize that if the bulk of my informants had fit this profile, my research questions and perspectives on market forces and the public good likely would have been different, as the very poor often suffer the most from structural adjustment and benefit most directly from social safety nets. The causes and consequences of deep poverty are worthy of study, and there are undeniably pockets of extreme poverty in Cuba, as well as increasing social stratification, even within a socialist welfare state whose very aim is a just distribution of resources to the population.

8. This said, an anthropology of the American "middle class" has developed in the past decade (see Overbey and Dudley 2000 and Kenny 2000; see also Pattillo-McCoy 1999 on the black middle class). In her ethnography of the politics of what she frames as "middle-class daily life" in Brazil, O'Dougherty (2002: 207) writes this relevant note: "Without belaboring the issue of resistance to studying middle classes per se (but see Burris 1986), I would note that Nader's (1969) call to 'study up' rather than limit themselves to studying poor people, has seldom been interpreted to mean study the middle classes."

9. Marxist and world systems theory paradigms follow the classic lead of Redfield (1941, 1947, 1955, 1956) and Steward (1949, 1955); and more recently, E. Wolf (1982); Mintz (1985); Nash (1993, 1994); Taussig (1983); and Starn (1994). See also discussion in Roseberry (1995). NSM is put forward by Castells (1983) and Melucci (1988); summarized by Alvarez, Dagnino, and Escobar (1998); and represented by Latin American–based ethnographies such as Warren (1998); Starn (1999); Edelman (1999); Nash (2001); Paley (2001); and Sawyer (2004); among others in this genre.

10. See, for example, Gabriel and Lang (1995); Cairncross, Goodlad, and Clapham (1996); Broad and Antony (1999); Vissol (1999); L. Cohen (2003); Spring (2003); Landau (2004); McGovern (2006). For scholars with non-Western foci, see García-Canclini (2001) on Latin American cities; Lukose (2005) on south India, and Garon and Maclachlan (2006) on East and Southeast Asia.

11. While consumption per se in the developing world has received attention (particularly Appadurai 1990; Abu-Lughod 1990; Lee 1993; Nash 1994; Wilk 1994; Pinches 1996, 1999), the developing world "citizen-consumer" has not, barring the work of García Canclini (2001). That said, the citizen-consumer concept I present complements the small body of work exploring contemporary material coping mechanisms that Latin American citizens commonly apply to economic and political problems. These include *Latin America at the End of Politics* (Colburn 2002), *Consumption Intensified* (O'Dougherty 2002), *Grassroots Expectations of Democracy and Economy* (Powers 2001), and the more

controversial but highly influential *The Other Path* (De Soto 1989). Finally, and most broadly, this book also offers a contribution to the recent scholarship on the interface among citizenship, consumption, and statist regimes in the third world (Gough and Wood 2004; Lukose 2005; Rhodes 2006).

12. While Tilly goes on to describe the local repertoires of protest in Western Europe and North America in the seventeenth through nineteenth centuries (distant in time and space from the lives of my informants), his vivid vocabulary regarding desires and demands nevertheless leads to an important consideration of how the historical record of public opinion is formed.

13. Exceptions to this rule were (1) a life-history project I conducted with six informants, in which I presented each informant with a printed copy of the transcript and an audiocassette to keep as personal mementos; (2) three isolated incidents of writing down prices of standard products and services, as an informant dictated them to me; and (3) taking digital photos or video clips during in-home celebrations, if the informant so requested.

14. Goldstein (2002: 485) uses *desconfianza* to describe the common experience of a "feeling of mistrust and suspicion of the ethnographer among the people being studied" in Latin American personal and political contexts.

15. My personal point of comparison for unaccompanied fieldwork is based on my previous fieldwork projects as a single, childless woman in the inner-city United States, Latin America, and Africa, during which I was less successful in establishing rapport, slower at collecting data, and prone to gather data that I now see as of lower quality and less reliable than my Cuban data, despite my greater flexibility in my use of time in the field.

Chapter 1. Historical Overview: Tracing Discontent

1. A notable exception that documents in detail the difficulties of shopping and consumption during the early Special Period is *Cuba Diaries: An American Housewife in Havana* (Tattlin 2002).

2. Lewis and his team were expelled and much of their notes and recorded material confiscated, and Rosendahl was denied reentry into the country, despite her careful treatment of the revolution and its accomplishments in her book.

3. *Structural adjustment,* called by other names: *market-oriented reform, neoliberal reform,* and even in the most general terms *economic reform,* summarizes the following constellation of policy changes: "selling of public enterprises, eliminating subsidies to domestic producers, export promotion, trade and financial liberalization, tax reform, reducing state contributions to pension plans, shedding public workers and decreasing their legal rights vis-à-vis employers, and making state social service agencies more efficient via performance assessments, targeting benefits, and fee collection. The idea is to create a market-directed and outward-oriented economy which relies on national comparative advantages in the global economy and a small, efficient, fiscally disciplined state" (Clark 2001: 147). The Special Period exhibits features of structural adjustment, as does any transition into late socialism.

4. For definitions of *authoritarian* and *socialist* see notes 1 and 2 in the introduction.

5. While there was significant immediate out-migration on the eve of the revolution, the main wave of migration did not occur until later. From 1960 to 1962, as the contours of the regime became clearer to the public, net out-migration from Cuba is estimated to have been 200,000 citizens, an unprecedented number averaging more than 60,000 per year. This wave of migration was composed primarily of upper-middle- and middle-class elites such as professionals, managers, executives, and white-collar workers (Domínguez 1993: 100).

6. Fidel Castro, in addition being first secretary of the PCC, was also Cuba's head of state, head of government, and commander in chief of the armed forces. In March 2003, Castro announced his intention to remain in power for life, although severe intestinal problems forced him to step down and cede power for the first time in forty-seven years, on August 3, 2006, to his brother Raúl. Despite this historic event, at the time of this writing, informants report that there have been few notable changes in the governmental structure or style of leadership that affect citizens' everyday lives.

7. Members of the CMEA were the Soviet Union, Bulgaria, Czechoslovakia, the German Democratic Republic (East Germany), Hungary, Romania, Poland, Cuba, the Mongolian People's Republic, and Vietnam. Its goal was to extend and improve the cooperation and development of "socialist economic integration" of member countries.

8. The Torricelli Act, also known as the Cuban Democracy Act, prohibited American companies, including subsidiaries abroad, from engaging in any trade with Cuba, and prohibited Cuban Americans from sending any cash remittances to Cuba. This halted shipments to Cuba of food and medicine, with the exception of humanitarian aid. The Helms-Burton Act, also known as the Cuban Liberty and Democratic Solidarity Act of 1996, extended the territorial application of the initial embargo to foreign companies trading with Cuba, and penalized foreign companies having dealings with enterprises formerly owned by U.S. citizens but expropriated by Cuba after the Cuban Revolution.

9. For a working definition of capitalism, I use that put forth by Muller (2002: xvii): "a system in which the production and distribution of goods is entrusted primarily to the market mechanism, based on private ownership of property, on exchange between legally free individuals," though he presents this as an "ideal type that exists in reality only in imperfect forms." He notes that this definition "is not purely 'economic,' for 'private' property and 'legally free individuals' exist only because there are political mechanisms that protect individuals from having their persons and property seized by others."

10. See also Eckstein (1995) for an analysis of Special Period reforms, which she categorizes as (a) market-style reforms, such as those I have mentioned; (b) socialist strategies (e.g., the Food Program, which sought to make the island's food production as self-sufficient as possible and increased rationing to "equalize sacrifice" and volunteer worker brigades); and (c) "reverting" to "pre-socialist" strategies, such as increased use of manual labor, draft animals, and herbal medicines. Although all these reforms had an impact on daily life in some sectors, I argue that the market-style reforms were the most lasting, the ones that citizen-consumers now speak about the most, and those that have changed Cuban social structure most profoundly.

11. For more than a decade—1993 to 2004—the U.S. dollar was legal tender in Cuba. In November 2004, however, Cuban authorities eliminated the circulation of dollars and

any other "convertible currency" nationwide. The exchange of U.S. dollars for convertible pesos (*pesos convertibles,* or CUCs, also known locally as *kooks* or *chavitos*) bears a 10 percent tax. The tax applies to both nationals and foreign visitors in any business that accepts cash payments in U.S. dollars: stores, hotels, bars, cafeterias, taxis, rental car companies, and so on. Cuban salaries continue to be paid in "ordinary" (nonconvertible) Cuban pesos, which must then be converted for most purchases, losing their value; consequently, the statements I make here concerning the legalization of the dollar are also true for the convertible peso.

12. Cuban citizens do, however, vote via secret ballot at the national, provincial and municipal levels, though the electoral commission uses a simple show-of-hands vote to select the list of nominees for the municipal elections, and for half of the provincial legislative offices. The number of candidates listed on the ballot is exactly equal to the number of seats open in the provincial legislature and the National Assembly, but the candidates still must win 51 percent of the votes to get elected. For a thorough (and positively cast) description of the Cuban electoral process, see August 1999.

13. The petition, covered widely in the international press, was named for Father Félix Varela, a nineteenth-century priest prominent in Cuba's struggle for independence from Spain. Oswaldo Payá Sardiñas, along with other dissident leaders, presented a petition containing 11,020 signatures of Cuban citizens to the country's National Assembly on May 10, 2002. The document called for an island-wide referendum that, if approved by voters, would grant amnesty to political prisoners and give Cubans freedom of expression and association, free enterprise, and electoral reform and elections within one year. In response, the National Assembly approved a counter-referendum—proposed by Fidel Castro and backed by more than eight million signatures—declaring the socialist regime "irrevocable." It then organized a citizens' march at the Plaza de la Revolución in support of the current government. In April 2003, twenty-five members of Proyecto Varela were jailed for terms ranging from six to twenty-eight years.

14. *Jineterismo* is literally "jockeying" or "riding," but has come to mean hustling or prostitution in Cuba. A male *jinetero,* or more commonly a female *jinetera,* sells sex, companionship, goods, or services to foreigners in exchange for dollars, a meal, a night out, desired goods, and sometimes even marriage (see Rundle 2001; Lundgren 2003; Kummels 2005; or Valle 2006 for overviews). Since *jineteros/as* are such willing and accessible informants and subjects, and are walking targets in tourist areas, I believe an overfocus on *jineterismo* has developed in reportage.

15. However, since the summer of 2005, the Cuban health-care system has been under considerable staffing strain as 20 percent of Cuban doctors have been sent to Venezuela to expand an aid mission started in 2003, commonly referred to as an "oil for doctors" deal. The Venezuelan government, under the leftist, populist leadership of President Hugo Chávez, claims that the program includes 30,000 medical professionals, 600 comprehensive health clinics, 600 rehabilitation and physical therapy centers, 35 high-technology diagnostic centers, and 100,000 ophthalmologic surgeries, making it by far the biggest "medical cooperation" project ever attempted by Cuba. Venezuela now ships Cuba 90,000 barrels of oil a day under preferential terms, a deal creating the strongest economic support for Cuba since the fall of the Soviet bloc. This project is also part of

Bolivian Alternative for the Americas (ALBA) to unite and integrate Latin America in a "social justice-oriented trade and aid block" under Venezuela's lead (S. Collins 2005; Feinsilver 2006, 2008).

16. It is estimated that eighty buildings a year collapse in Havana. See Coyula and Hamberg (2003) on Havana's "substandard" housing, and Corbett's (2002) chapter "Paradise Crumbling," on housing collapse.

17. Here I borrow Tilly's definitions of state as distinct from government: "*government* [is] any organization that controls the chief coercive means within some substantial territory, reserving the name *state* for those governments that (a) do not fall under the jurisdiction of any other government, (b) receive recognition from other governments in the same situation" (1997: 599, emphasis my own).

18. Cuba hosted 1.4 million tourists in 1998. In 1999 1.9 million visited, and tourism reached an all-time high of 2.3 million in 2005. Tourism in 1996 surpassed the sugar industry—the main source of hard currency in Cuba—at $1.4 billion (Ernst & Young 2006). This is a radical increase from pre–Special Period data. International tourism was nearly abandoned in the 1960s and 1970s, and few tourism-related data from that time exist. One meager estimate states that in 1974, 8,400 visitors from capitalist countries came to Cuba. Cuba opened its first nationalized tourist institute (INTUR) in 1976, but attempts at promoting tourism did not start in earnest until the Special Period (for further detail, see Espino 2000).

Part I. Private

1. By "neoliberal project," I refer to discussions concerning the intensification of individualization and marketization of the "neoliberal subject," who is expected to be entrepreneurial and involved in auto-regulation or auto-correction, autonomy, personal responsibility, and choice, with the individual ability to provide for one's own needs and services. Such analyses are usually framed by the Foucauldian concept of governmentality (see Burchell, Gordon, and Miller 1991; Cruikshank 1999; Rose 1998, 1999). While this framework has served as a valuable tool for analyzing the exercise of political power, it does not sufficiently illuminate what I am calling the "citizen's-eye view."

Chapter 2. Private Space

1. Following the revolution, whole areas in the wealthiest sections of Havana were deemed *áreas congeladas* (frozen zones), where luxurious mansions were kept closed, clearly not for redistribution to citizens and maybe not even for public use. Local lore around Havana is that Castro was saving the properties to be given to loyal Party members as gifts. While it is difficult to confirm the ownership of buildings, informants believe that some upper-level Party members have as many as five properties, and they told me rumors are that some are wastefully left vacant, fully furnished and utterly uninhabited, while Havana's public housing infrastructure crumbles around them.

2. José Martí was the leader of the Cuban independence movement as well as an esteemed poet and writer.

3. See S. Moore (1987) for a relevant discussion of how systems are maintained, and Bell (1992: 221) on "ritualized agents who understand ways of acting that both maintain and qualify the complex relations of power."

4. See Oring's (2004: 221) definition of "kitchen table" or "kitchen conversations" (*besedi na kukhnye*) in Soviet Russia, "candid conversations with close relatives and friends often lasting deep into the night," covering "'everything that it was risky to say.' People complained, people criticized, people expressed themselves without inhibition."

5. When Cubans refer to Fidel or El Partido in a negative way, they use either silent gestures (such as stroking a beard, tapping imaginary epaulettes on the shoulder), or for Fidel specifically, apply a variety of code names, most commonly *Él* (He), but also *el caballo* (the horse), *el Jefe* (the boss), or *el Loco* (the crazy man).

6. See Haddad (2003) and Wirtz (2004) on the *doble moral* in Cuba. Also see Havel's related discussion concerning the model of state socialism in the Eastern Europe of the 1970s (Havel and Keene 1986); Kharkhordin (1999) in the context of the USSR; and Verdery's (2002) definitions of "social schizophrenia," "doubling," "duplicity," or "split self," a phenomenon that she claims is universal in socialist societies.

7. In literature, propaganda, print media, and educational material published in Cuba, *Revolution* is consistently capitalized, as it is when Cubans themselves write the word. In attempting to capture this essence, I have likewise capitalized *Revolution* and *Revolutionary* when I quote informants' spoken words. This is how they would expect to see their words transcribed.

8. In the last several years there has been more published information on Cuba and the Internet, though Cuba has been officially connected to the Internet with very limited access since 1996. See Coté (2005) for a brief history of the lively black market in selling Internet codes that emerged in 2000, "Cuba Inches into the Internet Age" (2006) for updates on current Internet politics in Cuba, and Voeux and Pain (2006) on modes of censorship. It is difficult to know what percentage of Cubans have Internet access, but some estimates are as low as 1.7 percent, placing Cuba on par with Myanmar and Iran (though a 2007 report from Internet World Stats estimates 2.1 percent access). A crackdown on Internet use by the general public in Cuba occurred in 2004 (see Snow 2006); in 2006, Guillermo "Coco" Fariñas, a forty-one-year-old Cuban psychologist, went on a hunger strike demanding Internet access, and later in 2008, Yoani Sánchez received international recognition for winning the Ortega y Gasset prize for digital journalism in Spain for her "Generación Y" blog, both of which drew further international attention to the Internet situation in Cuba (see also the epilogue). For a comparative, book-length description of the politics of the Internet in Cuba and Costa Rica, see Hoffman (2004). Finally, see Kurlantzick (2004) for an important general discussion of why Internet access does not serve as an index of democratization of information.

9. Established in 1983 under the Reagan administration, Radio Martí is a radio and television broadcast based in Miami and funded by the U.S. government. It transmits short- and medium-wave broadcasts to Cuba, with the self-proclaimed mission to offer "a contrast to Cuban media and provide its listeners with an uncensored view of current events" (Office of Cuba Broadcasting n.d.). Former political prisoners, human-rights activists, and Cuban exiles often speak on Radio Martí, and on Saturdays, a Spanish ver-

sion of the U.S. president's weekly radio address is broadcast. Although the radio broadcasts are relatively easy to tap into in Cuba, viewing the television broadcasts requires a special satellite dish for reception not widely available (or legal) to most Cubans. The station's opponents view it as extremely right-wing, interventionist, propagandistic, and colonialist, although Elena perceived it as an important channel of self-expression and was grateful to have had the opportunity to use it.

10. In 1994, Joseph Sullivan, former head of the U.S. Interests Section, wrote a memo to the State Department, the Central Intelligence Agency, and the Immigration and Naturalization Service (INS), drawing a sharp distinction between economic and political refugees from Cuba. It is an important statement in light of the difference between citizens and consumers. The memo, leaked to the Cuban public in March of that year, stated:

> The processing of refugee applicants continues to show weak cases. Most people apply more because of the deteriorating economic situation than a real fear of persecution. Cases presented by human rights activists proved particularly difficult for USINT [U.S. Interests Section in Havana] officers and INS members. Although we have tried hard to work with those human rights organizations on which we exert greater control to identify activists truly persecuted by the government, human rights cases represent the weakest category of the refugee program. (Granma International, March 2004, available online at www.nowaroncuba.org/Documentation/Hypocrisy_memo_on_Human_Rights_in_Cuba.htm)

Chapter 3. Private Experience

1. Padre Varela was a Cuban-born philosopher and priest who lobbied for self-rule within the Spanish Empire and an end to slavery. In recent years Varela's name has become associated with the highly controversial Proyecto Varela (see chapter 2).

2. This situation is beginning to change with the introduction of a limited number of Internet blogs coming out of Cuba since 2007. See the epilogue for recent changes.

3. *Palabra nueva* has been published by the Havana Archdiocese since 1992. Forty-eight pages long and issued monthly, it is the longest and most frequently printed publication of the Catholic press in Cuba. Topics include religion and general news about the church, the economy, culture and films, science, and sports. Church members print it on a flatbed offset press, and it takes five people three weeks to collate and staple by hand, using private resources (and funding from a German Christian nongovernmental organization). *Palabra nueva* has an official distribution of around 10,000 copies, but as the editor, Orlando Márquez, explains, "The magazine is growing and is literally passed from one person to another" (see Cubanet 1998; Lionet 2003). I also witnessed this firsthand in the neighborhood where I lived. Notably, *El vitral* (The Church Window), distributed by the Diocese of Pinar del Río, had the reputation of being more direct and radical, but it was not generally available in Havana, and its publication was discontinued in April 2007. For a more general history of the importance of the Catholic Church in Cuba, see Kirk (1989).

4. Warner's (2002: 89) comment is relevant here: "activities that are part of reading,

but do not fit its idealized image as a practice of silent, private, replicable decoding— curling up, mumbling, fanaticizing, gesticulating, and writing marginalia, for example— are bereft of counterparts in public agency."

5. In December 1993, just months after the legalization of self-employment, 70,000 Cubans had obtained small business licenses. By February 1994, the number reached 150,000, peaking in 1995 at 208,000, at which time Cuba imposed its first income tax in thirty-seven years. Since that time, the number of legally self-employed has declined, hovering at around 150,000 or fewer (B. Smith 1999; Peters 2006).

6. Iris had been a middle-class worker before the revolution, living comfortably and already benefiting from free health care under the Batista regime (see essays in Bethell 1993 for a discussion of revolutionary reforms that were merely expansions of existing systems). Many of the revolutionary reforms, and certainly the consistently publicized ones, most benefited Cuba's very poorest and most rural citizens. The reforms were not particularly impressive to the urban middle class, however, a point well expressed in Oscar Lewis's trilogy (Lewis, Lewis, and Rigdon 1977–78). While the Lewis project abruptly ended when the government confiscated many of the researchers' tapes and notes and forced the team to leave, the resulting trilogy of ethnographic material still provides extensive detail concerning the lives of ordinary, middle-class Cubans just after the revolution.

7. David and Tatiana, like many ordinary Cubans, do not even have their own bank account, not wanting their private financial matters to be known at the whim of the state or for a sudden leap in income to be noted by officials.

8. Not all CDR presidents turn a blind eye to such unlicensed activities. In the two other neighborhoods in which I had direct contact with the CDR presidents, they seemed to take their task more seriously and certainly had a more visible neighborhood presence. For example, they would knock on the doors of neighbors who were late for meetings and would organize block parties.

9. Another important factor is Cuba's demographic transition. The country's population has been growing at less than 1 percent per year since 1980 and has a projected annual growth rate of less than 0.2 percent between now and 2025 (see Gonzalez and McCarthy 2004; McCarthy 2004). During the 1960s and 1970s, Cuba's annual birthrate was about 250,000. In 2005, there were slightly more than 120,000 births, despite Cuba's one million women of reproductive age (*Miami Herald* Staff 2006). One result is the shrinking number of preschoolers in Cuba in general (and Havana in particular), and consequently, the modified role of state-run daycare centers.

10. In speaking with Martina, a Party member and upper-level administrator of the mass organization Federación de Mujeres Cubanas, I asked about this problem of overfull state day care. (The FMC, or Federation of Cuban Women, is a mass organization.) Typical of official Party discourse, she began rattling off triumphs, statistics, objectives, and challenges. When I mentioned the rise of the private option, she told me flatly, "There's nothing like that here," her expression blank, her eye contact hazy. When I asked Petra later about Martina's response, she said that Martina was "ciega, ciega, ciega" (blind, blind, blind), although she indicated with some resentment that Martina also liked nice things, and was always asking to borrow Petra's clothes and enjoy her large TV.

Petra griped, "Next time she asks to borrow a skirt of mine, I'm going to say, 'Why don't you go ask Vilma?'" (The Vilma Espín Guillo, Raúl Castro's wife, president of the FMC, and sometimes referred to as "Cuba's first lady," was still alive at the time Petra made this comment.) Such remarks highlight perceived differences between socialist realties and socialist ideals as experienced by citizen-consumers.

11. See related categorizations in J. Hill's (2001) discussion of public/private boundaries in U.S. folk theory, and in Mansvelt's (2005) presentation of geographies of consumption.

12. See González Febles (2006) on *susurro urbano* in Havana. Oring (2004: 58) also identifies "anti-regime" humor and anecdote throughout the world as having become labeled as "underground humor," "whispered anecdotes," or "Flüsterwitze" (citing Draister 1989; Lipman 1991).

13. Examples of "embedding" are a public official selling goods on the private market; the private space of a *sala* (living room) serving as a safe space to discuss public, political problems; or a public speech intimately addressing and intimately affecting private individuals.

Part II. Means

1. Barrio Belén is a rundown but historically rich Old Havana neighborhood and home to the Our Lady of Belén Convent (1718), which is undergoing massive restoration funded with foreign donations. "Belén" also means "bedlam" or "in a fix."

2. Means, or *alcance,* as translated, refers to an available agent, a method for achieving a desired result, and also to financial resources. Common uses, for example, are "No tengo alcance comprarlo" (I don't have the means to buy it), or "Mantenga fuera del alcance de los niños" (Keep out of the reach of children.)

Chapter 4. Words and Means: The Special Period Lexicon

1. A common use of the term in the sanctioned sense, based on the source of the object discourse, is "luchando por la Revolución" (fighting for the revolution). See Rosendahl (1997: 89) for her definition of *lucha* as a word that expresses the pedagogical and moral role of the Party; *lucha* is also part of the "principal aspect of the Party program" according to the *Programa del PCC* (1987: 56–65), whose role is the "education of workers to a higher political consciousness." Also consider the specific application of *luchar* as it appears in the Cuban Constitution, highlighting sacrifice and political struggle:

por los obreros, campesinos, estudiantes e intelectuales que lucharon durante mas de cincuenta años contra el dominio imperialista, la corrupción política, la falta de derechos y libertades populares, el desempleo y la explotación impuesta por capitalistas y terratenientes.

[For the workers, peasants, students, and intellectuals who struggled over more than fifty years against imperial domination, political corruption, lack of rights and ordinary freedoms, unemployment, and exploitation imposed by capitalists and landowners.]

2. That recipients of social insurance "earn a bit on the side" is not a national or regional peculiarity. See Edin and Lein (1997) and Snel and Staring (2001) for a discussion of "coping strategies" under various welfare systems internationally. See also De Soto (1989), Tokman (1992), and Rakowski (1994) for discussions of the type, scale, and pervasiveness of the phenomenon of the informal sector at the regional level in Latin America. See Böröcz (2000), Humphrey (2002), Mandel and Humphrey (2002), and Ledeneva (2006) for similar phenomena in the former Soviet bloc.

3. As informants put it on multiple occasions, "In Cuba, there are no *communistas*, only *Fidelistas*" (people still willing to follow the dream of their charismatic leader). But in the current economic situation, no one is adhering strictly to communist principles. This statement resonated with how self-proclaimed communists described themselves.

4. The party had a membership of more than 780,000 when the fifth Party Congress was held in 1997 (the most recent Party Congress to date). This was actually an increase in membership from previous years, due in large part to the prohibition on party membership for religious believers being lifted. The process for choosing new party members was also streamlined so that more members could be drawn from work centers, based on votes from their coworkers (LeoGrande 2002: 9).

5. This meant that I, like many academics conducting research in contemporary Cuba, would have to complete my research over a series of return trips and without formal permission from the Cuban government.

6. There are, of course, many Cubans who are more concerned about procuring subsistence items, and since the Special Period there have been instances of nutritional deficiencies. These, however, are not the problems generally experienced by my pool of informants.

7. This conversation took place during six months of fieldwork in Costa Rica in 2003, during which time I conducted a study of Cuban migrants to Costa Rica. See also chapter 7.

8. While the U.S. embargo is often depicted as absolute, in the last several years there have been some surprising changes, particularly in the increasing amount of food imports coming directly from the United States. Since 2002, the United States has been Cuba's largest supplier of food and agricultural products. From 2004 through 2006, U.S. agricultural exports to Cuba have averaged more than $350 million, and the United States has remained Cuba's most important food and agricultural product supplier, accounting for up to 30 percent of Cuba's food imports, more than from any other country (CBS Broadcasting 2006; FAS/USDA 2008).

Chapter 5. What Goods Mean in Cuba

1. The exact quantity of eggs and other items on the ration book has varied from year to year, and even from season to season during the Special Period and beyond. Fourteen was quite a generous quantity, as Cubans may receive as few as seven to twelve per month.

2. Poly-Vi-Sol and Tri-Vi-Sol are leading brands of children's vitamins in the United States; they were not available for sale on the Cuban market in 2003, at the time of this conversation.

3. "*Pero, bueno*" is a common transitional phrase to neutralize one's own preceding negative comment, often used when someone does not want to complain too openly for personal or political reasons.

4. "Sábado gigante" is a Spanish-language variety show extremely popular throughout the Hispanic world. Its broadcast studios are now based in Miami. In many homes throughout Latin America, watching it is a Saturday-night family tradition.

5. Havana's joint-venture projects and concomitant renovation (most often cosponsored by Spain, Italy, Canada, or UNESCO) are elusive, causing further dissatisfaction and sense of deprivation among citizens, as well as curiosity about government logic. Buildings, primarily those in the old city, are restored not as living spaces for Cubans, but as "boutiques selling items Cubans can't afford and foreigners can buy cheaper and better at home, or bleak, expensive, empty bars, or bad, expensive restaurants, or offices for joint-venture capitalists that the government thinks will come, lured by 51-percent-for-the-government, 49-percent-for-them deals" (Tattlin 2002: 96).

6. There are various estimates of how much of Cuba's gross national product (GNP) comes from remittances. One estimate is that a massive US$700 million to US$1 billion is received annually from Cubans living abroad (CEPAL 1999, 2002), later revised to $900 million in 2003 (CEPAL 2004). The most recently published range is US$300 million to more than US$1 billion (D. Fernández 2005: xvi; discussion and overview of estimates and methods in Pérez-López and Díaz-Briquets 2005). These amounts represent about one-fifth of the island's GNP. Regardless, remittances rival tourism as Cuba's main source of hard currency (Betancourt 1996). The irony remains that while family members sending remittances to Cuba have abandoned the revolution, Cuba couldn't survive without them.

Changes in the last five years governing how remittances can be sent are likely to affect these estimates. As of this writing, due to restrictions imposed by the embargo, any remittances wired from the United States to a Cuban national who is not next of kin must be processed through costly, third-party cash-transfer agencies (usually located in Europe or Canada). These cash-transfer processing fees, along with taxes levied by the Cuban government on remittances entering the country through formal channels, reduce the cash-in-hand amount to the Cuban recipient. Informal and illegal ways around these fees and taxes have been developed, primarily in Miami, and involve paying commissioned *mulas* (mules) to hand-deliver wads of cash to Cuba.

7. Housing micro-brigades, falling under the state categorization of a mass movement are building-construction projects in which volunteer workers are provided with construction materials to build their own homes and those of their neighbors.

8. But see Frederick's contrasting essay on the *campesino* as the icon of essential Cuban identity as "true, uncontaminated, authentic and of *pura cepa*" (pure root, pure stock). She describes the state promotion of *campesino* morals and the *campesino* soul as the super–New Man of contemporary times, representing "humility, stamina . . . communist in his modesty and loyalty . . . and a philosophy of national patriotism of the united Latin American struggle against imperialist domination." (Fredrick 2005: 403).

9. John and Jean Comaroff (1999: 19) describe "millennial capitalism" as "capitalism

invested with salvific force; with intense faith in its capacity, if rightly harnessed, wholly to transform the universe of the marginalized and disempowered . . . in its more mundane manifestation, it accords the market itself an almost mystical capacity to produce and deliver cash and commodities."

10. This perspective stands in contrast to other political-economic ethnographies of globalization that portray it as an "external threat" to the autonomy of the indigenous (see Warren 1998) and working class in Latin America as "producers" in a "worldwide division of labor," as presented by June Nash, a long-standing and influential voice in Latin American anthropology (Nash 1981: 416; see also Nash 2001).

11. This is with the exception of globally circulating music coming from Cuba and, to a lesser degree, Cuban film (see R. Moore 2006 for further discussion).

12. As Bourdieu states of any classificatory system, it "continuously transforms necessities into strategies, constraints into preferences, and, without any mechanical determination, it generates the set of 'choices' constituting lifestyles, which derive their meaning, i.e., their value, for the position in a system of oppositions and correlations" (Bourdieu 1984: 175).

13. A related sentiment expressed in the assessment of transformation in Eastern Europe is interesting to consider in the context of the present conversation about goods and citizen-consumers:

> The Berlin Wall did not fall simply because the Soviet Union was militarily and economically bankrupt, nor even because the citizens of the East longed to be free. It fell because those citizens said, "Screw this" to communism's utopian message. They wanted video recorders, not the dictatorship of the proletariat. They wanted Michael Jackson albums. They wanted motorcycles. They wanted *Penthouse* magazine, combination washer-dryers, twenty-four hour convenience stores, rave music, and a lot of Ecstasy to go with it. Communism provided none of that. (Berlinski 2006: 70)

Chapter 6. Dollars, Means, and the New Cuban Class System

1. See Mesa-Lago (2002: table 1) for calculations of the monthly incomes in Havana for various state and private-sector occupations.

2. China offers an interesting cross-national comparison for room rental on the black market. See Liu (2005) for her description of the "Black Gold" regime in China's public housing development projects, in which room rental to foreigners is central to the shadow economy.

3. Other locally very popular Cuban-produced or -coproduced films that address "Special Period issues" include *Alicia en el Pueblo de las Maravillas* (Alice in Wondertown, 1991), *Fresa y chocolate* (Strawberry and Chocolate, 1993), *Madagascar* (1994), *La vida es silbar* (Life Is to Whistle, 1998), *Lista de espera* (Waiting List, 2000), *Habana Blues* (2005), and *Páginas del diario de Mauricio* (Pages from Mauricio's Diary, 2006). See also Fernandes (2006) for an analysis of how the Cuban government has allowed criticism of the state to be expressed within the realm of the arts.

4. Ordinary Cubans cannot legally buy new vehicles and are pushed into a second-

hand market in which prices have been artificially inflated by government restrictions on imports and permits to buy, and there is a massive demand but limited supply. David noted, shaking his head in disbelief, the absurdity of a fifteen-year-old Russian motorbike costing $3,000 more than a new European or Japanese model or a common used car such as the notoriously unreliable Lada, which cost US$4,500–$5,000.

5. Falcoff (2003: 105) refers to an "officers' class" that has access to ample foreign currency, presumably to ensure their continued political loyalty, but I have yet to see an analysis of Cuba's Burguesía Roja by that name.

6. Here I apply Craig Calhoun's (1992) general definition of civil society; see also Gray and Kapcia (2008) for an updated discussion of the Cuban case.

7. Differential access to dollars by race would be considered counter to the goals of the Communist Party. Furthermore, because conducting surveys or social research on sensitive topics requires government permission that is rarely granted, claims about differential access to dollars remain in need further empirical investigation.

8. As I have mentioned previously, estimates of remittances vary wildly, since there are no official records and many transfers are delivered by hand, not through official channels that can be tracked.

9. I did not identify informants by race in the appendix, but I will note that nine of the fifty or so households listed there might be considered Afro-Cuban in a census context or would contain at least one Afro-Cuban adult. As I state early on in the book, Afro-Cubans are a minority in my research, but are not completely unrepresented (see also note 3 in the introduction).

10. They did not, however, live in the neighborhood where I lived; if they had, my relationship with them would have aroused suspicions about my loyalty and trustworthiness among some of my most important informant families.

Chapter 7. Un-migration

1. Restrictions on freedom of movement, including selective denial of exit permits to thousands of citizens, has become a concern of Cuban dissidents within Cuba and of international human rights activists. "The freedom to leave and return to one's own country at will" is considered a "basic human right" (Albright and Havel 2006, para. 3; see also United Nations General Assembly 1948).

2. Specifically, migrants must pay processing fees (approximately $180 [4,500 pesos] for exit permission, $66 [1,650 pesos] for a passport, and $30 [750 pesos] in airport tax) that amount to approximately twenty-three months' salary for the average citizen. Prospective migrants to the United States face an additional charge of approximately $720 (18,000 pesos or five years' salary) for adults and $480 (12,000 pesos) for children. This leaves some potential migrants unable to leave the country because of inability to pay exit fees, even after they have received an official permit to exit (and a visa to enter the receiving country) (Bureau of Democracy, Human Rights, and Labor 2006).

3. Cuban citizens take to the sea in makeshift boats (*yomas*) and rafts that are often "dangerously overloaded, unseaworthy or otherwise unsafe" (Department of Homeland Security 2006a). Between one and two thousand Cubans are interdicted at sea by the

U.S. Coast Guard annually. The number of Cuban migrants who successfully make it to the United States by sea varies by year, ranging from the hundreds to thousands. For example, 303 Cubans reached U.S. soil in 2003 and 6,356 Cubans did so in 2005 (Gomez 2006). The cost, quality and safety of vessels vary tremendously, ranging from the inexpensive, individual makeshift variety to expensive high-speed, "go-fast" boats (known locally as *botes* or *lanchas*), to yachts which can cost upwards of $15,000 and requires the mutual trust of a large number of people to coordinate plans and resources without getting reported.

4. Despite the perennial popularity of the Florida Straits as a route to escape, in recent years, the Caribbean Sea, on the south side of the island, has also become an exit option. Cubans most commonly make it to Santo Domingo in the Dominican Republic, where they are then smuggled to San Juan, Puerto Rico, across the ninety-mile-wide Mona Passage (and then to the United States from there). The Mona Passage, where the Caribbean Sea and the Atlantic Ocean meet, is an extremely rough body of water, not suitable for the small, often handmade boats that carry migrants over. Nevertheless, identifying the Cuban migrant population is a burgeoning enterprise for Dominican *coyotes* (human smugglers), and a *coyote* business network walks through Santo Domingo, listening for distinctively Cuban accents to recruit potential clients. The U.S. Coast Guard claims the number of migrants coming through this passage has increased fivefold since 2003 (Gomez 2006; Robles 2006).

5. In his book, *To Die in Cuba: Suicide and Society* (2005), Louis Pérez Jr. provides a historical perspective on why the per-capita rate of suicide in Cuba is the highest in Latin America and among the highest in the world. Among his interpretations are Cubans' need to affirm personal agency or protest injustice. He explains that "voluntary death," is often frequently viewed as a logical response to economic, political, or social affliction.

6. The average number of daily international telephone calls into Cuba increased from 500 in 1995 to 50,000 in 1997 with the lifting of the telecommunication embargo by the U.S. government (*Cubanews,* July 1997, most recent publicly available estimate). High volumes of incoming calls continue, although they are costly and it is almost universally acknowledged that phone lines are tapped by the Cuban government to monitor counterrevolutionary activity. Most phone conversations therefore remain relatively short and free of explicitly political content. Occasionally, people send handwritten letters back and forth with trusted travelers. The few who have Internet access are very careful about the tone and content of their e-mail messages, assuming that they could be read by a third party (see also comments on "private communication" in chapter 3).

7. Temporary work contracts differ from open-ended work contracts and letters of invitation to work outside of the country, which might actually allow, in rare and seemingly arbitrary circumstances, legal migration out of Cuba. (See also note 17 in this chapter for further detail.)

8. One notable exception is the boom of doctors sent to Venezuela and, to a lesser degree, to Bolivia, in what some have called the "oil-for-doctors" trade. There are also much smaller programs in other third-world Latin America and African countries (Cuban Ministry of Public Health 2005; Feinsilver 2006, 2008).

9. Since 1963, Cuba has provided civilian assistance and "medical diplomacy" to third-world countries to build solidarity and political alliances. According to (contested) Cuban sources, between 1985 and 1990, Cuba supplied more than 46,000 civilian aid workers per year—including doctors, teachers, and construction crews—in thirty-seven African and Middle Eastern countries, thirteen Asian and Oceanic countries, and ten Latin American and Caribbean countries (Feinsilver 1993).

10. See Loss's provocative essay, "Wandering in Russian." In it, she describes how Cubans in the Special Period who came of age in the more liberal 1980s, reinvent their own personal experiences with the intimately exotic sphere of "things Russian" in order to savor the dissonance of its language, literature, and foods as a form of escape from the present (Loss 2009). While some of the biggest exchange programs were with the USSR, there were also opportunities for Cuban students to attend universities and obtain degrees in every Central and Eastern European socialist country (except for Yugoslavia and Albania), often taking them out of the country for approximately five years.

11. Africa and poorer parts of Latin America serve as an important counterexample for Cubans, because although Cuban unsatisfied citizen-consumers would initially claim "I'd live anywhere but here," if I named less-developed countries that would potentially allow them to live with more civil liberties, they would not consider those as permanent destinations, because of the lack of economic development and access to the lifestyle they were seeking.

12. Elena's opinions about "other Cubans" were important, in that they drove many of her dissatisfactions and actions, though I must note that her distaste for other Cubans was more extreme than that of most informants. Complaining about other Cubans does however represent a "safe" and acceptable repertoire of complaint because it does not directly criticize the government, but still allows for the release of frustrations about local conditions.

13. Notably, the 1980s (specifically the years 1981–1987) were considered the glory years for the revolution, when things were at least tolerable because it was popularly considered an *abertura* (aperture). People who stayed were rewarded for staying. Bookstores were full, there was plenty of food in the *bodegas,* there were no acute crises, and people were permitted to travel and return home.

14. Depending on the speaker, these metaphors might be used with more or less equivocation, some qualifying the metaphors with, "You can't compare, but . . . ," while others drew the associations more directly.

15. See Good and Good 1980; Good 1994; Csordas 1990; and Merleau-Ponty 1962, who classically address bodily metaphors, semiotics, and the social-psychological meaning of symptoms.

16. Of course, I am not arguing that people living in nation-states with economic and political problems have higher than average rates of asthma (current research shows that high concentrations of asthma are usually correlated with high levels of pollution), but rather intend to point out that Cubans talk about and experience asthma in a particular way.

17. This interview with Tristan also took place during fieldwork in Costa Rica in 2003, during which time I conducted a study of Cuban migrants there. Tristan, like most Cubans in Costa Rica, was able to migrate because he had been offered a coveted work contract and letter of invitation for a specific position, and because he had a specific skill (such contracts are most difficult to obtain for work in the United States, but can be procured somewhat more easily for work in Latin America and Spain). In Tristan's case, his contract was provided by an upper-level Cuban manager at a hotel outside of San José who was seeking a Cuban chef to cook classic Cuban cuisine and who had known Tristan personally since his childhood. This practice of bringing, or "lifting," migrants through work contracts is called *llevando*. Arranging for family reunification, another legal migration option, is called *reclamando* (reclaiming). Laws concerning both types of legal migration to Costa Rica and other countries change often, are becoming increasingly restrictive, and are enforced by the Cuban government in a way Cuban citizens perceive as arbitrary.

18. For an overview, see Zeitlin (1966); Amaro and Portes (1972); Aguirre (1976); Portes, Clark, and Bach (1977); Bach, Bach, and Triplett (1981–82); Rieff (1983); Portes (1984); J. Clark (1975); Pedraza (1995); Masud-Piloto (1996); and Henken (2005).

19. The four main waves of migration are considered (1) Cuba's elite in 1959–1960, immediately after Castro's government took power; (2) Lyndon B. Johnson's "refugees from communism," primarily the petite bourgeoisie, in 1965–1974; (3) the Mariel Boat Lift involving Cuba's "undesirables" (mental patients, homosexuals, criminals, or anyone who was perfectly willing to be labeled as such in order to escape; also an unprecedented number of blue-collar, working-class, and black Cubans), in 1980; and (4) the *balsero* (rafter) crisis in 1994, at the height of Cuba's economic collapse and material shortages, which was the first wave to contain a majority of black Cubans and represented the poorest migrants of any of the waves. See Pedraza (1995: 312) for complete analysis of these groups, along with a discussion of how each wave of migration has been characterized by a very different social composition of migrants, and of how "vintages" of migrants (defined by attitudes) may or may not be the same as "waves" of migrants (defined by timing).

20. See Portes, Guarnizo, and Landolt (1999); Portes (1999); Menjívar (2000); Al-Ali and Koser (2001); Levitt (2001); Miles (2004); Massey (2005); and R. Smith (2006), though this segment of the migration literature is not wholly applicable to contemporary Cuba because of Cuba's unusually strict laws on exit and return.

21. Abdelmalek Sayad published from the 1950s to 1999 on how the sociology of migration must start by exploring the structure and contradictions of the sending communities. In his culminating work, *The Suffering of the Immigrant,* he writes, "immigration here and emigration there are the two indissasociable sides of the same reality, which cannot be explained the one without the other" (Sayad 1999: 15).

22. What took me aback was what seemed at the time to be unpredictable turns that would lead to an announcement of intent to leave the country. These "unpredictable turns" were attributable to my genuine naïveté as an ethnographic observer without a predetermined agenda. In retrospect, and with the knowledge, typologies, and patterns

of discourse and behavior I have devised in the time since these pivotal conversations, I now find quite *un*surprising the people who "suddenly" announced their plan to migrate.

23. While the trajectory I present from unsatisfied citizen-consumer to migrant is my own, there are related discussions in the literature. Most notable are B. Roberts's (1991, 1994) considerations of "survival strategies" (living frugally, meeting individual needs, earning off-the-books, and adhering to patterns of the local community), versus "social mobility strategies," which are larger in scope (such as ensuring education of one's children or regional or international migration), and which reflect the usual paths to success in the larger society.

24. It is a common practice to attempt to migrate to one country legally through a work contract (particularly to a Latin American country where it is less complicated to obtain such a contract), and then shortly thereafter make one's way to the United States as a final destination.

25. Futurelessness (*sin futuro*) is a common theme or justification in talking about migration from Cuba, and is sometimes a harbinger for the announcement of a move. As Felina put it:

Yo deseo irme de este país. No hay nada, y esto no me gusta. De verdad. Yo, en el futuro—allá, no aquí. Cualquier. Mira: Aquí, para la juventud, no hay ningún futuro. Tú me entiendes? Aquí no hay nada. Nada de nada. No hay nada. Eso es mi sueño, salir. [I'm hoping to get myself out of this country. There is nothing and I don't like it. Really. Me, in the future—I'm over there, not here. Wherever. Look: here, for the youth, there is *no* future. Do you understand me? Here there is nothing. Absolutely nothing. There is nothing. That's my dream, to leave.] (Transcribed from life history interview, 2003, translation by the author.)

26. Lucius Walker is a Baptist minister and activist who founded Pastors for Peace, an NGO that provides humanitarian aid caravans to assist citizens in Latin America who are negatively affected by U.S. foreign policy. His caravans to Cuba, which are called "Friendshipments," are organized as a public challenge to the U.S. government's economic embargo and travel ban against Cuba.

27. Elena has permitted me to reproduce these e-mails with pseudonyms for my research. I have omitted the dates that they were sent to further protect her anonymity.

28. Referring to the court-ordered death penalty carried out against three Cuban men who hijacked a Cuban government yacht in order to migrate to the United States (April 2003).

29. *El bombo* is the Cuban name for the pervasive local alternative to undocumented migration or seeking refugee status. The United States has adopted a lottery system, officially called *el sorteo,* by which Cubans who do not qualify as refugees or immigrants can seek to enter the United States through obtaining a ticket from the U.S. interest section in Havana. (This system, separate from the "international diversity lottery" is unique to Cuba.) It seemed everyone I knew had applied for the *bombo*—everyone on his block had, confirmed David, including his own family. To qualify for a *bombo* ticket, Cubans must be between eighteen and fifty-five years of age and have two of the following three characteristics: (1) completion of higher-level education or secondary education,

(2) three years of work experience, or (3) relatives in the United States. Participants are randomly selected and are "paroled" into the United States (Department of Homeland Security 2006b).

Since the 1994 migration agreement between the United States and Cuba (an attempt to halt an uncontrolled exodus of 30,000 Cuban rafters fleeing to the United States), the United States has conducted three visa lottery open seasons to implement the Special Cuban Migration Program and is willing to take a quota of 20,000 Cubans to the United States annually. The three open seasons were at two-year intervals: fiscal years 1994, 1996, and 1998. The number of qualifying lottery applicants has increased each year, from 189,000 in 1994, to 433,000 in 1996, and to 541,000 in 1998. Cubans qualifying through the 1998 lottery are still being paroled into the United States. Once selected through the lottery, the successful applicants are given parole status with a visa that is valid for six months. The medical examination required of all potential immigrants is good for one year. Spouses and minor children may accompany the successful registrants (U.S. Department of State, Havana Interests Section, 2008). The barriers the Cuban government erects against potential parolees, such as exorbitantly priced medical exams and exit visa fees, and repercussions for family members who remain in Cuba, remain a concern those who have applied for the bombo.

30. Following the March 2003 arrests and summary trials of seventy-five dissidents (in a season of crackdowns, now referred to as the "Black Spring"), speculation arose that George W. Bush's administration would apply new penalties against Cuba. While there was much anticipation of an announcement of new sanctions in the circles in which I was moving, the most feared threat was that of no longer being able to receive remittances directly.

31. *Quedarse* (to stay), in Cuban Spanish, has come to signify leaving Cuba for another country and staying there. For example, "Ella se fue para México, y se quedó" (She left for Mexico, and she stayed), or simply, "se quedó" (glossed as "he/she migrated").

Chapter 8. Freedom Offstage

1. In this chapter, I borrow Hirschman's (1970) terms from his classic "exit, voice, and loyalty" model for analyzing public responses to a state in decline. It is important to note, particularly in reference to the prior chapter on migration, that the presence of an "exit" alternative can also "tend to atrophy the development of the art of voice" (Hirschman 1970: 43).

2. In their analysis of civil society and politics in Africa, Chazan et al. (1992) as filtered by Gledhill (2000: 100) use the phrase "forms of popular protest" to discuss a constellation of phenomena that are also relevant to the Cuban experience. They describe "legal and illegal economic activity beyond the range of state control, job absenteeism and tax evasion," among other activities (Chazan et al. 1992: 207).

> Chazan et al. also argue that such forms of "protest" are largely "coping mechanisms" and express themselves as much through "quiet alienation and passivity" as confrontation. Nevertheless, the authors feel that these activities have the objective consequence of wearing down the African continent's political fabric. States cannot really control such dissidence: it is too disorganized and sporadic to respond to systematic repression. (Gledhill 2000: 100)

The question remains whether such popular protests simply "underscore disintegration" or whether they are powerful enough to spark "a broader process of democratization" (Chazan et. al 1992: 207).

3. While joking about a leader's appearance on TV is certainly an offstage form of resistance, it may still be a litmus for deep-seated discontent with the regime, if not a harbinger of regime change (see Oring 2004).

4. Although the *cuentos* I have enumerated are not jokes per se, some reflect a form of humor, and many of the features that Brandes (1977) and Oring (2004) discuss in relation to jokes hold true for *cuentos* as well and shed light on their meaning.

5. Like an anecdote in English, the Russian *Anekdot*, which can be roughly glossed as "joke," is a humorous story relating an actual personal experience, or a short fictional story or dialogue with a punch line.

6. *Granma* is named after the yacht used to transport Fidel and his comrades of the 26th of July Movement from Mexico (where various revolutionary camps and training centers were located throughout the country) to Cuba in 1956, to begin the process of overthrowing the Batista regime.

7. In this case, a giant rally had been organized to demonstrate against Spain and Italy in front of their consulates. The "spontaneous" protests followed these countries' cancellation of aid and plans for joint projects with Cuba following what was perceived internationally as the Cuban government's summary execution of three Cubans who had attempted to steal a government yacht in order to defect in April 2003.

8. "Authoritative discourse" may be described in the following way: it "coheres around a strict external idea or dogma . . . and occupies a particular position within the discursive regime of the period. . . . [I]t is sharply demarcated from all types of discourse that coexist with it, which means that it does not depend on them . . . all other types of discourse are organized around it, having to refer to it, quote it, praise it, interpret it, apply it, and so forth" (Yurchak 2005: 14–15, citing Bakhtin 1994: 342–43).

9. Though see the discussion of Yoani Sánchez and her "Generación Y" blog in the epilogue.

10. The contrasts between this series of tape-recorded interviews versus the wholly informal chats I usually engaged in highlighted the difference in content and tone of naturally occurring discourse as opposed to that which had the potential circulate to a wider audience.

11. This is the only instance in this book where I use the real name of an interlocutor. Mariela has been receiving increasing press since Fidel's illness. Of note, despite her adherence to socialist and nationalist principles, Mariela is known for being a rebel within her family. For example, she was supportive of Soviet perestroika in the 1980s, and she has an international reputation for being progressive, even radical, because of her leadership in encouraging the acceptance of homosexuality, bisexuality, transvestism, and transsexualism. In 2005, she publicly proposed allowing transgendered people to receive sex reassignment surgery and change their legal gender. Nevertheless, as I illustrate here, she appears quite committed to talking about Cuba and Cubans in a way that is loyal to the Party.

12. Many acts of resistance on this list are also common in other socialist states in transition, as defined by Verdery (2000).

Chapter 9. Conclusion: Citizens, Consumers, and Shadow Publics in Time and Space

1. The important distinction between citizenship-as-legal-status ("full membership in a particular political community") and citizenship-as-desirable-activity ("the extent and quality of one's citizenship is a function of participation in that community") is laid out most clearly in Kymlica and Norman's survey article on citizenship theory (1994: 353) and in Stewart (1995).

2. For an overview of relative deprivation, see Walker and Smith (2002). Here, I use the term in its simplest definition: the experience of being deprived of something to which one thinks one is entitled.

3. For another relevant but somewhat contrasting definition of citizenship, consider that of García Canclini (2001: 20): "social and cultural practices confer a sense of belonging, provide a sense of difference, and enable the satisfaction of the needs of those who possess a language and organize themselves in certain ways."

4. Holston and Appadurai go on to say that "formal membership in the nation-state is increasingly neither a necessary nor sufficient condition for substantive membership" (1996: 190). Furthermore, "procedural liberalism" produces passive citizens who can also slide easily into spectators who vote or citizens whose citizenship is managed by an unelected bureaucracy (p. 193), reflecting the Cuban case.

5. Gough and Wood (2004), frame citizen strategies to ensure well-being in Asia, Latin America, and Africa more benignly, as alternative forms of "welfare delivery" or "informal security regime."

6. Although I must note here that there is no possibility of unsatisfied citizen-consumers constituting a "social movement," particularly if we are to apply Tarrow's solid definition of a social movement as "collective challenges based on common purposes and social solidarities, in sustained interaction with elites, opponents and authorities" (Tarrow 1998: 4).

7. Migration literature has dealt with the phenomenon of relative deprivation, but generally in the framework of "migration motivation" (most notably Stark 1984; Stark and Yitzhaki 1988; Stark and Taylor 1989, 1991; and Massey 1989; Massey et al. 1993) rather than the collective lived experience of citizens or communities who remain in the sending country, as discussed in chapter 7.

8. Again, these types also articulate smoothly with Hirschman's (1970) widely applied "exit, voice, and loyalty" model. In figure 9.1, ideal type diagrams 1 and 2 reflect loyalty; diagram 3, voice; and diagrams 5 and 6, exit through withdrawal and departure, respectively.

9. See Strauss (2006) for an overview of the ways the imaginary has been applied by Castoriadis, Lacan, Anderson, and Taylor, and how the term has come to replace *cultural beliefs*.

10. Therefore, they lack the vital "variegated array of journals, bookstores, film and video distribution networks, lecture series, research centers, academic programs, conferences conventions, festivals or local meeting spaces" mentioned by Fraser in her case example of feminist subaltern counter-publics (Fraser 1992: 85).

11. My term *shadow public* is different from but related to Bruno Latour's concept

of a phantom public, which also addresses the problem of identifying and solidifying multitudes. As Latour (2005: n.p.) explains, "We might be more connected to each other by our worries, our matters of concern, the issues we care for, than by any other set of values, opinions, attitudes or principles."

12. O'Donnell describes "brown areas" as territorially based systems of rule in which mafia-like legal systems mix in complex forms with state legality.

13. De Soto obtained a modest grant and brought in "an obscure American anthropologist" (not mentioned by name) who had written what de Soto thought was the only perceptive thing he had been able to find on Lima's squatters, and who taught de Soto how to "walk a shantytown" (M. Miller 2001).

14. For an extended (and perhaps comparative) discussion of the production of political apathy, silence, and civic disengagement in the United States, see Nina Eliosoph's *Avoiding Politics: How Americans Produce Apathy in Everyday Life* (1998).

15. This trend has ostensibly been demonstrated most notably in Venezuela, Bolivia, and recently Nicaragua, but also in Peru, Argentina, Brazil, Chile, Uruguay, and Ecuador—all of which have elected left-leaning leaders since 2000. What this so-called "pink tide" really means in terms of policy, and moreover, how it plays out for citizens on the ground, remains to be seen, since with the possible exception of Venezuela's Chávez, the other left-leaning leaders are decidedly more open to "market solutions" (with all these entail for the themes discussed here) than their 1970s counterparts were.

16. The term *Ostalgie,* a German play on words combining *east* and *nostalgia,* captures this revivalist trend.

17. For scholarly works that address the politics of nostalgia in various levels of depth, see Boym (2002), particularly her section on Moscow and St. Petersburg; Scribner (2003) on political implications of post-socialist literature and art; Eckman and Linde (2005) on opinion polls and actual desire to return to communist rule in Eastern and Central Europe; and Pickering and Keightley (2006) for a general appraisal of the concept and modalities of nostalgia.

18. *Da vueltas* means literally "turns" or "goes in circles" and the phrase *la vida da tantas vueltas* implies that "life is a lottery" and full of surprises. The quotation is transcribed from a life-history interview, Havana, June 2003.

Epilogue

1. There is continued debate regarding whether Ávila was arrested or detained. Though the video clip was never aired on Cuban TV, the Cuban media felt the need to respond, assuming it had been viewed by many Cubans, and within a month, interviews with Ávila were conducted in which he attempted to clear his name by declaring himself revolutionary and the victim of media manipulation.

2. Despite the drain on staff, the doctor-patient ratio has remained significantly higher in Cuba than in the market-driven, democratic OECD (Organization for Economic Cooperation and Development) member countries, and the broad distribution of Cuba's medical staff around the island contributes to relatively equitable treatment.

Literature Cited

Abu-Lughod, Lila. 1986. *Veiled Sentiments: Honor and Poetry in a Bedouin Society*. Berkeley: University of California Press.
———. 1990. "The Romance of Resistance: Tracing Transformations of Power through Bedouin Women." *American Ethnologist* 17(1): 41–55.
Acheson, James. 1972. "Limited Good or Limited Goods?: Response to Economic Opportunity in a Tarascan Pueblo." *American Anthropologist* 72(11): 52–69.
Acosta, Nelson. 2006. "Vintage US Cars Keep Chugging in Cuba but Face Threat." Reuters.com, May 12. Electronic document, http://today.reuters.com/News/newsArticle.aspx?type=hinDepthNews&storyID=2006 (accessed December 14, 2006).
Agha, Asif. 2000. "Register." *Journal of Linguistic Anthropology* 9(1–2): 216–19.
Aguirre, Benigno E. 1976. "The Differential Migration of Cuban Social Classes." *Latin American Research Review* 11: 103–24.
Al-Ali, Nadje S., and Khalid Koser. 2001. *New Approaches to Migration: Transnational Communities and the Transformation of Home (Transnationalism)*. London: Routledge.
Alarcón de Quesada, Ricardo. 2000. *Cuba y la lucha por la democracia*. Havana: Editorial por las Ciencias Sociales.
Albright, Madeleine, and Vaclav Havel. 2006. "Cuba: Human Rights à la Havana." InternationalHeraldTribune.com., July 20. Electronic document, www.iht.com/articles/2006/07/20/opinion/edallbright.php (accessed December 14, 2006).
Alicia en el pueblo de las maravillas. 1991. Rolando Díaz Torrez, dir. 93 min. Havana: Instituto Cubano de Arte e Industria Cinematografía.
Alvarez, José. 2004. *Cuba's Agricultural Sector*. Gainesville: University Press of Florida.
Alvarez, Sonia E., Evelina Dagnino, and Arturo Escobar, eds. 1998. *Cultures of Politics, Politics of Cultures: Re-Visioning Latin American Social Movements*. Boulder, Colo.: Westview Press.
Alvarez, Sonia E., and Arturo Escobar. 1992. *The Making of Social Movements in Latin America: Identity, Strategy, and Democracy*. Boulder, Colo.: Westview Press.
Amaro, Nelson, and Alejandro Portes. 1972. "Una sociología del exilio: situación de los grupos cubanos en los Estados Unidos." *Aportes* 23: 6–24.
Andrews, Geoff. 1991. *Citizenship*. London: Lawrence and Wishart.
Appadurai, Arjun, ed. 1986. *The Social Life of Things: Commodities in Cultural Perspective*. Cambridge: Cambridge University Press.

———. 1990. "Disjuncture and Difference in the Global Cultural Economy." *Public Culture* 2(2): 1–24.

———. 1996. *Modernity at Large: Cultural Dimensions of Globalization.* Minneapolis: University of Minnesota Press.

Arce M., Daniel G. 1999. "The Political Economy of the Neoliberal Transition." *Latin American Research Review* 34(1): 212–20.

Ariens, Ilva, and Ruud Strijp. 1989. *Anthropological Couples.* Theme Issue, *Focaal* 10.

Arrington, Vanessa. 2005. "Latest Cuba Census Reports 11.2M Residents." Cubanet.org, November 14. Electronic document, www.cubanet.org/CNews/y05/nov05/14e8.htm (accessed February 18, 2007).

Aschkenas, Lea. 2006. *Es Cuba: Life and Love on an Illegal Island.* Emeryville, Calif.: Seal Press.

Åslund, Anders. 1992. *Post-Communist Economic Revolutions: How Big a Bang?* New York: HarperCollins.

August, Arnold. 1999. *Democracy in Cuba and 1997–1998 Elections.* Havana: Editorial José Martí.

Austin, John L. 1962. *How to Do Things with Words: The William James Lectures Delivered at Harvard University in 1955.* J. O. Urmson, ed. Oxford: Clarendon.

Azicri, Max. 2000. *Cuba Today and Tomorrow: Reinventing Socialism.* Gainesville: University Press of Florida.

Azicri, Max, and Elsie Deal, eds. 2004. *Cuban Socialism in a New Century: Adversity, Survival, and Renewal.* Gainesville: University Press of Florida.

Bach, Robert L., Jennifer B. Bach, and Timothy Triplett. 1981–82. "The Flotilla 'Entrants': Latest and Most Controversial." *Cuban Studies* 11–12: 29–48.

Barbalet, J. M. 1988. *Citizenship: Rights, Struggle, and Class Inequality.* Minneapolis: University of Minnesota Press.

Barbassa, Juliana. 2005. "The New Cuban Capitalist." In *God, Capitalism and a Good Cigar,* Lydia Chávez, ed., pp. 17–30. Durham: Duke University Press.

Barber, Karin, and Christopher Waterman 1995. "Traversing the Global and the Local: Fuji Music and Praise Poetry in the Production of Contemporary Yoruba Popular Culture." In *Worlds Apart: Modernity through the Prism of the Local,* Daniel Miller, ed., pp. 240–63. London: Routledge.

Barberia, Lorena. 2002. "Remittances to Cuba: An Evaluation of Cuban and US Government Policy Measures." Rosemary Rogers Working Paper Series no. 15. Cambridge, Mass.: Massachusetts Institute of Technology. Electronic document, http://web.mit.edu/cis/www/migration/pubs/rrwp/15_remittances.doc (accessed October 9, 2008).

Barker, Adele Marie, ed. 1999. *Consuming Russia: Popular Culture, Sex, and Society since Gorbachev.* Durham, N.C.: Duke University Press.

Basch, Linda, Nina Glick Schiller, and Christina Szanton Blanc. 1994. *Nations Unbound: Transnational Projects, Global Predicaments and Deterritorialized Nation-States.* New York: Gordon and Breach.

Bell, Catherine. 1992. *Ritual Theory, Ritual Practice.* Oxford: Oxford University Press.

Bell, Dianne, Pat Caplan, and Wazir Jahn Karim. 1993. *Gendered Fields: Women, Men, and Ethnography.* London: Routledge.

Ben-Amos. Dan. 2000. Metaphor. *Journal of Linguistic Anthropology* 9(1–2): 152–54.

Berger, Peter L. 1997. "Four Faces of Global Culture." *Natural Interest* (49): 23–29.

Berlinski, Claire. 2006. *Menace in Europe: Why the Continent's Crisis Is America's, Too.* New York: Crown Forum.

Bernard, H. Russell. 2000. *Social Research Methods: Qualitative and Quantitative Approaches.* Thousand Oaks, Calif.: Sage Publications.

Berreman, Gerald D. 1962. *Behind Many Masks: Ethnography and Impression Management in a Himalayan Village.* Ithaca, N.Y.: Society for Applied Anthropology.

Betancourt, Roger R. 1996. "Growth Capabilities and Development: Implications for Transitions in Cuba." *Economic Development and Cultural Change* 44(2): 315–31.

Bethell, Leslie. 1993. *Cuba: A Short History.* Cambridge: Cambridge University Press.

Bhabha, Homi K. 1994. *The Location of Culture.* London: Routledge

———. 2001. "Locations of Culture: The Postcolonial and the Postmodern." In *Postmodern Debates,* Simon Malpas, ed., pp. 136–44. New York: Palgrave.

Blue, Sara A. 2007. "The Erosion of Racial Equality in the Context of Cuba's Dual Economy." *Latin American Politics and Society* 49(3): 35–68

Böröcz, Jozsef. 2000. "Informality Rules." *East European Politics and Society* 14(2): 348–80.

Boudy Sánchez, José. 1999. *Diccionario mayor de cubanismos.* Miami, Fla.: Ediciones Universales.

Bourdieu, Pierre. 1984. *Distinction: A Social Critique on the Judgment of Taste.* Cambridge, Mass.: Harvard University Press.

Boyer, Dominic. 2005. *Spirit and System: Media, Intellectuals, and the Dialectic in Modern German Culture.* Chicago: University of Chicago Press.

Boym, Svetlana. 2002. *The Future of Nostalgia.* New York: Basic Books.

Brandes, Stanley. 1977. "Peaceful Protest: Spanish Political Humor in a Time of Crisis." *Western Folklore* 36(4): 331–46.

Britannica Online Encyclopedia. 2006. "Citizenship." Electronic document, www.britannica.com (accessed November 13, 2006).

Broad, David, and Wayne Antony. 1999. *Citizens or Consumers?: Social Policy in a Market Society.* Halifax, Nova Scotia: Fernwood Publishing.

Brotherton, P. Sean. 2005. "Macroeconomic Change and the Biopolitics of Health in Cuba's Special Period." *Journal of Latin American Anthropology* 10(2): 339–69.

Brown, Matthew Hay. 2006. "Cuba: The Immigration Exception." Baltimoresun.com, May 21. Electronic document, www.baltimoresun.com/news/nationworld/balid.cuba21may21,0,5063695.story (accessed February 18, 2006).

Burchell, Graham, Colin Gordon, and Peter Miller, eds. 1991. *The Foucault Effect: Studies in Governmentality.* Chicago: University of Chicago Press.

Bureau of Democracy, Human Rights, and Labor. 2006. "Cuba: Country Reports on Human Rights Practices, 2006." Electronic document, www.cubanet.org/ref/dis/011906_e.htm (accessed March 17, 2007).

Butler, Barbara, and Diane Michalski Turner, eds. 1987. *Children and Anthropological Research.* New York: Plenum Press.

Cabrera Infante, Guillermo. 1992. *Mea Cuba.* Madrid: Alfaguara.

Cairncross, Liz, Robina Goodlad, and David Clapham. 1996. "Consumers or Citizens?" In *Housing Management, Consumers and Citizens*, Liz Cairncross, Robina Goodlad, and David Clapham, eds., pp. 26–50. London: Taylor and Francis.

Calhoun, Craig. 1994. *Habermas and the Public Sphere*. Cambridge, Mass.: MIT Press.

Carr, Stephen, Mark Francis, Leanne Rivlin, and Andrew Stone. 1992. *Public Space*. New York: Cambridge University Press.

Cassell, Joan, ed. 1987. *Children in the Field: Anthropological Experiences*. Philadelphia: Temple University Press.

Castells, Manuel. 1983. *The City and the Grassroots: A Cross-Cultural Theory of Urban Social Movements*. Berkeley: University of California Press.

CBS Broadcasting, Inc. 2006. "U.S. Companies Flock to Cuba: 37 U.S. States Export Food to Cuba, More Than Any Other Country." CBSNews.com, September 24. Electronic document, www.cbsnews.com/stories/2006/09/24/eveningnews/main2036729.shtml (accessed February, 18, 2007).

CEPAL [Comisión Económica para América Latina y el Caribe]. 1999. "Cuba: Evolución económica durante 1998." LC/MEX/L.392.

———. 2002. "Cuba: Evolución económica durante 2001." LC/MEX/L.525.

———. 2004. "Cuba: Evolución económica durante 2003 y Perspectivas para 2004." LC/MEX/L.622.

Chávez, Lydia. 2005. *Capitalism, God, and a Good Cigar: Cuba Enters the Twenty-First Century*. Durham, N.C.: Duke University Press.

Chazan, Naomi, Robert Mortimer, John Ravenhill, and Donald Rothchild. 1992. *Politics and Society in Contemporary Africa*. 2nd ed. Boulder, Colo.: Lynne Rienner Publishers.

Chiang, Lynnette. 2004. *The Handsomest Man in Cuba: An Escapade*. Sydney: Bantam.

Chomsky, Aviva, Barry Carr, and Pamela María Smorkaloff. 2003. *The Cuba Reader: History, Culture, Politics*. Durham, N.C.: Duke University Press.

Clark, Juan M. 1975. "The Exodus from Revolutionary Cuba (1959–1974): A Sociological Analysis." Ph.D. diss., Department of Sociology, University of Florida.

Clark, Mary A. 2005. *Where Men Are Wives and Mothers Rule: Santería Ritual Practices and their Gender Implications*. Gainesville: University Press of Florida

Cochran, Robert. 1989. "'What Courage!' Romanian 'Our Leader' Jokes. *Journal of American Folklore* 102(405): 259–74.

Codrescu, Andrei. 1999. *Ay, Cuba!: A Socio-Erotic Journey as Heard on NPR*. New York: Picador USA.

Cohen, Jeffrey. 2004. *The Culture of Migration in Southern Mexico*. Austin: University of Texas Press.

Cohen, Lizabeth. 2003. *A Consumer's Republic: The Politics of Mass Consumption in Postwar America*. New York: Knopf.

Colburn, Forrest D. 2002. *Latin America at the End of Politics*. Princeton: Princeton University Press.

Cole, Kenneth. 1998. *Cuba: From Revolution to Development*. London: Pinter.

Collins, Randall. 2004. *Interaction Ritual Chains*. Princeton, N.J.: Princeton University Press.

Collins, Sheila D. 2005. "Breaking the Mold? Venezuela's Defiance of the Neoliberal Agenda." *New Political Science* 27(3): 367–95.

Comaroff, Jean, and John L. Comaroff, eds. 2001. "First Thoughts on a Second Coming." In *Millennial Capitalism and the Culture of Neoliberalism*, Jean Comaroff and John L. Comaroff, eds., pp. 1–56. Durham, N.C.: Duke University Press.

Comaroff, John L., and Jean Comaroff. 1999. "Alien-Nation: Zombies, Immigrants and Millennial Capitalism." *CODESRIA Bulletin* 3–4: 17–26.

Corbett, Ben. 2002. *This Is Cuba: An Outlaw Culture Survives*. Cambridge, Mass.: West-view Press.

Coté, John. 2005. "Cubans Log on behind Castro's Back." In *Capitalism, God, and a Good Cigar: Cuba Enters the Twenty-First Century*, Lydia Chávez, ed., pp. 160–76. Durham: Duke University Press.

Coyula, Mario, and Jill Hamberg. 2003. "Urban Slums Reports: The Case of Havana, Cuba." *Capitalism Nature Socialism* 16(13): 7–25.

Crabb, Mary Katherine. 2001. "Socialism, Health, and Medicine in Cuba: A Critical Re-appraisal." Ph.D. diss., Department of Anthropology, Emory University, Atlanta, Ga.

Cruikshank, Barbara. 1999. *The Will to Empower: Democratic Citizens and Other Subjects*. Ithaca, N.Y.: Cornell University Press.

Csordas, Thomas J. 1990. "Embodiment as a Paradigm for Anthropology." *Ethos* 18(1): 5–47.

"Cuba Inches into the Internet Age." 2006. LATimes.com, November 19. Electronic document, www.latimes.com/technology/lafgcubanet19nov19,1,2828501.story?ctrack =1&cset=true (accessed February 18, 2007).

Cuban Ministry of Public Health. 2005. *Statistical Yearbook of the Cuban Ministry of Public Health*. Havana: Statistical Registers of the Central Medical Cooperation Units.

Cubanet. 1998. "Catholic Press in Cuba." Electronic document, www.cubanet.org/CNews/ y98/nov98/19e3.htm (accessed February 18, 2007).

Cupples, Julie, and Sara Kindon. 2003. "Far from Being 'Home Alone': The Dynamics of Accompanied Fieldwork." *Singapore Journal of Tropical Geography* 24(2): 211–28.

Daniels, Yvonne. 1995. *Rumba: Dance and Social Change in Contemporary Cuba*. Bloomington: Indiana University Press.

De Certeau, Michel. 1984. *The Practice of Everyday Life*. Berkeley: University of California Press.

De Jong, Gordon F., and James T. Fawcett. 1989. "Migration and Motivation: The Migrant's Perspective." *International Migration Review* 23(1): 96–102.

De la Fuente, Alejandro. 1998. "Recreating Racism: Race and Discrimination in Cuba's 'Special Period.'" Cuba Briefing Paper Series. Washington, D.C.: Caribbean Project, Center for Latin American Studies, Georgetown University.

———. 2000. "Race, Ideology and Culture in Cuba." *Latin American Research Review* 35(3): 199–210.

———. 2001. *A Nation for All: Race, Inequality and Politics in Twentieth-Century Cuba*. Chapel Hill: University of North Carolina Press.

De Soto, Hernando. 2000. *The Mystery of Capital: Why Capitalism Triumphs in the West and Fails Everywhere Else*. New York: Basic Books.

———. 2002. *The Other Path: The Economic Answer to Terrorism*. New York: Basic Books.

———. 2004. "Bringing Capitalism to the Masses." *Cato's Letter* 2(3).

Department of Homeland Security. 2006a. "U.S. Coast Guard Alien Migration Interdiction." Electronic document, www.uscg.mil/hq/g-o/g-opl/amio/AMIO.htm (accessed December 13, 2006).

———. 2006b. "USCIS Will Further Strengthen Measures That Support the Reunification of Families Separated by the Castro Regime." Electronic document, www.dhs.gov/xnews/releases/pr_1158350356206.shtm (accessed February 19, 2007).

Di Leonardo, Micaela. 1998. *Exotics at Home: Anthropologies, Others, and American Modernity*. Chicago: University of Chicago Press.

Díaz-Briquets, Sergio. 1983. "Demographic and Related Determinants of Recent Cuban Emigration." *International Migration Review* 17(1): 95–119.

Díaz-Briquets, Sergio, and Jorge Pérez-López. 2006. *Corruption in Cuba: Castro and Beyond*. Austin: University of Texas Press.

Dilla, Haroldo. 2003. Civil Society. In *The Cuba Reader: History, Culture, Politics*. Aviva Chomsky, Barry Carr, and Pamela Maria Smorkaloff, eds., pp. 650–60. Durham, N.C.: Duke University Press.

Dolores, María. 2003. "El entierro." *Cubanews de Costa Rica* 2(11): 11.

Domínguez, Jorge I. 1989. *To Make a World Safe for Revolution*. Cambridge, Mass.: Harvard University Press.

———. 1993. "Cuba since 1959." In *Cuba: A Short History*, Leslie Bethell, ed., pp. 95–149. Cambridge: Cambridge University Press.

Douglas, Mary, and Baron Isherwood. 1996. *The World of Goods: Towards an Anthropology of Consumption*. 2nd ed. New York: Routledge.

Dunn, Elizabeth C. 2004. *Privatizing Poland: Baby Food, Big Business, and the Remaking of Labor*. Ithaca, N.Y.: Cornell University Press.

Eckman, Joakim, and Jonas Linde. 2005. "Communist Nostalgia and the Consolidation of Democracy in Central and Eastern Europe." *Journal of Communist Studies and Transition Politics* 21(3): 354–74.

Eckstein, Susan Eva. 1994. *Back from the Future: Cuba under Castro*. Princeton, N.J.: Princeton University Press.

———. 1995. "Responses to Edelstein." *Latin American Perspectives* 22(4): 27–38.

Edelman, Marc. 1999. *Peasants against Globalization: Rural Social Movements in Costa Rica*. Stanford, Calif.: Stanford University Press.

Edin, Kathryn, and Laura Lein. 1997. *Making Ends Meet: How Single Mothers Survive Welfare and Low-Wage Work*. New York: Russell Sage Foundation.

Eliosoph, Nina. 1998. *Avoiding Politics: How Americans Produce Apathy in Everyday Life*. Cambridge: Cambridge University Press.

Emerson, Robert M., Rachel I. Fretz, and Linda L. Shaw. 1995. *Writing Ethnographic Fieldnotes*. Chicago: University of Chicago Press.

Erickson, Ken, and Donald Stull. 1998. *Doing Team Ethnography: Warnings and Advice*.

Qualitative Research Methods Series No. 42. Thousand Oaks, Calif.: Sage Publications.

Erisman, H. Michael. 2000. *Cuba's Foreign Relations in a Post-Soviet World.* Gainesville: University Press of Florida.

Erisman, H. Michael, and John M. Kirk. 2006. *Redefining Cuban Foreign Policy: The Impact of the Special Period.* Gainesville: University Press of Florida.

Erjavek, Ales, ed. 2003. *Postmodernism and the Postsocialist Condition: Politicized Art under Late Socialism.* Berkeley: University of California Press.

Ernst & Young. 2006. "A Business Guide to Cuba: A Presentation by Ernst & Young Caribbean Services, Ltd." Electronic document, www.ishav.org/2006%20-%20Ernst%20 &%20Young%20-%20A%20Business%20Guide%20to%20Cuba.pdf (accessed February 20, 2007).

Espina Prieto, Rodrigo, and Pablo Rodríguez Ruiz. 2006. "Raza y desigualdad en la Cuba actual." *Temas* 45: 44–54.

Espino, María Dolores. 2000. "Cuban Tourism during the Special Period." *Cuba in Transition* 10: 360–73.

Falcoff, Mark. 2003. *Cuba the Morning After: Confronting Castro's Legacy.* Washington, D.C.: AEI Press.

FAS/USDA, Office of Global Analysis. 2008. "Cuba's Food and Agriculture Situation Report," March 2008. Electronic document, www.fas.usda.gov/itp/cuba/CubaSituation0308.pdf (accessed December 9, 2008).

Feinsilver, Julie M. 1993. *Healing the Masses: Cuban Health Politics at Home and Abroad.* Berkeley: University of California Press.

———. 2006. "Cuban Medical Diplomacy: When the Left Has Got It Right." Council on Hemispheric Affairs website, November 1. Electronic document, www.coha. org/2006/10/30/cuban-medical-diplomacy-when-the-left-has-got-it-right (accessed February 19, 2007).

———. 2008. "Oil-for-Doctors: Cuban Medical Diplomacy Gets a Little Help from a Venezuelan Friend." *Nueva Sociedad* 216. Electronic document, www.nuso.org/upload/articulos/3537_2.pdf (accessed December 11, 2008).

Fernandes, Sujatha. 2006. *Cuba Represent!: Cuban Arts, State Power, and the Making of New Revolutionary Cultures.* Durham, N.C.: Duke University Press.

Fernández, Damián J. 1992. "Opening the Blackest of Black Boxes: Theory and Practice of Decision-Making in Cuba's Foreign Policy." *Cuban Studies* 22: 53–78.

———. 2000. *Cuba and the Politics of Passion.* Austin: University of Texas Press.

———, ed. 2005. *Cuba Transnational.* Gainesville: University Press of Florida.

Fernández, Nadine. 1996. "The Color of Love: Young Interracial Couples in Cuba." *Latin American Perspectives* 23(1): 99–117.

———. 2001. "The Changing Discourse on Race in Contemporary Cuba." *Qualitative Studies in Education* 14(2): 117–32.

Fischer, Edward F., and Peter Benson. 2006. *Broccoli and Desire: Global Connections and Maya Struggles in Postwar Guatemala.* Stanford, Calif.: Stanford University Press.

Flinn, Juliana, Leslie Marshall, and Jocelyn Armstrong, eds. 1998. *Fieldwork and Families:*

Constructing New Models for Ethnographic Research. Honolulu: University of Hawaii Press.

Foster, George. 1965. "Peasant Society and the Image of Limited Good." *American Anthropologist* 67(2): 293–315.

Foster, Robert J. 1991. "Making National Cultures in the Global Ecumene." *Annual Review of Anthropology* 20: 235–60.

Foucault, Michel. 1991. "Governmentality." In *The Foucault Effect: Studies in Governmentality*, Peter Miller, Colin Gordon, and Graham Burchell, eds., pp. 87–104. Chicago: University of Chicago Press.

Fraser, Nancy. 1992. "Rethinking the Public Sphere: A Contribution to the Critique of Actually Existing Democracy." In *Habermas and the Public Sphere*, Craig Calhoun, ed., pp. 109–42. Cambridge, Mass.: MIT Press.

Frederick, Laurie Aleen. 2005. "Cuba's National Characters: Setting the Stage for the *Hombre Novísimo*." *Journal of Latin American Anthropology* 10(2): 401–37.

Freeman, Gary P. 1986. "Migration and the Political Economy of the Welfare State." *Annals of the American Academy of Political and Social Science* 485 (1): 51–63.

Fresa y Chocolate. 1994. Tomás Gutiérrez Alea and Juan Carlos Tabio, dirs. 108 min. Havana: Instituto Cubano del Arte e Industria Cinematográficos.

Gabriel, Yiannis, and Tim Lang. 1995. "Consumer as Citizen." In *The Unmanageable Consumer: Contemporary Consumption and Its Fragmentation*, pp. 187–91. London: Sage Publications.

Gaidar, Y. 1990. *Ekonomicheskie Reformi i Ierarchicheskie Struktury*. Moscow, Russia: Nauka.

Gal, Susan. 2002. "A Semiotics of the Public/Private Distinction." *Differences* 13(1): 77–95.

———. 2005. "Language Ideologies Compared: Metaphors of Public/Private." *Journal of Linguistic Anthropology* 15(1): 23–37.

Gal, Susan, and Gail Kligman. 2000. *The Politics of Gender after Socialism*. Princeton, N.J.: Princeton University Press.

García, María Elena. 2005. *Making Indigenous Citizens: Identities, Education, and Multicultural Development in Peru*. Stanford, Calif.: Stanford University Press.

García Canclini, Néstor. 1995. *Hybrid Cultures: Strategies for Entering and Leaving Modernity*. Minneapolis: University of Minnesota Press.

———. 2001. *Consumers and Citizens: Globalization and Multicultural Conflicts*. Minneapolis: University of Minnesota Press.

Garon, Sheldon, and Patricia L. Maclachlan, eds. 2006. *The Ambivalent Consumer: Questioning Consumption in East Asia and the West*. Ithaca, N.Y.: Cornell University Press.

Garrido, José Luis, Enrique Ferrer, Dayan Abad, and Equis Alfonso. 2005. "Habaneando." From *Habana Blues* (soundtrack). New York: WEA International.

Geertz, Clifford. 1973. *The Interpretation of Cultures*. New York: Basic Books.

———. 1983. "'From the Native's Point of View': On the Nature of Anthropological Understanding." In *Local Knowledge: Further Essays in Interpretive Anthropology*, pp. 55–70. New York: Basic Books.

George, Kenneth M. 1993. "Lyric, History, and Allegory, or the End of Headhunting Ritual in Upland Sulawesi." *American Ethnologist* 20(4): 696–716.

Giddens, Anthony. 1984. *The Constitution of Society: Outline of the Theory of Structuration.* Cambridge: Polity Press.

Giese, Joan L., and Joseph A. Cote. 2000. "Defining Consumer Satisfaction." *Academy of Marketing Science Review.* Electronic document, www.amsreview.org/amsrev/theory/giese01-00.html (accessed February 19, 2007).

Gilmore, Sheila Seiler. 1998. "Both Ways through the Looking Glass: The Accompanied Ethnographer as Repositioned Other." In *Fieldwork and Families: Constructing New Methods for Ethnographic Fieldwork,* Juliana Flinn, Leslie Marshall, and Jocelyn Armstrong, eds., pp. 35–44. Honolulu: University of Hawaii Press.

Glaser, Barney G., and Anselm L. Strauss. 1967. *The Discovery of Grounded Theory: Strategies for Qualitative Research.* Chicago: Aldine.

Gledhill, John. 2000. *Power and Its Disguises: Anthropological Perspectives on Politics.* London: Pluto Press.

Goffman, Erving. 1974. *Frame Analysis.* New York: Harper and Row.

Golde, Peggy E. 1986. *Women in the Field: Anthropological Experiences.* 2nd ed. Berkeley: University of California Press.

Goldstein, Daniel M. 2002. "*Desconfianza* and the Problems of Representation in Urban Ethnography." *Anthropological Quarterly* 75(3): 485–517.

Gomez, Alan. 2006. "More Cubans Take Trip to USA Using Alternate Routes." USA Today.com, November 16. Electronic document, www.usatoday.com/news/world/2006-11-15-cuban-refugees_x.htm (accessed February 19, 2007).

Gonzalez, Edward, and Kevin F. McCarthy. 2004. *Cuba after Castro: Legacies, Challenges, and Impediments.* Santa Monica, Calif.: RAND Corporation. Electronic document, www.rand.org/pubs/monographs/2004/RAND_MG111.pdf (accessed October 8, 2008).

González Febles, Juan. 2006. "Susurro urbano." Cubanet.org. August 3, 2006. Electronic document, www.cubanet.org/CNews/y06/ago06/03a5.htm (accessed December 8, 2008).

Good, Byron J. 1994. *Medicine, Rationality, and Experience: An Anthropological Perspective.* Cambridge: Cambridge University Press.

Good, Byron J., and Mary-Jo DelVecchio Good. 1980. "The Meaning of Symptoms: A Cultural Hermeneutic Model for Clinical Practice." In *The Relevance of Social Science for Medicine,* Leon Eisenberg and Arthur Kleinman, eds., 165–96. Dordrecht, The Netherlands: D. Reidel Publishing.

Goodenough, Ruth Gallagher. 1998. "Fieldwork and Family: Perspectives over Time." In *Fieldwork and Families: Constructing New Methods for Ethnographic Fieldwork,* Juliana Flinn, Leslie Marshall, and Jocelyn Armstrong, eds., pp. 22–34. Honolulu: University of Hawaii Press.

Gordy, Katherine. 2006. "'Sales + Economy + Efficiency = Revolution?' Dollarization, Consumer Capitalism and Popular Response in Special Period Cuba." *Public Culture* 18(2): 383–412.

Gough, Ian, and Geof Wood, eds. 2004. *Insecurity and Welfare Regimes in Asia, Africa, and Latin America: Social Policy in Development Contexts.* Cambridge: Cambridge University Press.

Grant, Bruce. 1995. *In the Soviet House of Culture: A Century of Perestroikas.* Stanford, Calif.: Stanford University Press.

Gray, Alexander I., and Antoni Kapcia. 2008. *The Changing Dynamic of Cuban Civil Society.* Gainesville: University Press of Florida.

Greenberg, Jessica. 2006. " Noć Reklamoždera: Democracy, Consumption, and the Contradictions of Representation in Post-Socialist Serbia." *PoLAR: Political and Legal Anthropology Review* 29(2): 181–207.

Gutmann, Matthew C. 2002. *The Romance of Democracy: Compliant Defiance in Contemporary Mexico.* Berkeley: University of California Press.

Habana Blues. 2005. Benito Zembrano, dir. 110 min. Havana: Instituto Cubano del Arte e Industria Cinematográficos.

Habermas, Jürgen. 1974. "The Public Sphere: An Encyclopedia Article." *New German Critique* 3: 49–55.

———. 1984. *The Theory of Communicative Action.* Vol. 1, *Reason And the Rationalization of Society.* Trans. T. McCarthy. Boston: Beacon Press.

———.1987a. *The Philosophical Discourse of Modernity: Twelve Lectures.* Trans. F. Lawrence. Oxford: Basil Blackwell.

———. 1987b. *The Theory of Communicative Action.* Vol. 2, *Lifeworld and System: A Critique of Functionalist Reasoning.* Trans. T. McCarthy. Boston: Beacon Press.

———. 1989. *The Structural Transformation of the Public Sphere: An Inquiry into a Category of Bourgeois Society.* Trans. F Lawrence. Cambridge, Mass.: MIT Press.

Haddad, Angela T. 2003. "Critical Reflexivity, Contradictions and Modern Cuban Consciousness." *Acta Sociologica* 46(1): 51–68.

Hagedorn, Katherine J. 2001. *Divine Utterances: The Performance of Afro-Cuban Santeria.* Washington, D.C.: Smithsonian Institution Press.

Halliday, M.A.K. 1964. "Comparison and Translation." In *The Linguistic Sciences and Language Teaching,* M.A.K. Halliday, Angus McIntosh and Peter Strevens, eds. London: Longman.

———. 1978. *Language as Social Semiotic: The Social Interpretation of Language and Meaning.* London: Edward Arnold.

Hann, C. M., ed. 2002. *Postsocialism: Ideals, Ideologies and Practices in Eurasia.* New York: Routledge.

Hannerz, Ulf. 1989. "Notes on the Global Ecumene." *Public Culture* 1(2): 66–75

Havana Journal. 2008. "Sticky Chronological List of President Raúl Castro's Reform Initiatives—updated June 11." March 11. Electronic document, http://havanajournal.com/politics/entry/chronological-list-of-president-raul-castros-reform-initiatives/#14723 (accessed July 8, 2008).

Havel, Vaclav, and John Keene eds. 1986. *The Power of the Powerless: Citizens against the State in Central-Eastern Europe.* Armonk, N.Y.: M. E. Sharpe.

Heater, Derek. 1990. *Citizenship: The Civic Ideal in World History, Politics, and Education.* London: Longman.

Henken, Ted. 2002a. "Condemned to Informality: Cuba's Experiments with Self-Employment during the Special Period." Ph.D. diss,, Department of Sociology, Tulane University, New Orleans, La.

——. 2002b. "*Vale Todo* (Anything Goes): Cuba's *Paladares.*" *Cuba in Transition* 12: 344–53.

——. 2004. "Between Ideology and Pragmatism: The Revolution and the Private Sector before the Special Period, 1959–1990." *Cuba in Transition* 14: 212–23.

——. 2005. "*Balseros, Boteros,* and *El Bombo*: Post-1994 Cuban Immigration to the United States and the Persistence of Special Treatment." *Latino Studies* 3: 393–416.

Hernández, Rafael. 2003. *Looking at Cuba: Essays on Culture and Civil Society.* Dick Cluster, trans. Gainesville: University Press of Florida.

Hernández Díaz, Alejandro. 1998. *La Milla.* Trans. Dick Cluster. Pittsburgh, Pa.: Latin American Literary Review Press.

Hernandez-Reguant, Ariana. 2004. "Copyrighting Ché: Art and Authorship under Cuban Late Socialism." *Public Culture* 16(1): 1–29.

——. 2005. "Cuba's Alternative Geographies." *Journal of Latin American Anthropology* 10(2): 275–313.

——. 2006. "Havana's *Timba*: A Macho Sound for Black Sex." In *Globalization and Race: Transformations in the Cultural Production of Blackness,* Kamari Clarke and Deborah A. Thomas, eds., pp. 249–78. Durham, N.C.: Duke University Press.

—— ed. 2009. Cuba in the Special Period: Culture and Ideology in the 1990s. New York: Palgrave MacMillan.

Hill, Jane. 2001. "Mock Spanish, Covert Racisms, and the (Leaky) Boundary between Public and Private Spheres." In *Languages and Publics: The Making of Authority*, Susan Gal and Kathryn Woolard, eds., pp. 83–102. Manchester, UK: St. Jerome's Press.

Hill, Matthew J. 2007. "Reimagining Old Havana: World Heritage and the Production of Scale in Late Socialist Cuba." In *Deciphering the Global: Its Spaces, Scalings, and Subjects*, Saskia Sassen, ed. London: Routledge.

Hirschman, Albert O. 1970. *Exit, Voice, and Loyalty: Responses to Decline in Firms, Organizations, and States.* Cambridge, Mass.: Harvard University Press.

Ho Tai, Hue-Tam, ed. 2001. *The Country of Memory: Remaking the Past in Late Socialist Vietnam.* Berkeley: University of California Press.

Hoffman, Bert. 2004. *The Politics of the Internet in Third World Development: Challenges in Contrasting Regimes with Case Studies of Costa Rica and Cuba.* New York: Routledge.

Holston, James, and Arjun Appadurai. 1996. "Cities and Citizenship." *Public Culture* 8(2): 187–204.

Howes, David. 1996. "Introduction: Commodities and Cultural Borders." In *Cross-Cultural Consumption: Global Markets, Local Realities*, David Howes, ed., pp. 1–18. London: Routledge.

Humphrey, Caroline. 2002. *The Unmaking of Soviet Life: Everyday Economies after Socialism.* Ithaca, N.Y.: Cornell University Press.

Hunt, Christopher. 1998. *Waiting for Fidel.* Boston: Houghton Mifflin.

Hyman, Herbert H. 1960. "Reflections on Reference Groups." *Public Opinion Quarterly* 24(3): 389–96.

————. 1980. *The Psychology of Status*. Manchester, N.H.: Ayer Publishing.

Internet World Stats. 2007. Electronic document, www.internetworldstats.com/car/cu.htm (accessed December 9, 2008).

Kandel, William, and Douglas S. Massey. 2002. "The Culture of Mexican Migration: A Theoretical and Empirical Analysis." *Social Forces* 80(3): 981–1004.

Karanova, Marta. 2003. "Socialist Nostalgia: Fad or Here to Stay?" *Business Hungary* 17(11): 33–35.

Keane, John. 1998. *Civil Society*. Stanford, Calif.: Stanford University Press.

Kearney, Michael. 1986. "From the Invisible Hand to Visible Feet: Anthropological Studies of Migration and Development." *Annual Review of Anthropology* 15: 331–61.

————. 1995. "The Local and the Global: The Anthropology of Globalization and Transnationalism." *Annual Review of Anthropology* 24: 547–65.

Kenny, Lorraine Delia. 2000. *Daughters of Suburbia: Growing Up White, Middle Class, and Female*. New Brunswick, N.J.: Rutgers University Press.

Kharkhordin, Oleg. 1999. *The Collective and the Individual in Russia: A Study of Practices*. Berkeley: University of California Press.

Kildergaard, Ann, and Roberto Orro Fernández. 2000. "Dollarization in Cuba and Implications for the Future Transition." Papers and Proceedings of the 9th Annual Meeting of the Association for the Study of the Cuban Economy (ASCE). *Cuba in Transition* 9: 25–35.

Kirk, John M. 1983. *José Martí: Mentor of the Cuban Nation*. Gainesville: University Presses of Florida.

————. 1989. *Between God and the Party: Religion and Politics in Revolutionary Cuba*. Tampa: University of South Florida Press.

Kirk, John M., and Leonardo Padura Fuentes. 2001. *Culture and the Cuban Revolution*. Gainesville: University Press of Florida.

Kittay, Eva Fedder. 1987. *Metaphor: Its Cognitive Force and Linguistic Structure*. Oxford: Clarendon.

Kittrell, Elizabeth L. 2004. "Defying Theoretical Predictions: The Non-Emergence of Popular Dissidence in Cuba's Post-Soviet Era." Paper presented at the Comparative Politics Graduate Research Seminar, Princeton University, Princeton, N.J., February 27.

Kozol, Jonathan. 1978. *Children of the Revolution: A Yankee Teacher in Cuban Schools*. New York: Delacorte Press.

Kummels, Ingrid. 2005. "Love in the Time of Diaspora: Global Markets and Local Meaning in Prostitution, Marriage, and Womanhood in Cuba." *Iberoamericana* 20: 7–26.

Kurlantzick, Joshua. 2004. "Dictatorship.com: The Web Won't Topple Tyranny." *New Republic* Online, April 10. Electronic document, www.tnr.com/doc.mhtml?pt=oGG%2BvQEIjJRNjHGlOJiX4X%3D%3D (accessed February 20, 2007).

Kutzinski, Vera M. 1993. *Sugar's Secrets: Race and the Erotics of Cuban Nationalism*. Richmond: University of Virginia Press.

Kymlica, Will, and Wayne Norman. 1994. "Return of the Citizen: A Survey of Recent Work on Citizenship Theory." *Ethics* 104(2): 352–81.

Latour, Bruno. 2005. "From Realpolitik to Dingpolitik—or How to Make Things Public." Electronic document, www.bruno-latour.fr/articles/article/96-DINGPOLITIK2. html (accessed February 20, 2007).

La vida es silbar. 1998. Fernando Pérez, dir. 106 min. Havana: Instituto Cubano del Arte e Industria Cinematográficos.

Lacey, Marc. 2008. "Stores Hint at Change under New Castro. NYtimes.com, May 2. Electronic document, www.nytimes.com/2008/05/02/world/americas/02cuba.htm (accessed July 9, 2008).

Lakoff, George, and Mark Johnson. 1980. *Metaphors We Live By.* Chicago: University of Chicago Press.

Lampland, Martha. 1995. *The Object of Labor: Commodification in Socialist Hungary.* Chicago: University of Chicago Press.

Lancaster, Roger N. 1992. *Life Is Hard: Machismo, Danger and the Intimacy of Power in Nicaragua.* Berkeley: University of California Press.

Landau, Saul. 2004. *The Business of America: How Consumers Have Replaced Citizens and How We Can Reverse the Trend.* London: Routledge.

Latell, Brian. 2005. *After Fidel: The Inside Story of Castro's Regime and Cuba's Next Leader.* New York: Palgrave Macmillan.

Laughlin, Charles Jr. 1974. "Deprivation and Reciprocity." *Man* 9(3): 380–96.

Ledeneva, Alena V. 2006. *How Russia Really Works: The Informal Practices That Shaped Post-Soviet Politics and Business.* Ithaca, N.Y.: Cornell University Press.

Lee, Martyn J. 1993. *Consumer Culture Reborn: The Cultural Politics of Consumption.* London: Routledge.

Leiner, Marvin. 1974. *Children Are the Revolution: Day Care in Cuba.* New York: Penguin Press.

Lemon, Alaina. 2000. *Between Two Fires: Gypsy Performance and Romani Memory from Pushkin to Post-Socialism.* Durham, N.C.: Duke University Press.

LeoGrande, William. 2002. *The Cuban Communist Party and Electoral Politics: Adaptation, Succession and Transition.* Miami, Fla.: Cuban Transition Project, University of Miami.

León, Francisco. 1998. "Socialism and Sociolismo: Social Actors and Economic Change in 1990s Cuba." In *Toward a New Cuba?: Legacies of a Revolution,* Miguel Ángel Centeno and Mauricio Font, eds., pp. 39-51. Boulder, Colo.: Lynne Rienner Publishers.

Levinson, Sandra, and Carol Brightman. 1971. *Venceremos Brigade: Young Americans Sharing the Life and Work of Revolutionary Cuba.* New York: Simon and Schuster.

Levinson, Stephen C. 1999. "Maxim." *Journal of Linguistic Anthropology* 9(1–2): 144–47.

Levitt, Peggy. 2001. *Transnational Villagers.* Berkeley: University of California Press.

Lewis, Oscar. 1966. *La Vida.* New York: Knopf.

Lewis, Oscar, Ruth M. Lewis, and Susan M. Rigdon. 1977–78. *Living the Revolution: An Oral History of Contemporary Cuba.* 3 vols. Urbana: University of Illinois Press.

Linneken, Jocelyn. 1998. "Family and Other Uncontrollables: Impression Management in Accompanied Fieldwork." In *Fieldwork and Families: Constructing New Methods for Ethnographic Fieldwork,* Juliana Flinn, Leslie Marshall, and Jocelyn Armstrong, eds., pp. 71–83. Honolulu: University of Hawaii Press.

Lionet, Christian. 2003. "The Exception of the Church." Reporters without Borders, June

25. Electronic document, www.rsf.org/article.php3?id_article=7298 (accessed February 20, 2007).

Lista de espera. 2000. Juan Carlos Tabio, dir. 107 min. Havana: Instituto Cubano del Arte e Industria Cinematográficos.

Liu, Sian Victoria. 2005. "Mediating Civil Society: Housing Markets and Working Morality." Paper presented at the Annual American Anthropological Association Meeting, Washington, D.C., November 30.

López, Alfred J. 2006. *José Martí and the Future of Cuban Nationalisms.* Gainesville: University Press of Florida.

Loss, Jacqueline. 2009. "Wandering in Russian." In *Cuba in the Special Period: Culture and Ideology in the 1990s,* Ariana Hernandez-Reguant, ed., pp. 105–22. New York: Palgrave Macmillan.

Low, Setha M. 2000. *On the Plaza: The Politics of Public Space and Culture.* Austin: University of Texas Press.

Lukose, Ritty. 2005. "Empty Citizenship: Protesting Politics in the Era of Globalization." *Current Anthropology* 20(4): 506–33.

Lundgren, Silje. 2003. "'You're a Useless Person': The Understanding of Prostitution within a Cuban Context of Gender Equality and Machismo-Leninismo." Master's thesis, Department of Anthropology, Uppsala University, Sweden.

Luthar, Brenda. 2006. "Remembering Socialism: On Desire, Consumption and Surveillance." *Journal of Consumer Culture* 6(2): 229–59.

Macedo, Stephen. 1990. *Liberal Virtues: Citizenship, Virtue, and Community.* Oxford: Oxford University Press.

Madagascar. 1994. Fernando Pérez, dir. 50 min. Havana: Instituto Cubano del Arte e Industria Cinematográficos.

Maier, Charles. 1997. *Dissolution: The Crisis of Communism and the End of East Germany.* Princeton, N.J.: Princeton University Press.

Mañach, Jorge. 1991: *La crisis de la alta cultura en Cuba: indagación del choteo, indagación al choteo.* Miami: Ediciones Universal.

Mandel, Ruth, and Caroline Humphrey, eds. 2002. *Markets and Moralities: Ethnographies of Postsocialism.* New York: Berg Publishers.

Mansvelt, Juliana. 2005. *Geographies of Consumption.* London: Sage Publications.

Marcus, George E. 1998a. "Ethnography in and of the World System." In *Ethnography through Thick and Thin,* pp. 79–105. Princeton, N.J.: Princeton University Press.

———. 1998b. "The Uses of Complicity in the Changing Mise-en-Scène of Anthropological Fieldwork." In *Ethnography through Thick and Thin,* pp. 105–33. Princeton: Princeton University Press.

Marshall, T. H. 1965. *Class, Citizenship and Social Development.* New York: Anchor.

Martinez, Lisa M. 2005. "Yes We Can: Latino Participation in Unconventional Politics." *Social Forces* 84(1): 135–55.

Martinez-Alier, J. 1974. "Peasants and Labourers in Southern Spain, Cuba, and Highland Peru." *Journal of Peasant Studies* 1(2): 133–63.

Massey, Douglas S. 1989. "International Migration and Economic Development in Comparative Perspective." *Population and Development Review* 14(3): 383–413.

———. 2005. "Social and Economic Aspects of Immigration." In *Understanding and Optimizing Human Development: From Cells to Patients to Populations,* Stephen G. Kaler and Owen M. Rennert, eds., pp. 206–12 Annals of the New York Academy of Sciences vol. 1038. New York: New York Academy of Sciences.

Massey, Douglas S., Rafael Alarcón, Jorge Durand, and Humberto González. 1987. *Return to Aztlán: The Social Process of International Migration from Western Mexico.* Berkeley: University of California Press.

Massey, Douglas S., Joaquin Arango, Graeme Hugo, Ali Kouaouci, Adela Pellegrino, and J. Edward Taylor. 1993. "Theories of International Migration: A Review and Appraisal." *Population and Development Review* 26(3): 431–66.

———. 1998. *Worlds in Motion: International Migration at the End of the Millennium.* Oxford: Oxford University Press.

Massey, Douglas S., and María Aysa. 2005. "Social Capital and International Migration from Latin America." Expert Group Meeting on International Migration and Development in Latin America and the Caribbean. Population Division, Department of Economic and Social Affairs, United Nations Secretariat, November 21, 2005. Electronic document, www.un.org/esa/population/meetings/IttMigLAC/P04_Massey_Aysa.pdf (accessed December 9, 2008).

Masud-Piloto, Felix Roberto. 1996. *From Welcomed Exiles to Illegal Immigrants: Cuban Migration to the U.S., 1959–1995.* Lanham, Md.: Rowman and Littlefield.

McCarthy, Kevin F. 2004. "Cuba's Demographic Future and Its Implications: Appendix C." In *Cuba after Castro: Legacies, Challenges, and Impediments,* Edward Gonzalez and Kevin F. McCarthy, eds. Report TR-131 RC, 2004. Santa Monica, Calif.: RAND Corporation. Electronic document, www.rand.org/pubs/monographs/2004/RAND_MG111.pdf (accessed October 8, 2008).

McGovern, Charles F. 2006. *Sold American: Consumption and Citizenship, 1890–1945.* Chapel Hill: University of North Carolina Press.

Melucci, Alberto. 1988. *Nomads of the Present: Social Movements and Individual Needs in Contemporary Society.* Ed. John Keane and Paul Mier. Philadelphia, Pa.: Temple University Press.

Menjívar, Cecilia. 2000. *Fragmented Ties: Salvadoran Immigrant Networks in America.* Berkeley: University of California Press.

Merleau-Ponty, Maurice. 1962. *Phenomenology of Perception.* London: Routledge and Kegan Paul.

Mesa-Lago, Carmelo. 2000. *Market, Socialist, and Mixed Economies: Comparative Policy and Performance, Chile, Cuba, and Costa Rica.* Baltimore, Md.: Johns Hopkins University Press.

———. 2002. "Growing Economic and Social Disparities in Cuba: Impact and Recommendations for Change." Cuba Transition Project report. Miami: Institute for Cuban and Cuban-American Studies, University of Miami.

Mesa-Lago, Carmelo, and Horst Fabian. 1993. "Analogies between East European Socialist Regimes and Cuba: Scenarios for the Future." In *Cuba: After the Cold War,* Carmelo Mesa-Lago, ed., pp. 353–80. Pittsburgh, Pa.: University of Pittsburgh Press.

Miami Herald staff. 2006. "Cuba's Aging Society Is Straining Resources." MiamiHerald.

com, December 7. Electronic document, www.flacso.org/hemisferio/al-eeuu/bo-letines/01/53/pol_02.pdf (accessed February 20, 2007).

Miles, Ann. 2004. *From Cuenca to Queens: An Anthropological Story of Transnational Migration.* Austin: University of Texas Press.

Miles, Steven, Allison Anderson, and Kevin Meehan. 2002. *Changing Consumer: Markets and Meanings: Studies in Consumption and Markets.* New York: Routledge.

Miller, Daniel. 1995. *Acknowledging Consumption.* New York: Routledge.

———. 1998. *Material Cultures: Why Some Things Matter.* Chicago: University of Chicago Press.

———. 2001a. "The Poverty of Morality." *Journal of Consumer Culture* 1(2): 225–43.

Miller, Daniel, ed. 2001b. *Consumption: Critical Concepts.* London: Routledge.

Miller, Matthew. 2001. "The Poor Man's Capitalist: Hernando de Soto." *New York Times,* July 3. Electronic document, www.racematters.org/hernandodesoto.htm (accessed February 20, 2007).

Miller, Tom. 1992. *Trading with the Enemy: A Yankee Travels through Castro's Cuba.* New York: Basic Books.

Mintz, Sydney. 1985. *Sweetness and Power: The Place of Sugar in Modern History.* New York: Viking.

Monroe, Alexei. 2005. *Interrogation Machine Laibach and NSK.* Cambridge, Mass.: MIT Press.

Moore, Robin. 1997. *Nationalizing Blackness: Afrocubanismo and Artistic Revolution in Havana, 1920–1940.* Pittsburgh, Pa: University of Pittsburgh Press.

———. 2006. *Music and Revolution: Cultural Change in Socialist Cuba.* Berkeley: University of California Press.

Moore, Sally Falk. 1987. " Explaining the Present: Theoretical Dilemmas in Processual Ethnography." *American Ethnologist* 14(4): 727–36.

Moses, Catherine. 2002. *Real Life in Castro's Cuba.* Wilmington, Del.: SR Books.

Mouffe, Chantal. 1992. *Dimensions of Radical Democracy: Pluralism, Citizenship, and Community.* London: Routledge.

Muller, Jerry Z. 2002. *The Mind and the Market: Capitalism in Western Thought.* New York: Anchor Books.

Nash, June. 1981. "Ethnographic Aspects of the World Capitalist System." *Annual Review of Anthropology* 10: 393–423.

———. 1993. *We Eat the Mines and the Mines Eat Us: Dependency and Exploitation in Bolivian Tin Mines.* New York: Colombia University Press.

———. 1994. "Global Integration and Subsistence Insecurity." *American Anthropologist* 96(1): 6–30.

———. 2001. *Mayan Visions: The Quest for Autonomy in an Age of Globalization.* New York and London: Routledge.

Oboler, Regina S. 1986. "For Better or for Worse: Anthropologists and Husbands in the Field." In *Self, Sex, and Gender in Cross-Cultural Fieldwork,* Tony Larry Whitehead and Mary Ellen Conaway, eds., pp. 28–51. Urbana: University of Illinois Press.

O'Donnell, Guillermo. 1993. "On the State, Democratization, and Some Conceptual Problems: A Latin American View with Glances at Some Postcommunist Countries." *World Development* 21: 1355–69.

O'Dougherty, Maureen. 2002. *Consumption Intensified: The Politics of Middle-Class Daily Life in Brazil.* Durham, N.C.: Duke University Press.

Office of Cuba Broadcasting. n.d. "Misión: Oficina de Transmisiones para Cuba." Electronic document, www.martinoticias.com/mision.asp (accessed December 2, 2006).

Ojito, Mirta. 2005. *Finding Mañana: Memoirs of a Cuban Exodus.* New York: Penguin.

Oldfield, Adrian. 1990. *Civic Republicanism and the Modern World.* London: Routledge.

Olwig, Karen Fog. 2007. *Caribbean Journeys: An Ethnography of Migration and Home in Three Family Networks.* Durham, N.C.: Duke University Press.

Ong, Aiwa. 1999. *Flexible Citizenship: The Cultural Logics of Transnationality.* Durham, N.C.: Duke University Press.

Oring, Elliott. 2004. "Risky Business: Political Jokes under Repressive Regimes." *Western Folklore* 63(3): 209–37.

Ortony, Andrew, ed. 1979. *Metaphor and Thought.* Cambridge: Cambridge University Press.

Overbey, Margaret, and Kathryn Marie Dudley. 2000. "Anthropology and Middle-Class Working Families: A Research Agenda." Washington, D.C.: American Anthropological Association.

Oxhorn, Phillip D. 1995. *Organizing Civil Society: The Popular Sectors and the Struggle for Democracy in Chile.* University Park: Pennsylvania State University Press.

Páginas del diario del Mauricio. 2006. Manuel Pérez, dir. 135 min. Havana: Instituto Cubano de Arte e Industria Cinematografía.

Paley, Julia. 2001. *Marketing Democracy: Power and Social Movements in Post-Dictatorship Chile.* Berkeley: University of California Press.

Pastor, Manuel Jr. 1996. "Cuba and Cuban Studies: Crossing Boundaries During a 'Special Period.'" *Latin American Research Review* 31(3): 218–33.

Pattillo-McCoy, Mary. 1999. *Black Picket Fences: Privilege and Peril among the Black Middle Class.* Chicago: University of Chicago Press.

Pedraza, Silvia. 1995. "Cuba's Refugees: Manifold Migrations." *Cuba in Transition* 5: 311–25.

Pérez, Gina. 2004. *The Near Northwest Side Story: Migration, Displacement, and Puerto Rican Families.* Berkeley: University of California Press.

Pérez, Louis A. Jr. 1999. *On Becoming Cuban: Identity, Nationality, and Culture.* Chapel Hill: University of North Carolina Press.

———. 2005. *To Die in Cuba: Suicide and Society.* Chapel Hill: University of North Carolina Press.

Pérez-López, Jorge, and Sergio Díaz-Briquets. 2005. Remittances to Cuba: A Survey of Estimates and Methods. In *Cuba in Transition,* vol. 15, 396–409. Washington, D.C.: Association for the Study of the Cuban Economy.

Pérez Roque, Felipe. 1999. "Foreign Affairs Minister Felipe Pérez Roque Speaks at the United Nations Assembly General." September 24. Radio Havana, Cuba. Electronic document, www.nnc.cubaweb.cu/discur/ingles/24sept99.htm (accessed February 11, 2007).

Pérez Sarduy, Pedro, and Jean Stubbs. 2000. *Afro-Cuban Voices: On Race and Identity in Contemporary Cuba.* Gainesville: University Press of Florida.

Perna, Vincenzo. 2005. *Timba: The Sound of the Cuban Crisis*. London: Ashgate Publishers.

Peters, Phillips. 2006. "Cuba's Small Entrepreneurs: Down but not Out." Lexington Institute, September 2006. Electronic document http://lexingtoninstitute.org/docs/cubas_small_entrepreneurs.pdf. (accessed December 12, 2008).

Petryna, Adriana. 2002. *Life Exposed: Biological Citizens after Chernobyl*. Princeton, N.J.: Princeton University Press.

Pickering, Michael, and Emily Keightley. 2006. "The Modalities of Nostalgia." *Current Sociology* 54(6): 919–41.

Pinches, Michael. 1996. "The Philippines' New Rich: Capitalist Transformation amidst Economic Gloom." In *The New Rich in Asia: Mobile Phones, McDonalds, and Middle Class Revolution*, Richard Robinson and David S. G. Goodman, eds., pp. 105–37. London: Routledge.

———, ed. 1999. *Culture and Privilege in Capitalist Asia*. New York: Routledge.

Piore, Michael J. 1979. *Birds of Passage: Migrant Labor in Industrial Societies*. Cambridge: Cambridge University Press.

Portes, Alejandro. 1984. "The Rise of Ethnicity: Determinants of Ethnic Perceptions among Cuban Exiles in the United States." *American Sociological Review* 49(3): 383–97.

———. 1995. "Economic Sociology and the Sociology of Immigration: A Conceptual Overview." In *The Economic Sociology of Immigration: Essays on Networks, Ethnicity, and Entrepreneurship*, Alejandro Portes, ed., pp. 1–41. New York: Russell Sage Foundation.

———. 1999. "Immigration Theory for a New Century: Some Problems and Opportunities." In *The Handbook of International Migration: The American Experience*, C. Hirschman, P. Kasinitz, and J. DeWind, eds., pp. 21–31. New York: Russell Sage Foundation.

Portes, Alejandro, Juan M. Clark, and Robert L. Bach. 1977. "The New Wave: A Statistical Profile of Recent Cuban Exiles to the United States." *Cuban Studies* 7: 1–32.

Portes Alejandro, Luis E. Guarnizo, and Patricia Landolt. 1999. "The Study of Transnationalism: Pitfalls and Promise of an Emergent Research Field." *Ethnic and Racial Studies* 22(2): 217–37.

Portes, Alejandro, and Rubén G. Rumbout. 2006. *Immigrant America. A Portrait*. 3rd ed. Berkeley: University of California Press.

Powers, Nancy R. 2001. *Grassroots Expectations of Democracy and Economy: Argentina in Comparative Perspective*. Pittsburgh, Pa.: University of Pittsburgh Press.

Price, Scott L. 2002. *Pitching around Fidel: A Journey into the Heart of Cuban Sports*. New York: HarperCollins.

Programa del PCC. 1987. Havana: Editora Política Habana.

Purvis, Andrew. 2006. "Nostalgia Isn't What It Used to Be." Time.com, May 21. Electronic document, www.time.com/time/magazine/article/0,9171,901060529-1196386,00.html (accessed February 20, 2007).

Rakowski, Cathy A., ed. 1994. *Contrapunto: The Informal Sector Debate in Latin America*. Albany: State University of New York.

Randall, Margaret. 1974. *Cuban Women Now*. Toronto: Dumont Press Graphix.

———. 1981. *Women in Cuba: Twenty Years Later*. New York: Smyrna Press.

Redfield, Robert. 1941. *The Folk Cultures of the Yucatan*. Chicago: University of Chicago Press.

———. 1947. "The Folk Society." *American Journal of Sociology* 52(4): 293–308.

———. 1955. *The Little Community*. Chicago: University of Chicago Press.

———. 1956. *Peasant Society and Culture: An Anthropological Approach to Civilization*. Chicago: University of Chicago Press.

Renzetti, Claire M., and Raymond M. Lee, eds. 1992. *Researching Sensitive Topics*. Thousand Oaks, Calif.: Sage Publications.

Rhodes, Sybil. 2006. *Social Movements and Free Market Capitalism in Latin America: Telecommunications Privatization and the Rise of Consumer Protest*. Albany: State University of New York.

Ribas, Armando. 1998. "Freedom from What? Where To? And the Role of the Cuban-Americans." *Cuba in Transition* 8: 538–45.

Ricoeur, Paul. 1977. *The Rule of Metaphor: Multi-disciplinary Studies of the Creation of Meaning in Language*. Toronto: University of Toronto Press.

Rieff, David. 1993. *The Exile: Cuba in the Heart of Miami*. New York: Simon and Schuster.

Ries, Nancy. 1997. *Russian Talk: Culture and Conversation during Perestroika*. Ithaca, N.Y.: Cornell University Press.

Roberts, Bryan R. 1991. "Household Coping Strategies and Urban Poverty in Comparative Perspective." In *Urban Life in Transition*, Mark Gottdiener and Chris G. Pickvance, eds., pp. 135–68. London: Sage Publications.

———. 1994. "Informal Economy and Family Strategies." *International Journal of Urban and Regional Research* 18: 6–23.

Roberts, Kenneth. 1997. "Beyond Romanticism: Social Movements and the Study of Political Change." *Latin American Research Review* 32(2): 137–51.

———. Forthcoming. *Changing Course: Parties, Populism, and Political Representation in Latin America's Neoliberal Era*. Cambridge: Cambridge University Press.

Robles, Frances. 2006. "Island Newest Portal to U.S. for Cubans." MiamiHerald.com, September 11. Electronic document, www.cubanet.org/CNews/y06/mar06/22e12.htm (accessed February 20, 2007).

Roman, Peter. 2003. *People's Power: Cuba's Experience with Representative Government*. Lanham, Md.: Rowman and Littlefield.

Rosaldo. 1989. *Culture and Truth: The Remaking of Social Analysis*. Boston: Beacon Press.

Rose, Nicolas. 1998. *Inventing Our Selves: Psychology, Power, and Personhood*. Cambridge: Cambridge University Press.

———. 1999. *Powers of Freedom: Reframing Political Thought*. Cambridge: Cambridge University Press.

Roseberry, William. 1995. "Latin American Peasant Studies in a 'Postcolonial' Era." *Journal of Latin American Anthropology* 1(1): 150–77.

Rosenberg, Amelia G. 1995. "The Changing Face of Cuban Political Propaganda: Tracing the Transformation of the Socialist Revolutionary Message, 1959–1994." B.A. honors thesis, Department of Anthropology and Sociology, Earlham College, Richmond, Ind.

Rosendahl, Mona. 1997. *Inside the Revolution: Everyday Life in Socialist Cuba.* Ithaca, N.Y.: Cornell University Press.

Rumbaut, Reuben G., and Lisandro Pérez. 1999. "¿Pinos Nuevos?: Growing up American in Cuban Miami." *Cuban Affairs/Asuntos Cubanos* 5(1–2): 22.

Rundle, Mette Louise B. 2001. "Tourism, Social Change and *Jineterismo* in Contemporary Cuba." In *The Society for Caribbean Studies Annual Conference Papers,* vol. 2, Sandra Courtman, ed. Electronic document, www.caribbeanstudies.org.uk/papers/2001/olv2p3.pdf (accessed October 10, 2008).

Safa, Helen. 2005. "The Matrifocal Family and Patriarchal Ideology in Cuba and the Caribbean." *Journal of Latin American Anthropology* 10(2): 314–38.

Sanday, Peggy R. 1976. *Anthropology and the Public Interest: Fieldwork and Theory.* New York: Academic Press.

———. 1998. "Opening Statement: Defining Public Interest Anthropology. Symposium Defining a Public Interest Anthropology." Paper presented at the annual American Anthropological Association meeting, Philadelphia, Pa., December 3.

———. 2004. "Public Interest Anthropology: A Model for Engaged Research and Action." Electronic document, www.sas.upenn.edu/~psanday/PIE.05.htm (accessed December 9, 2008).

Sánchez, Yoani. 2008. "'De la casa a la nación': Generación Y." February 7. Electronic document, http://desdecuba.com/generaciony/?m=200802 (accessed December 12, 2008).

Sapir, J. David, and J. Christopher Crocker, eds. 1977. *The Social Use of Metaphor: Essays on the Anthropology of Rhetoric.* Philadelphia: University of Pennsylvania Press.

Sassen, Saskia. 2006. *Territory, Authority, and Rights: From Medieval to Global Assemblages.* Princeton, N.J.: Princeton University Press.

Sawyer, Mark Q. 2005. *Racial Politics in Post-Revolutionary Cuba.* Cambridge: Cambridge University Press.

Sawyer, Suzana. 2004. *Crude Chronicles: Indigenous Politics, Multinational Oil, and Neoliberalism in Ecuador.* Durham, N.C.: Duke University Press.

Sayad, Abdelmalek. 1999. *La double absence. Des illusions de l'émigré aux souffrances de l'immigré.* Edited and with a preface by Pierre Bourdieu. Paris: Editions du Seuil.

———. 2004. *The Suffering of the Immigrant.* Cambridge: Polity Press.

Schweizer, Kristen. 2006. "Old Communist Brands Don't Die, They Go 'Retro.'" *International Herald Tribune,* October 26. Electronic document, www.iht.com/articles/2006/10/26/business/east.php (accessed February 20, 2007).

Scott, James C. 1979. *The Moral Economy of the Peasant: Rebellion and Subsistence in Southeast Asia.* New Haven, Conn.: Yale University Press.

———. 1990. *Domination and the Arts of Resistance: Hidden Transcripts.* New Haven, Conn.: Yale University Press.

Scribner, Charity. 2003. *Requiem for Communism.* Cambridge, Mass.: MIT Press.

Serra, Ana. 2007. *The "New Man" in Cuba: Culture and Identity in the Revolution.* Gainesville: University Press of Florida.

Sewell, William H. 1999. "The Concepts of Culture." In *Beyond the Cultural Turn: New Directions in the Study of Culture and Society*, Victoria E. Bonnell and Lynn Hunt, eds., pp. 35–61. Berkeley: University of California Press.

Sherraden, Michael, Deborah Page-Adams, and Gautam Yadama. 1995. Assets and the Welfare State: Policies, Proposals, Politics, and Research. *Research in Politics and Society: The Politics of Wealth and Inequality* 5: 241–68.

Shevchenko, Olga. 2002. "'In Case of Fire Emergency': Consumption, Security and the Meaning of Durables in a Transforming Society." *Journal of Consumer Culture* 2(2): 147–70.

Sierra, Christine Marie, Teresa Carrillo, Louis DeSipio, and Michael Jones-Correa. 2000. "Latino Immigration and Citizenship." PSOnline September: 535–40.

Silverman, Sydel F. 1966. "An Ethnographic Approach to Social Stratification: Prestige in a Central Italian Community." *American Anthropologist* 68(4): 899–921.

Simmel, George. 1978. *The Philosophy of Money*. London: Routledge.

Skidmore, Thomas E., and Peter H. Smith. 2004. *Modern Latin America*. 5th ed. New York: Oxford University Press.

Smith, Benjamin. 1999. "The Self-Employed in Cuba: A Street-Level View." *Cuba in Transition* 9: 49–59.

Smith, Robert. 2006. *Mexican New York: The Transnational Lives of New Immigrants*. Berkeley: University of California Press.

Snel, Erik, and Richard Staring. 2001. "Poverty, Migration and Coping Strategies: An Introduction." *Focaal: European Journal of Anthropology* 38: 7–22.

Snow, Anita. 2006. "Cuban Writer Can't Return, Won't Defect." October, 20, 2006. Washingtonpost.com. Electronic document www.washingtonpost.com/wp-dyn/content/article/2006/10/20/AR2006102000701_pf.html (accessed December 12, 2008).

Spring, Joel H. 2003. *Educating the Consumer Citizen: A History of the Marriage of Schools, Advertising, and Media*. Mahwah, N.J.: Lawrence Erlbaum Associates.

Stark, Oded. 1984. "Migration Decision-Making: A Review Article." *Journal of Development Economics* 14: 251–59.

Stark, Oded, and J. Edward Taylor. 1989. "Relative Deprivation and International Migration." *Demography* 26(1): 1–14.

———. 1991. "Migration Incentives, Migration Types: The Role of Relative Deprivation." *Economic Journal* 101(408): 1163–78.

Stark, Oded, and Shlomo Yitzhaki. 1988. "Labor Migration as a Response to Relative Deprivation." *Journal of Population Economics* 1(1): 57–70.

Starn, Orin. 1994. "Rethinking the Politics of Anthropology: The Case of the Andes." *Current Anthropology* (35)1: 13–38.

———. 1999. *Nightwatch: The Politics of Protest in the Andes*. Durham, N.C.: Duke University Press.

Starrs, Paul F., with Carlin F. Starrs, Genoa I. Starrs, and Lynn Huntsinger. 2000. "Fieldwork . . . with Family." *The Geographical Review* 91(1–2): 74–87.

Stephen, Lynne. 2007. *Transborder Lives: Indigenous Oaxacans in Mexico, California, and Oregon*. Durham, N.C.: Duke University Press.

Steward, Julian. 1949. "Cultural Causality and Law: A Trial Formulation of the Development of Early Civilizations." *American Anthropologist* 51(1): 1–27.

———. 1955. *Theory of Culture Change: The Methodology of Multilinear Evolution.* Urbana: University of Illinois Press.

Stewart, Angus. 1995. "Two Conceptions of Citizenship." *British Journal of Sociology* 41: 63–78.

Strauss, Claudia. 2006. "The Imaginary." *Anthropological Theory* 6(3): 322–44.

Suite Habana. 2003. Fernando Pérez, dir. 80 min. Havana: Instituto Cubano de Arte e Industria Cinematografía.

Tanuma, Sachiko. 2007. "Post-Utopian Irony: Cuban Narratives during the 'Special Period' Decade." *PoLar* 30(1): 44–66.

Tarrow, Sidney. 1998. *Power in Movement: Social Movements and Contentious Politics.* 2nd ed. New York: Cambridge University Press.

Tattlin, Isadora. 2002. *Cuba Diaries: An American Housewife in Havana.* New York: Broadway Books.

Taussig, Michael. 1983. *The Devil and Commodity Fetishism in South America.* Chapel Hill: University of North Carolina Press.

Taylor, Charles. 1995. *Philosophical Arguments.* Cambridge, Mass.: Harvard University Press.

———. 2004. *Modern Social Imaginaries.* Durham, N.C.: Duke University Press.

Thomas, Deborah A. 2004. *Modern Blackness: Nationalism, Globalization, and Politics of Culture in Jamaica.* Durham, N.C.: Duke University Press.

Thomas, John F. 1967. "Cuban Refugees in the United States." *International Migration Review* 1(2): 46–57.

Thompson, Richard W., and Roy E. Roper. 1976. "Relative Deprivation in Buganda: The Relation of Wealth, Security and Opportunity to the Perception of Economic Satisfaction." *Ethos* 4(2): 155–87.

Tilly, Charles. 1983. "Speaking Your Mind without Elections, Surveys or Social Movements." *Public Opinion Quarterly* 47(4): 461–78.

———. 1997. "A Primer on Citizenship." *Theory and Society* 26(4): 599–602.

Tokman, Victor E. 1992. *Beyond Regulation: The Informal Economy in Latin America.* Boulder, Colo.: Lynne Rienner Publishers.

Trouillot, Michel-Rolph. 1995. *Silencing the Past: Power and the Production of History.* Boston: Beacon Press.

———. 2001. "The Anthropology of the State in the Age of Globalization." *Current Anthropology* 4: 125–38.

Turner, Brian. 1990. "Outline of a Theory of Citizenship." *Sociology* 24(2): 189–217.

United Nations General Assembly. 1948. "Universal Declaration of Human Rights." Resolution 217A(III). Article 13. Electronic document, www.un.org/Overview/rights. html (accessed February 27, 2007).

United States Interests Section, Havana. 2006. "Immigrant Visas: The Special Program for Cuban Migration." Electronic document, http://havana.usinterestsection.gov/immigrant_info.html (accessed February 27, 2007).

Urban, Greg. 1991. *A Discourse-Centered Approach to Culture: Native South American Myths and Rituals.* Austin: University of Texas Press.

———. 2001. *Metaculture: How Culture Moves through the World.* Minneapolis: University of Minnesota Press.

U.S. Department of Agriculture, Foreign Agriculture Service. 2004. "Fact Sheet: Cuba's Poultry Market." Electronic document, www.fas.usda.gov/info/factsheets/cuba/poultry.html (accessed February 28, 2007).

U.S. Department of State. 2001. "Cuban Labor Practices, Fact Sheet: Bureau of Western Hemisphere Affairs." September 13. Electronic document, www.state.gov/p/wha/rls/fs/2001/fsjulydec/4889.htm (accessed February 27, 2007).

U.S. Department of State, Bureau of Consular Affairs. 2007. "Consular Information Sheet: Cuba." January 8. Electronic document, http://travel.state.gov/travel/cis_pa_tw/cis/cis_1097.html (accessed February 27, 2007).

U.S. Department of State, Havana Interests Section. 2008. "U.S. Refugee Admissions Program." Electronic document, http://havana.usinterestsection.gov/refugee_page.html (accessed December 9, 2008).

U.S. Immigration and Naturalization Service, Office of Policy and Planning. 2003. "Estimates of Unauthorized Immigrant Populations Residing in the United States." Electronic document, www.dhs.gov/xlibrary/assets/statistics/publications/Ill_Report_1211.pdf (accessed February 27, 2007).

Valdez, Rosa Tania. 2006. "Family Urges Ailing Castro Not to Attend Birthday." Reuters.com. Electronic document, www.puenteinfocubamiami.org/NoticiasSINA/Cuban%20News%20December%2001%202006.htm#a4 (accessed February 11, 2007).

Valentine, Gill. 1999. "Doing Household Research: Interviewing Couples Together and Apart." *Area* 31(1): 67–74.

Valle, Amir. 2006. *Jineteras*. Bogota, Colombia: Editorial Planeta.

Venegas, Cristina. 2009. "Filmmaking with Foreigners." In *Cuba in the Special Period: Culture and Ideology in the 1990s*, ed. Ariana Hernandez-Reguant, pp. 37–50. New York: Palgrave Macmillan.

Verdery, Katherine. 1996. *What Was Socialism, and What Comes Next?* Princeton: Princeton University Press.

———. 2000. *The Political Lives of Dead Bodies: Reburial and Postsocialist Change*. New York: Columbia University Press.

———. 2002. "Anthropology of Socialist Societies." In *International Encyclopedia of the Social and Behavioral Sciences*, Neil Smelser and Paul B. Baltes, eds., pp. 14496–500. Amsterdam: Pergamon Press.

———. 2003. *The Vanishing Hectare: Property and Value in Postsocialist Transylvania*. Ithaca: Cornell University Press.

Verdery, Katherine, and Michael Buroway. 1999. *Uncertain Transition: Ethnographies of Change in the Post-Socialist World*. Lanham, Md.: Rowman and Littlefield.

Vissol, Thierry, ed. 1999. *The Euro: Consequences for the Consumer and the Citizen*. Dordrecht, The Netherlands: Kluwer Academic Publishers.

Voeux, Claire, and Julien Pain. 2006. "Going Online in Cuba: Internet under Surveillance." Paris: Reporters Without Borders—Internet Desk. Electronic document, www.rsf.org/IMG/pdf/rapport_gb_md_1.pdf (accessed February 27, 2007).

Vogel, Ursula, and Michael Moran. 1991. *The Frontiers of Citizenship*. New York: St. Martin's Press.

Wald, Karen. 1978. *The Children of Ché: Education and Day Care in Cuba*. New York: Rampart Press.

Wallerstein, Immanuel. 1974. *The Modern World-System*. Vol. 1: *Capitalist Agriculture and the Origins of the European World-Economy in the Sixteenth Century*. New York/ London: Academic Press.

Walker, Iain, and Heather J. Smith, eds. 2002. *Relative Deprivation: Specification, Development and Integration*. Cambridge: Cambridge University Press.

Wanner, Catherine. 1998. *Burden of Dreams: History and Identity in Post-Soviet Ukraine*. University Park: Pennsylvania State University Press.

Warner, Michael. 2002. *Publics and Counterpublics*. New York: Zone Books.

Warner, W. Lloyd, Marchia Meeker, and Kenneth Eels. 1949. *Social Class in America: A Manual of Procedure for the Measurement of Social Status*. Chicago: Science Research Associates.

Warren, Kay B. 1998. *Indigenous Movements and Their Critics: Pan-Maya Activism in Guatemala*. Princeton, N.J.: Princeton University Press.

Wedel, Johan. 2003. *Santería Healing: A Journey into the Afro-Cuban World of Divinities, Spirits, and Sorcery*. Gainesville: University Press of Florida.

Weintraub, Jeff, and Krishan Kumar, eds. 1997. *Public and Private in Thought and Practice: Perspectives on a Grand Dichotomy*. Chicago: University of Chicago Press.

Whitehead, Tony Larry, and Laurie Price. 1986. "Summary: Sex and the Fieldwork Experience." In *Self, Sex, and Gender in Cross-Cultural Fieldwork*, Tony Larry Whitehead and Mary Ellen Conaway, eds., pp. 289–304. Urbana: University of Illinois Press.

Whitfield, Esther. 2006. "Havana and the Ideology of Ruins." Paper presented at the Center for Latin American Studies Faculty Forum, Brown University, Providence, R.I., February 13.

———. 2008. *Cuban Currency: The Dollar and "Special Period" Fiction*. Minneapolis: University of Minnesota Press.

Wilk, Richard. 1994. "Consumer Goods as Dialog about Development: Colonial Time and Television Time in Belize." In *Consumption and Identity*, Jonathan Friedman, ed., pp. 97–118. Amsterdam: Harwood Academic Publishers.

Willis, Paul. 2000. *The Ethnographic Imagination*. Cambridge: Polity Press.

Winchie, Diana B., and David W. Carment. 1988. "Intention to Migrate: A Psychological Analysis." *Journal of Applied Social Psychology* 18(9): 727–36.

Wirtz, Kristina. 2004. "Santeria in Cuban National Consciousness: A Religious Case of the 'Doble Moral.'" *Journal of Latin American Anthropology* 9(2): 409–38.

Wolf, Diane L. 1996. "Situating Feminist Dilemmas in Fieldwork." In *Feminist Dilemmas in Fieldwork*, Diane L. Wolf, ed., pp. 1–55. Boulder, Colo.: Westview Press.

Wolf, Eric R. 1982. *Europe and the People without History*. Berkeley: University of California Press.

Wunderlich, Annelise. 2005. "Hip Hop Pushes the Limits." In *Capitalism, God and a Good Cigar: Cuba Enters the Twenty-First Century*, Lydia Chávez, ed., pp. 65–78. Durham, N.C.: Duke University Press

Yurchak, Alexei. 1997. "The Cynical Reason of Late Socialism: Power, Pretense, and the Anekdot." *Public Culture* 9(2) 161–88.

———. 2005. *Everything Was Forever Until It Was No More: The Last Soviet Generation.* Princeton, N.J.: Princeton University Press.

Zeitlin, Maurice. 1966. "Political Generations in the Cuban Working Class." *American Journal of Sociology* 71(5): 493–508.

Zhang, Li. 2001. "Migration and Privatization of Space and Power in Late Socialist China." *American Ethnologist* 28 (1): 179–205.

Index

Page numbers set in *italic* typeface indicate illustrations.

Accompanied fieldwork, 13, 199n15

Activism, 25, 141, 142–59, 181

Adaptation: private, 183–85; to shortages, 67

Afro-Cubans. *See* Race/ethnicity

Agency, 81, 166

Agrarian Reform Act of 1961, 22

Agriculture, 45, 72, 185–86

Alarcón, Ricardo, 181

Alcance. See Means

Allegiance, horizontal/vertical, *163*, 164

Alternate moral universe, 151

Analytic paradigm, for Latin America, 7, 169

Anthropology, 6–7, 151, 161, 172, 198n8, 218n13

Aphorisms, 148–52

Appadurai, Arjun, 166

Appliances, 185

Arrendador inscritos. See Rental houses

Art, mass-produced, 84

Asphyxiation, 126–28

Asthma, 127, 212n16

Authoritarian regime, 2, 21, 197n1; discourse of, 152, 153, 158, 216n8; Latin American history/changes in, 170

Ávila, Eliécer (student), 181, 218n1

Balloons, 86

Balsero migration, 22, 200n5, 213n19, 214n29

Bank accounts, 57, 205n7

Barrios. See Neighborhoods

Batista, Fulgencio, 21, 147, 216n6

Beatriz (informant/child-care provider), 88–89, 187, 191

Benny (informant/taxi driver), CDR meeting and, 175–76, 187, 191

Berlin Wall, 176–77, 209n13

Billboards, 41

Binary socialism, 33–34, 37, 60

Birth control, 5

Birth rate, 205n9

Black market, 13, 46, 57, 63, 87, 203n8, 209n2; irony of, 67; privatization and, 55. *See also* Double life/double standard; Micro-enterprises

Blackouts, 182

Blessing, *resolver* meaning as, 71

Blogs, 155, 181

Boats, 210n3, 213n19

Bodegas. *See* Store(s)

Bourgeois households, 4

Brand names, awareness of, 85–87

Brazil, 172

Breastfeeding, mandatory year off for, 157

Breathing, emotional health and, 127–28

Buses, Chinese, 182

Bush, George W., 102, 215n30

Busts, José Martí, 39, *40*, 202n2

Calhoun, Craig, 141

Campesinos (farmers/peasants), 91–93, 208n8

Canclini, Garcia, 96

Capitalism, 22, 29–30, 94–95, 97, 170, 200n9, 208n9, 209n10; intimacy of goods and, 94–95, 208n9; late, 30–31

Caribbean Sea, 211n4

Carolos Tercero Mall, 31

Casas particulares (private homes), 60, 78, 183

Castro, Fidel, 21, 25, 45, 67, 147, 148–50, 203n5; CDRs and, 45, 47; ceding power to brother,

142; death date predicted for, 174–75; gesture of reference to, 102; health of, 158; jokes about, protest as, 216n3; length of rule, 144; media and, 144; nicknames for, 45, 203n5; senility of, 149–50; Special Period reforms justified by, 23, 200n10; television appearance of, 144–46

Castro Espín, Mariela, 156–58, 216n11

Castro Ruz, Raúl, 21, 25, 175; conversation with daughter of, 156–58, 216n11; new commander in chief, 180; reforms introduced by, recent, 182, 185–86

Catholic Church, 4, 52, 53–54, 204n3

CDR. See Comité de Defensa de la Revolución

CENESEX, 156, 182

Censorship, videotape, 88

Che, 31, 72, 156

Chickens, 72, 148

Child-care centers (círculos infantiles), 14, 57–59, 88, 205n10

Children, 33; fieldwork contributions by own, 15, 16; informant rapport enhanced by, 12–13; wealth indicated by number of, 184

Chile, 138

China, 31–32, 209n2

Chinese buses (Yutongs), 192

Chronic obstructive pulmonary disease, 127, 212n16

Círculos particulares. See Child-care centers

Citizen(s): consumers replacing, 8; dissatisfied, uncounted, 161–62; exit permits for world, 122–24; nostalgia of, 177–79; recent reforms not representing, 182; resolver/resolviendo context of, 70–72, 80; Soviet, 154; suspended, 141; tourist places off limits to, 42; unaware of "other half," 102–4

Citizen-consumer, 7–9, 198n11; older, 56–57

Citizen-consumers, unsatisfied, 2–9, 168–69, 217n11; constituency of, 6–7, 198n6; documentation of, 9–16; families as, 4–5; isolation feelings of, 91, 95; Latin America's, 170–74; migration announcements of, 133–39; migration trajectory of, potential, 131, 131–33; as new category for scholarship focus, 16–17; as overlooked, 16–17; as prospective migrants, 169; social class of, 105

Citizen's-eye view, 37, 202n1

Citizenship, 18, 160–63, 171, 217n4; "bad," 164;

contractual classic, 162–63; criminality factor in, 139–40; Cuban, 162–63; definition of good, 160–63; flexible, 161; lateral nature of, 164

Citizen-state relationships, 163, 163–65

Civic participation, 7

Civil society, public sphere and, 168–69

Clotheslines, 1

CMEA. See Council for Mutual Economic Assistance

Codrescu, Andrei, 178

Colburn, Forrest D., 171, 172

Collective criticism, 41–42

Collins, Randall, 153, 154

Comaroff, John/Jean, 94, 208n9

Comecon. See Council for Mutual Economic Assistance

Comité de Defensa de la Revolución (CDR), 25, 41, 111; as bridge between public/private space, 45–47; love of hating, 176; march attendance and, 153; meetings, 175–76, 179, 187, 191; micro-enterprises tolerated by, 205n8; presidents of, 45–46, 57, 113, 205n8

Commodity fetishization, 93–94

Communication: freedom and, 115, 145; goods coded for, 95–96; telecommunications embargo, 211n6

Communism: capitalism and, vague place between, 29–30; nostalgia for, 176–77; peso poor and, 108–9

Communist Manifesto, discarding of, 54

Communist Party, 19, 36; barrios activities reported to, 45; publications of, 53; race and, 111; "real communists" in, 69; Red Bourgeoisie and, 103–4; two-toilet regulation by, 78

Community life, 14

Competitor, welfare state as, 78

Complaints: in conversations, 85; about other Cubans, 124–26, 212n12; hierarchy of vocalizable, 115; radius of, 91; secrecy of, 101–2

Compromise, values-economics, 6–7

Confederation of Cuban Workers, 25

Confrontation, student-state official, 181, 218n1

Consiguiendo (finding/acquiring), 65–66, 72–75

Consumer(s): blending citizens with, 7–9; citizens replaced by, 8; frustrations of, personal, 83–85, 207n1; nostalgia of, 176–77, 178; *resolver* context of, 69–70, 80

Consumer rights, 67

Consumption, 5, 28, 199n1; campesino desire and, 91–93, 208n8; imagined normal, 64; local in global setting, 96; loosening of restrictions on, 185

Contracts, work, 182, 211n7, 213n17, 214n24

Conversations: with Raúl Castro's daughter, 156–58, 216n11; complaints in, 85; freedom as topic of, 115, 145; private/with foreigners, 47; telephone, 211n6; unofficial, 166

Cootacracy, 144–46

Corrective action, 162

Corruption, 27, 29

Costa Rica, 74, 127, 134, 175, 213n17

Council for Mutual Economic Assistance (CMEA), 22, 200n7

Criminality, citizenship and, 139–40

Criticism, of state, 51, 81; aphorisms/sayings as, 148–50; collective, 41–42; complaints about other Cubans as, 124–26, 212n12; detecting, 146–47; films as channel for state, 102–3, 209n3; scholarship on, 146–47; shadow opposition, 146–47; Special Period lexicon allowing, 81; U.S. dollar access allowing open, 107. *See also* Complaints

Cuba: citizenship in, 162–63; comparison to Moscow/China, 31–32; ethnographies on, 20; former internationalism of, 122, 212nn9,10; future of, 174–75; isolation of, 95, 120; "real," 4, 42; representation of, 4, 42, 155–56; visits to, 10, 180–83; winds of change in, 185–86. *See also* Fieldwork; *specific topics*

Cuban(s): Afro-, poverty of, 108, 109–13; Fidel Castro referred to by, 45, 203n5; distancing of other, 124–26, 212n12; as Islanders of the mind, 124; "ordinary," 19; in popular imagination, 174; U.S. migrant, 128, 214n29

Cuban Adjustment Act, 27

Cuban convertible peso (CUC): freedom and, *106*; as only legal currency, 98; struggle to attain, 186; student's question about, 181

Cuban National Assembly, 181

Cuban-style divorce, migration and, 120

CUC. *See* Cuban convertible peso

Cuentos. See Aphorisms

Cultural diversity, global capitalism as destroying, 97, 209n10

Culture: blended categories of, 34; "culture as usual," 158–59; flash drive, 180–81; historic transition in, 187; language use in understanding, 81; meta-, 81; of migration, 130; neoliberalism, 37, 94, 202n1, 208n9

Currency, 73, 98, 185, 186, 210n5; civil liberties and, *106*. *See also* Dollars, U.S.

Daily life: Cuban v. Soviet Union, 175; details as litmus test, 186–87; documentation of, 180–81; of other half, 102–4; state intimacy tension in, 147–48; struggle, 65–69, 80, 158–59, 186, 206n1

Dairy farmer, 91–93, 208n8

David (key informant), 44–45, 66–67, 103–4, 183, 187, 191; concern of Cuban representation, 155; flash drives of, 180–81; freedom according to, 122–24; job switching of, CDR fear with, 46–47; migration intention of Tatiana and, 133–35; as world citizen, 122–23

Defection, 121, 216n7

Defense, 155

De la Fuente, Alejandro, 110

Delegalization, U.S. dollar, 98

Democracy, 170, 175

Dentists, private, 102

Deprivation, relative, 217n7

Desconfianza. See Mistrust

De Soto, Hernando, 172, 218n13

Diaspora, 32–33

"Dictatorship of the Proletariat," 21

Digital Information, 180–82

Disclosure, migration and, 132

Discrimination, tourist industry employment, 108

Dissatisfaction, 1, 19–34; consumer v. citizen, 8–9; desires and, 91–93, 208n8; "materialism" gloss of, 173; relatives abroad fueling, 91; silent majority/shadow opposition and, 146–47; Soviet Union v. Latin American, view of, 173–74; space between enjoyment-desire, 93; under theorized, 161–62; U.S. dollar lack of access, 24–25. *See also* Citizen-consumers, unsatisfied; Migration

Dissent, 142–43; Catholic press channel for, 52–53, 204n3. *See also* Activism; Protest
Distribution, 26, 109, 186; income, 98; wealth, 130
Divorce, Cuban-style, 120
Doble vida. See Double life/double standard
Doctors, 102, 182, 211n8, 218n2
Documentation, 9–16; daily hardships, 180–81
Dollar dogs, 99–104, *105*
Dollars, U.S., 10, 23, 105–6; benefits of earning, *106*, 107; delegalization of, 2004, 98; dollar dogs and, 99–104; "dollarization," 23; lack of access to, 24–25; legalization of, 55–56; medicine and, 102; psychosis of, 107; race and, 107–12, 210n7
Dollar stores, 23, *24*, 24
Dominican migration, 119
Double life/double standard (*doble vida/doble moral*), 45, 112–13, 132, 140–41, 151, 158, 203n6

Economic crisis, 29, 157; Brazil's, 172
Economic reform. *See* Structural adjustment
Economics, compromise of values for, 6–7
Economy, 145; two-tiered, 23, 100, 109; underground, 20, 26, 66, 67, 132, 172, 201n14, 207n2
Editorials, 152
Education, 4, 5, 6, 26, 109, 111, 156, 183–84; migration and, 183, 214n29; sexual health, 157–58
El bombo, migration lottery ticket, 214n29
Elections, 25, 152, 201n12
Electronics, 185
Elite, 1959-1960 migration of, 213n19
El Partido. *See* Communist Party
Email Elena (informant), 35, 83–84, 100, 187–88, 192; benefactor of, 125–26, 135–37; emails of, 47–50, 136–38, 214n27; migration announcement of, 135–38; other Cubans distanced by, 124–26, 212n12; resistance activities of, 50–51, 55; Stuart and, 100–101; travel of, 125, 212n13
Embargo. *See* Telecommunications embargo, lifting of; Trade embargo, U.S.
Embeddings, public-private, 61, 206n13
Emotional health, 127–28
Employment: civil liberties/dollars and, *106*; highest-paying, 183; legal, 65; migration motivation, 132; state, 22, 40, 109, 111, 157, 185; tourist industry, 108, 110; work contracts abroad, 211n7, 213n17, 214n24. *See also* Self-employment
Escape: psychological, 27, 126. *See also* Migration
Ethical duality, 140–41
Ethnographies: informants of existing Cuban, 20; of Latin American migration, 172–73; post-socialism, 33–34. *See also* Scholarship
Exchange programs, migration and, 121, 212n10
Exit permits, 117, 120, 122–24, 210nn1,2

Faith (fe), 107–10
Falcoff, Mark, 91
Families: abroad, 88; income, 66, 67, 198n4, 207n2; informant, 11; providing for, 4–5; size of, 5
Family fieldwork, 12–16, 199n13
Farmers. *See* Campesinos
Fe (faith), remittances and, 107–10
Federation of Cuban Women, 25
Fernandes, Sujatha, 142
Fernández, Damián, 80
Fetishes, goods as, 93–94
Fieldwork: accompanied, 13, 199n15; Elena's emails contributing to, 49–50; family, 12–16, 199n13; methodology, 11–13, 199n13; social class focus of, 3
Films, criticism of state through, 102–3, 209n3
Finding/acquiring (*consiguiendo*), 65–66, 72–75
Flash drives, 180–81
Florida Straits, *117*, 119, 211n4
Foods, 66, 74, 75, 76–77, 83, 84, 138, 182, 207nn1,8; shortages of, 74; unavailability of Cuban, 74
Foreigners, conversations with, 47
Fredrich/Felina (informants/cigar factory), 78–80, 144, 188, 214n25
Freedom, 122–24; to assemble, 152; communicating about, 115, 145; dollars and, 105–6, *106*; economic v. political, 145; migration equated with, 120, 139–41; offstage, 142–59; representation and, 155–56; self-employment affording, 147; travel in 1980s, 125, 212n13

Free market, 185
Friendshipments, 214n26
Fuel, 182
Fula (delegalization of U.S. dollar), 98
Futurelessness, motivation for migration, 214n25

García, Cristina, 41
Gay rights, 182
Gender roles, 15
Gifts, 59
Global capitalism, 94–95, 97, 208n9, 209n10
Globalization, 31–33, 87–89, 172–73
Glory years, Revolution, 212n13
GNP. *See* Gross national product
Good-bye Lenin!, 176
Goods, 1, 178–79; availability of everyday, 73–74, 182–83; awareness of unavailable, 2; communication coded by, 95–96; *conseguir* and, 65–66, 72–75; contraband, 183; as fetishes, 93–94; inaccessibility/sociality and, 93; intimacy of, 85–87, 94–95, 208n9; legalized purchase of, 185; as lifestyle proxy, 87, 96; as local symbols, 95–97; meaning of, 83–97, 207n1, 208n9; rationing of, 8, 26, 83, 207n1; *resolver* as finding, 69–70; self-esteem connected to, 87; shortages of, 2, 65, 182; social class and, 103, 209n4; value and, 93–97
Government, state v., 202n17
Granma, 53, 144, 152, 185, 216n6
Greenberg, Jessica, 178
Gross national product (GNP), 208n6
Guevara, Che. *See* Che

Habana Blues, "Habaneando" from, 63
Hagedorn, Katherine, 142
Haitian migration, 119
Havana, 102–3; Carolos Tercero Mall in, 31; hidden, 63–64; joint-venture projects in, 208n5; labor migration to, 110, *111*; old, *33*; pre-Revolutionary, 90; primary school in, sign to Fidel Castro, *179*; U.S. Interests Section in, 51, 203n10
Health: Castro, F.'s, 158; emotional, 127–28
Health care, 4, 26, 60, 201n15
Hegemony, 173
Hernandez-Reguant, Ariana, 103, 142

History/overview, sources/perspectives on, 19–21
Holidays, 153
Horizontal allegiance, *163*, 164
Household income, 66, 67, 198n4, 207n2
Housing, 79, 111–12, 202n1; inspectors, 183; public, 202n1. *See also* Private property
Hungary, 175
Hussein, Saddam, 102, 126
Hustling, 20, 26, 201n14

Identity: campesinos, 91–93, 208n8; informant, 12; prospective migrant, 169
Immigrants, Cuban, racial percentages in U.S., 108
Income, 66, 67, 198n4, 207n2; distribution, 98; -generating strategies, 66, 67, 139–40, 207n2. *See also* Underground economy
Inequality, 185
Informants: Raúl Castro's daughter viewed by, 157; ethnographies and, existing Cuban, 20; family, 11; identity of, 12; key, 44–45; migration announcements of, 133–39; migration of, 133–39, 187–89, 213n22; mistrust of, 11–13; poverty v. condition of, 5, 198n7; profiles of, 191–95; race of, 3, 197n3, 210n9; rapport with, 1, 12–14; social class of, 3–4, 10; tape-recorded interviews of, 155–56, 216n10; updates on key, 187–89. *See also specific informants*
Ingrid/Humberto (informants), 78, 188
Inspectors, housing, 183
International Human Rights Day, 142
Internationalism, 122, 212nn9,10
Internet access, 48–51, 99, 155–56, 203n8, 211n6
Interviews, tape-recorded, 155–56, 216n10
Intimacy of goods, 85–87, 94–95, 208n9
Inventing (*Inventando*), 65, 76–80, 93
Iris (informant/landlady), 56–57, 188, 192
Islanders of the mind, Cubans as, 124
Isolation, 91, 95, 120

Jamaica, local-global in, 96–97
Jineterismo. *See* Hustling
Jinori/Stan (informant), 188, 193
Johnson, Lyndon B., 213n19
Joint-venture projects, Havana's, 208n5
Jokes, 41, 77, 151, 216n3
Juventud, 152

Karlos (informant/wrestler), 112–13, 138–39,
188, 193

Labor, 22; migration, Special Period, 110
Language: new, 80; Special Period lexicon as
new, 64, 65–82; street, 67; understanding
culture through, 81
Late capitalism, 30–31
La Telenovela sin Parar (The Never-Ending
Soap Opera), 149
Late socialism, 29–34; acts of resistance in,
158–59; aphorisms on, 148–50; citizenship
models for, 160–63; communism-capitalism
vagueness and, 29–30; definition of, 3,
197n2; *doble vida/doble moral* of, 45, 112–13,
132, 203n6; future for, 33–34; global context
for, 31–33; irony in, 31; the private valued in,
61; resistance as culture as usual in, 158–59;
social class analysis for, 104–7, *105–6*; transition as, 29–34
Latin America: analytic paradigm for, 7, 169;
capitalism of, 170; citizenship in, 164; end
of politics in, 170–74; migration and, 119,
172–73; welfare model of, 28–29
Latour, Bruno, 217n11
Laws, forced violation of, 139–40. *See also*
Underground economy
Leadership: as old/cootocracy, 144–46; pink
tide/left-leaning, 218n15; voicing of opinions
over future, 158
Legalization/legality: employment, 65; gay
marriage, talk of, 182; goods/electronics
purchase, 185; inventing loopholes around,
77–78; private enterprise, 55–56, 57, 77–78,
99–104, 205n8; self-employment, 55–56,
77–78, 205n5; shifting, 77–78
Legal means, dollar dogs and, 99–104, *105*
Legislation, 22, 27, 200n8; billboard, 41;
citizens banned from tourist places, 42;
migration, 17–18, 118–19, 214n29; private
enterprise legalization, 55–56; remittance,
215n30
Letter of invitation, 134
Lewis, Oscar, 20
Lewis, Ruth M., 20
Lexicon, Special Period, 64, 65–82; *conseguir*
(to find), 65–66, 72–75; *inventar*, 65, 76–80;

luchar (to struggle), 65–69, 206n1; *resolver*
(to resolve), 65–66, 69–72, 80
Liberalism, procedural, 217n4
Lifestyles: media not reporting different,
102–4; social class analysis and, *106*; U.S.,
good as proxy for, 87, 96
Lines, waiting in, 75, 76–77
Lottery ticket, migration, 214n29
Low, Setha, 42
Loyalty, 8, 93; Afro-Cuban, 110, 112–13; poverty
and, 109
Luchar (to struggle), 65, 66–69, 80, 206n1
Luxury, 83
Lyric discourse, 151

Malecón Riot, 110–11
Mansions, 39–40, 202n1
Marches, state-organized, 112, 153–55
Marginalia, silent, 53–54, 204n4
Mariel Boat Lift, 213n19
Marriage of convenience, 138–39
Martí, José, busts of, 39, *40*, 202n2
Marx, Karl, 104
Mass participation, 154–55
Materialism, dissatisfaction glossed by accusa-
tion of, 173
Maya (daughter), chocolate "resolved" by,
69–70
Meals, *inventando* and, 76–77
Means (*alcance*), 63–64, 206n2; illegal, 6; legal,
dollar dogs and, 99–104, *105*; scope of term,
17. *See also* Micro-enterprises; Underground
economy
Media, 102–4, 110–11, 144–46, 152, 174, 184;
Catholic Church, 52, 203n3
Medical diplomacy, 212n9
Medicine, private, 102
Meetings: CDR, 175–76, 179, 187, 191; town
hall, 181
"Mesa Redonda" (Round Table) news show, 152
Messages, state-sponsored, 41–42, 68
Metaculture, 151; Special Period lexicon allow-
ing, 81
Metaphors, for feeling trapped, 126–28. *See
also* Aphorisms
Methodology, 9–12, 199n13; family fieldwork,
12–13, 199n13

Miami, 85, 109

Micro-enterprises, 57, 77–78, 88, 205n8; CDR presidents tolerating, 57; as unlicensed, 57, 205n8. *See also* Black market; Means; Underground economy

Middle class, 3, 4, 6–7, 10, 56–57, 91, 172, 198n8

Migrants: prospective, 128, 130, *131*, 131–33, 162, 169; U.S. Coast Guard on, 210n3, 211n4

Migration, 32–33, 117–41, 161, *163*, 169, 200n5, 213nn17,19,21; *Balsero*, 22, 200n5, 213n19, 214n29; citizenship and, 161–62; to Costa Rica, 213n17; culture of, 130; cumulative push factors, 139; education and, 183, 214n29; exchange programs and, 121, 212n10; exit permits for, 117, 120, 122–24, 210nn1,2; freedom as, 120, 139–41; global, in the 1990s, 161; to Havana, 110, *111*; human rights and, 119, 139–40, 210n1; informants, 133–39, 187–89, 213n22; labor, 110, *111*; Latin American, 119, 172–73; legislation/constraints on, 17–18, 118–19, 214n29; letter of invitation for, 134; lottery ticket for, 214n29; major waves of, 128, 213n19; medical diplomacy program of, 212n9; motivation for, 129–30, 132, 214n25; not taken/unactualized, 129; potential, 128, 130, *131*, 131–33, 162; processing fees for, 210n2; progressive revelation preceding, 132–33, 213n22; by raft, 22, 118, 200n5, 210n3; relatives abroad, 91; scholarship on, 129–30, 214nn23,25, 217n7; signs/symptoms of dissatisfaction leading to, 140; social class and, 213n19; social imaginary and, 129; of teachers from public to private schools, 183; transnational, 172–73; turning points in decision for, 133–39; un-, 129; wet-foot/dry-foot policy on, 118–19; white, 107–8; work contracts for, 182, 211n7, 213n17, 214n24

Minda (informant/child-care center owner), 58

MINFAR (Cuba's Ministry of Defense), 155

Ministry of Defense (MINFAR), 155

Mistrust (*desconfianza*), 11–13, 55, 155–56

Modernization, 97

Mona Passage, 211n4

Moscow, 31–32

Motherhood persona, 13–14

Musician, state-sponsored, 72

National Center for Sex Education (CENESEX), 156

Neighborhoods, 183; *barrios*, 45–46; names of, 3, 197n4; policing of, 46; scenes from, 43–44

Neoliberalism, 37, 94, 202n1, 208n9

News show, 152

New York Times, 185

Nostalgia, 109, 170, 175–79

O'Dougherty, Maureen, 96, 171–72

Oil-for-doctors program, 182, 211n8, 218n2

Ojito, Mirta, 90

Oring, Elliott, 151

Ortega, Jaime, 52

Outlaws, ordinary, 6–7

Ownership, 55, 57

Paco/Pratha (informant/musician), 56–57, 72, 128, 188, 194

Palabra nueva, 52–54, 204n3

Pantyhose, 84–85

Party People, Red Bourgeoisie as, 103–4

Pastors for Peace, 214n26

Paternalistic citizen-state relationship, *163*

Peasants. *See* Campesinos

Performative shift, 154

Performers/athletes, 103, *105*, 121, 209n4

Peso, value of, 186

Peso poor, *15*, 104; as communist, 108–9; gratitude for revolution expressed by, 155–56; informants, 108–9, 112; race and, 110

Petra (informant/mother of migrated son), 115, 145, 183, 189, 194

Phantom public, Latour's, 217n11

Pink tide, 218n15

Plastic bags, state message on, 68

Pleasant appearance (*presencia agradable*), 108

Poetry, 151

Poland, 175

Policing, neighborhood, 46

Political discourse, complaints about goods as replacement for, 85

Political rituals, shadow, 152–55

Politics, 36, 145; aphorisms in light of, 150–52; end of, Latin American, 170–74
Population growth, 205n9
Post-socialism, 30, 33–34
Poverty, 5, 198n7; Afro-Cuban, 108, 109–12; historical legacies and, 109–12; media and, 174; race and, 108; Revolutionary/postrevolutionary, 111, 111–12. See also Peso poor
Predictions, 174–75
Presencia agradable (pleasant appearance), 108
Presidents, CDR, 45–46, 57, 113, 205n8
Prices, 1, 23–24, 85–86, 185; chicken, 72; internet access, 49; private medicine/doctor/dentist visit, 102; vehicle, 209n4
Primary school sign, homage to Fidel Castro, 179
The private, 35–37, 59
Private education, 183–84
Private enterprises, 57, 77–78, 88, 205n8; dollar dogs operating, 99–104; legality of, 55–56, 57, 77–78, 99–104, 205n8; medicine as, 102; number of, 56, 205n5; teachers, 183. See also Means; Micro-enterprises
Private property, 43–44, 60, 78, 183; homes/casas particulares, 60, 78, 183
Private public, 54–55
Private space, 37–51, 59–60, 183–85; CDR and, 45–47; embedding of public and, 61, 206n13; mistrust and, 55; neighborhood scenes and, 43–44; as non-political, 36; the private and, 35–37, 59; private circulation/silent marginalia, 53–54, 204n4; reading in, 53–55, 204n4; social sciences and, 36–37; state control context for, 17, 36; virtual, 48–51
Privatization, 55–59
Procedural liberalism, 217n4
Profiles: informant, 191–95; potential migrant, travel denied based on, 120
Property: assessors, 183; private, 43–44, 60, 78, 183
Prostitution, 20, 26, 201n14
Protest, 54, 110–11, 144, 147, 164, 204n4, 217n6; coping mechanism as form of silent, 172, 215n2; fear behind lack of, 147; Malecón Riots, 110–11; shadow opposition as, 146–47; Soviet Union v. Cuban, 175
Psychological escape, 126
Publications/texts, 52–55, 152, 204n3; church, 52–54, 204n3; Communist Party, 53;

marking of, 54, 204n4; non-state, 52–54, 204nn3,4. See also Granma
Public buildings, 39–40, 202n1
Public opinion, 81–82
Public sphere, 45–47, 183–84; absence of activity in, 40; civil society and, 168–69; communists not part of general, 69; definitions of, 166; dissent expressed in, 142–43; faking, 152–55; private, 54–55; public-private embedding, 61, 206n13

Quincy (informant), 101–2, 194

Race/ethnicity, 3, 109–10, 197n3; access to U.S. dollars and, 107–12, 210n7; Afro-Cubans, 108, 109–13; CDR leadership and, 111; Communist Party, 111; Cuban immigrants in U.S., 108; informants, 3, 197n3, 210n9; tourist industry employment and, 108; urban school tensions and, 184
Radio Martí, 51, 203n9
Rafts, 22, 118, 200n5, 210n3, 213n19, 214n29
Rationing, 8, 26, 83, 207n1
Reading, as private act, 53–55, 204n4
Red Bourgeoisie, 103–4, 105, 105
Reforms, 22, 23, 157, 200n10; recent, 182, 185–86. See also Structural adjustment
Refugees, 51, 204n10
Relative deprivation, 217n7
Relatives: dissatisfaction fueled by migrated, 91; separation from, 115, 119–21
Remittances, 26, 88, 91, 107–10, 125–26, 208n6, 215n30
Rental houses, 78, 99, 100, 209n2
Representation, 4, 42, 155–56, 182
Research visas, 71–72, 157, 207n5
Resistance: acts of, 158–59; dollars as, 107; Elena's, 50–51, 55; migration and, 141; visibility of, 158–59. See also Activism; Protest
Resolver (to resolve), 65–66, 69–72, 80; blessing, meaning of, 71
Responsible Parenthood Movement, 156
Revolution, 19, 20, 154, 199n2; Castro Espín's view of, 157; glory years of, 212n13; gratitude for, 155–56; Havana before, 90; middle-class changes from, 56–57; poster advertising, 30; poverty and, 111, 111–12; racial equality and, 109–10; to Special Period, 21–29
Rigdon, Susan M., 20

Rights: 2003–2008, non-change in, 183; citizenship and, 164, 171, 217n4; consumer, 67; gay, 182; Radio Martí and, 51, 203n9; social, 139–40, 161; spatial, 42; three basic, 67, 207n2; U.S. dollar v. pesos/CUCs and, *106*. *See also* Migration

Riots. *See* Protest

Ritual: failure, 155; shadow political, 152–55

"Round Table" news show, 152

Saízo family (informants), 108–9, 112

Salaries/wages, 53–54, 109, 183, 185; discrepancies in, 90; migrant processing fees in relation to, 210n2

Sánchez, Yoani, 181

Sayings. *See* Aphorisms

Scholarly exchange programs, 121, 212n10

Scholarship: citizen-consumer dissatisfaction in previous, 16–17; dissatisfaction/criticism, 146–47; middle-class, 6–7, 198n8; on migration, 129–30, 214n23, 214n25, 217n7; post-Soviet, 32. *See also* Ethnographies

Sea, 118–19, 211n4

Secrecy, 101–2, 134–35

Self-disclosure, two-way, 15

Self-employment, 5–6, 22, 77, 147; legalization of, 55–56, 77–78, 205n5; privatization and, 55–57

Self-esteem, goods and, 87

Self-representation, 155–56

Senility, Fidel Castro's, 149–50

Separation, from relatives, 115, 119–21

Sex education, Cuba's national center for, 156

Shadow public, 2, 9, 16, 217n11; adaptation of, 183–85; aphorisms circulating among, 148–50; Catholic press/publications of, 52, 53, 204n3; collective criticism, 41–42; digital information, 181–82; discourse of, aphorisms as, 151–52; everyday outlaws of, 68; forms of struggles of, 158–59; marches not attended by, 153; as metaculture, 81; neighborhood context for, 3–4; opposition of, 146–47; political rituals and, 152–55; voice of, 142. *See also* Private space

Shopping, 84, 85–87

Shortages, 2, 65, 73, *73*, 93, 178; adaptation to, 67; foodstuff, chronic, 74; staples, 182

Simmel, George, 93

Smugglers, human, 211n4

Social class, 56–57, 91, 104, 172, 184, 198n8; analysis of late socialism, 104–7, *105*, *106*; citizens unaware of "other half," 102–4; dollar dogs, 99–104, *105*; emerging, 98–113; goods access and, 103, 209n4; informants, 3–4, 10; performers/athletes category of, 103, *105*, 209n4; Red Bourgeoisie, 103–4, 105, *105*

Social imaginary, 129, 161, 166

Socialism, *30*; binary, 33–34, 37, 60; older citizen-consumers' view of change to, 56–57; social class analysis/access to dollars and, *106*. *See also* Late socialism

Socialist bureaucracy, 3. *See also* Late socialism; Revolution

Socialist nostalgia, 109, 170, 175–79

Sociality: *consiguiendo* and, 74–75; shortages creating, 93

Social movement, *163*, 164, 217n6

Social sciences, private space and, 36–37

Social semiotic, language as, 81

Solidarity, group, 141, 153

Soviet Union, 3, 22, 32, 122, 154, 173, 212n10; dissatisfaction in Latin America v., view of, 173–74; protest waves in 1980s/1990s, 175

Special Cuban Migration Program, 214n29

Special Period, 17, 20, 200n10; act of protest during, 54; labor migration at beginning of, 110, *111*; lexicon of, 64, 65–82; from revolution to, 21–29; social class since, 104–7, *105*, *106*

Stalin, Joseph, 32

Stan/Jinori (informants), 91–93, 188, 208n8

Staples, shortages of, 182

State, 9; child-care circles run by, 58, 205n10; collective independence from, 70; dependency/protest and, 147; employment, 22, 40, 109, 111, 157, 185; freedom to assemble under, 152; government v., 202n17; loyalty as weapon of, 110; marches organized by, 112, 153–55; messages posted by, 41–42, 68; private space in context of, 17, 36; publications owned/censored by, 52; *resolviendo* between citizens and, 70–72, 80; shadow public view of, 142; "stealing" from, 67, 207n2; stores run by, 23, 24, *24*, *73*, 183; struggle to make a living reminder of, 67–68; subsidized education, 6; surveillance, 27, 41, 45–47, 56; tension in daily life intimacy with, 147–48;

State—*continued*
under-the-table realm of governance, 164.
See also Citizen-state relationships; Criticism, of state
State official, confrontation between student and, 181, 218n1
Stealing, new word for, 66–67, 207n2
Store(s), *73*, 157, 183; dollar, 23, 24, *24*; playing, 70
Structural adjustment, 20, 199n3
Struggle (*luchar*), 65–69, 80, 158–59, 186, 206n1
Stuart (informant/dollar dog), 189, 194; Email Elena and, 100–101; legal means of, 99–102
Student, confrontation between state official and, 181, 218n1
Suicide rate, 211n5
Suite Havana, 102–3
Surveillance, 27, 41, 45–47, 56

Tatiana (key informant/David's wife), 69, 85–87, 127–28, 133–35, 187, 191
Taxation, 56, 99, 161
Taxis, 76
Taylor, Charles, 97, 152, 166
Teachers, migration from public to private schools, 183–84
Telecommunications embargo, lifting of, 211n6
Telephones, 43; calls, 211n6
Television (TV), 112; Fidel Castro on, 144–46; news show on, 152; satellite, 87; social class awareness and, 103
Texts. *See* Publications/texts
Thomas, Deborah, 96–97
Tilly, Charles, 9, 199n12
Torricelli Act, 22, 200n8
Tourist apartheid, 185
Tourist industry, 20, 22, 42, 76, 108, 110
Trabajadores, 152
Trade embargo, U.S., 22, 25, 32, 42, 123, 207n8
Transnational comparison shopping, 85–87
Transportation, 182
Travel, 27, 87, 88, 118, 120, 210n1; 1980s freedom to, 125, 212n13; performers/athletes allowed to, 121
Tristan (informant/Costa Rican migrant), 127
TV. *See* Television
Two-tiered economy, 23, 100, 109. *See also*

Double life/double standard; Underground economy

Underground economy, 20, 26, 172, 201n14; two-tiered economy as, 23, 100, 109. *See also* Black market; Double life/double standard; Micro-enterprises
United States (U.S.), 32, 80; Cuban immigrants in, racial percentages for, 108; migration to, 88, 117, 128, 214n29; telecommunications embargo lifted by, 211n6; trade embargo, 22, 25, 35, 42, 123, 207n8; visa lotteries of, 214n29
Urban schools, tensions in, 184
U.S. Coast Guard, 210n3, 211n4
U.S. Interests Section, Havana, 51, 203n10

Valle, Amir, 119
Varela, Padre Félix, 25, 52, 201n13, 204n1
Vehicles, *36*, 76, *77*, 103, 182, 209n4
Venezuela, 26, 201n15, 211n8
Vertical allegiance, *163*, 164
Videos, 57, 88
Virtual private space, 48–51
Visas, 88, 120, 134, 161–62, 214n29; research, 71–72, 157, 207n5
Voting, 25, 152, 201n12

Walker, Lucius, 214n26
Warner, Michael, 53, 54
Wealth: migration based on distribution of, 130; number of children indicating, 184
Welfare state, 28–29, 67, 207n2; as competitor, 78; critique of, 147–48; paternalistic style of, 148–50
Wet-foot/dry-foot policy, 118–19
White migration, 1960s, 107–8
Women, 25; post-partum, 157
Word-of-mouth, *consiguiendo*, 74–75
Work contracts, 182, 211n7, 213n17, 214n24

Yugoslavia, 178
Yurchak, Alexei, 33–34, 151, 154
Yutongs (Chinese buses), 182

Zemmi (informant/peso poor), 155–56, 195

Amelia Rosenberg Weinreb is a lecturer in the Department of Anthropology at the University of Texas at Austin. Her current fieldwork is in a remote desert town in the Negev Highlands.